Solving Critical Design Problems

Solving Critical Design Problems demonstrates both how design is increasingly used to solve large, complex, modern-day problems and, as a result, how the role of the designer continues to develop in response. With 13 case studies from various fields, including program and product design, Tania Allen shows how types of design thinking, such as systems thinking, metaphorical thinking, and empathy, can be used together with methods, such as brainstorming, design fiction, and prototyping. This book helps you find ways out of your design problems by giving you other ways to look at your ideas, so that your designs make sense in their setting.

Solving Critical Design Problems encourages a design approach that challenges assumptions and allows designers to take on a more critical and creative role. With over 100 images, this book will appeal to students in design studios, industrial and product design, as well as landscape and urban design.

Tania Allen is an Associate Professor of Art and Design and Design Studies at North Carolina State University in Raleigh, North Carolina, USA.

"This book is written from the perspective of an individual who has studied, practiced, and taught design. It is the interaction of these experiences that cause her to adopt a Socratic underpinning to the act of design. She inspires the reader to consider the act of design in the context of questions that stimulate thoughts of culture and place to enrich the utilitarian aspects of a design project. This approach opens the path toward inter and transdisciplinary approaches defining the act of design as a means to pose a way of seeing design as a rhetorical activity. It is this connection between the realization of artifacts and the role of design in the definition of culture that distinguishes this book. There is real substance in this monograph for the experienced design professional and it serves as an inside insight for those who are new to the design activity. It is worthy to be required reading in the classroom and is a must read for those who are seeking to understand the design culture."

Marvin J. Malecha, FAIA, DPACSA
President, NewSchool of Architecture and Design, San Diego, California

Solving Critical Design Problems

Theory and Practice

Tania Allen

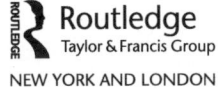
Routledge
Taylor & Francis Group
NEW YORK AND LONDON

First published 2019
by Routledge
52 Vanderbilt Avenue, New York, NY 10017

and by Routledge
2 Park Square, Milton Park, Abingdon, Oxon, OX14 4RN

Routledge is an imprint of the Taylor & Francis Group, an informa business

© 2019 Taylor & Francis

The right of Tania Allen to be identified as author of this work has been asserted by her in accordance with sections 77 and 78 of the Copyright, Designs and Patents Act 1988.

All rights reserved. No part of this book may be reprinted or reproduced or utilised in any form or by any electronic, mechanical, or other means, now known or hereafter invented, including photocopying and recording, or in any information storage or retrieval system, without permission in writing from the publishers.

Trademark notice: Product or corporate names may be trademarks or registered trademarks, and are used only for identification and explanation without intent to infringe.

Library of Congress Cataloging-in-Publication Data
Names: Allen, Tania, author.
Title: Solving critical design problems : theory and practice / Tania Allen.
Description: New York : Routledge, 2019. | Includes bibliographical references and index.
Identifiers: LCCN 2019002231| ISBN 9780367025830 (hardback) | ISBN 9780367025847 (pbk.) | ISBN 9780429398872 (e-book)
Subjects: LCSH: Design. | Problem solving.
Classification: LCC NK1510 .A58 2019 | DDC 745.4—dc23
LC record available at https://lccn.loc.gov/2019002231

ISBN: 978-0-367-02583-0 (hbk)
ISBN: 978-0-367-02584-7 (pbk)
ISBN: 978-0-429-39887-2 (ebk)

Typeset in Franklin Gothic and Garamond
by Swales & Willis Ltd, Exeter, Devon, UK

To Todd, Owen and Calvin: Who always make me want to be better.

Contents

Foreword ix
Preface xiii

1 Introduction: defining the drivers of design theory and practice   1

Part 1. Design and usability: if a design falls in the forest . . .   **7**
2 Design and usability: from universal to individual experiences   9
3 Experiential and adaptive design thinking   19
4 Design as dialogue: case studies of experiential design thinking   39

Part 2. Design and technology: not if, but when   **57**
5 Reciprocity and impact   59
6 Networked design thinking   71
7 Visualizing the invisible: case studies of networked design thinking   85

Part 3. Design and sustainability: killing messengers   **109**
8 Paradigm shifts: designing resilient systems   111
9 Ecological design thinking   121
10 Creating resilient futures: case studies of ecological design thinking   137

Part 4. Design and morality: do the right thing   **157**
11 Making change, design as moral mediator   159
12 Narrative design thinking   171
13 Creating stories together: case studies of narrative design thinking   185

14 Conclusion: putting it all together—design futures   197

References   205
Index   215

Foreword

Normally I am wary of another book on design thinking. It has become a subject of continuing debate including much advocacy and considerable derision. It seems to me that this is true because so many of the authors are not writing from the intensely personal position of being an active designer. There is a kind of voyeurism at work that manifests itself when design thinking is posited as another liberal arts position. So much of the literature impresses me as written by individuals looking in to a story written by others. This text is different. Associate Professor Tania Allen understands as an active practitioner that a designer must think "expansively and narrowly: broadly and deeply: generatively and selectively; and to operate both as insiders and outsiders." She understands the connection between need and experience and further incorporates the intimate connection between theory and practice in her observations. For Tania, design is a metacognitive activity that not only asks what is the best design for an artifact, but also if there is a need for the artifact at all. She sees design as a malleable experience that matches ethical and moral questions with a predilection for action. Because of her experience, she urges the reader to consider challenging themselves to think about his or her work differently, looking beyond the traditional sources of inspiration to a rich and exhilarating set of disciplines. Her strategy in this text is to explore four distinct paradigms; design and usability, design and technology, design and sustainability, and design and morality. Through these four paradigms, she encourages the reader to accept the patterns of each that will impact the others. It is the critical interrelationship between them that characterizes design thought.

So strong is the connection between self-identity and process that when Frank Gehry was asked to explain how he begins teaching a studio, he noted that he asks the students to design their own signature. This exercise underlines the importance of understanding that there is no right or wrong regarding the outcome beyond the preference of the individual. His identification of his work with his signature is a powerful example of the relationship between design of a project or experience with the design of self that is always underway.

Several years ago, following the completion of the Whitney Museum of American Art in New York, Renzo Piano (2015), the building's architect, was interviewed by an NPR

Foreword

reporter for a whimsical summer story about spending time on the beach during the month of August with his grandchildren. What was intended to be a public interest story became profound as he articulated the lessons of building a sandcastle. He addressed the necessity of understanding the properties of water and the ebb and flow of the waves, and the resultant impact on the design of the castle. He further wondered about what it meant to design a castle at the water's edge and he reflected that he was able to observe 1,000 years of erosion in an afternoon. In the process, the entire experience became a wonderful adventure to get to know his grandchildren and for them to get to know him. But for him, his focus on a life of design caused him to draw deep lessons from the experience. The sandcastle had become something more than playful diversion. Just as with any of his buildings, the sandcastle became an exploration of self. Like the signature project of Frank Gehry, Renzo Piano had found a way for the intense self-reflection that should be a part of everyone's search for renewal that time away affords.

Every project is defined by aspects of a story to be communicated through metaphor, interpretation, and demonstration. It is given further definition by the system that must be addressed through relevant information, application, and analysis. Between story and system, the playfulness of iteration is found to be measured by each. This is true whether it is a signature, a sandcastle, a skyscraper, or a human experience. Each of these elements are found throughout Associate Professor Tania Allen's text. Her ability to unwrap them to discover their essence is a valuable aspect of this text.

Ultimately, the individual who is a creative spirit comes to realize the discipline of the design process defines them not only as artists, creative thinkers, and design professionals, but also as people. It is no exaggeration to observe that for the creative spirit, design thought is as much a search for self as it is for new places and products. From project to project, users and user experience, defining project-based learning is an amazing tool to understand one's self. This is the source of the cutting-edge ideas that flow forward from such an awareness. This deep understanding of self is a prerequisite for design. Tania Allen approaches this through her assertion of user experience defined by knowledge, affordances, and schemas. Through this, she approaches the subject that has come to be known as human-centered design. The focus on knowing the human experience is further explored by her connection between usability as a cultural experience articulated by signs, symbols, and codes. Her assertion that "by designing objects, technologies and systems, we are in fact designing cultures of the future," is precisely the intention of design inquiry. The exploration in design research envisioned by Associate Professor Allen is a precise guide for the imperative to foster an evidence-based process in design thought. For too long this has been an evident weakness among design professionals. The iterative process that has long characterized the work of creative individuals has too often depended on a "do it, and do it again" experience with little or no recording of lessons learned. This has the unintended outcome of producing little to share and no measures by which the success of a project may be assessed. Tania Allen has provided in this text the beginning points of research from which the appropriate questions may be asked. Perhaps most importantly, she connects the process of discovery with the excitement of the creative experience. Her exploration of the impacts of new tools and technologies on thought and project development is an insightful embracing of our new reality. It is a further demonstration of the inclusive mentality she has already articulated earlier in the text. Supporting the evidence-based foundation of design thought are a series of case studies that explore a series of design ideas from sustainability to urban design. These case studies are the substantive articulation of the four paradigms.

I have long believed that the design thinking experience is perhaps the most gregarious of theoretical pursuits. The networks and patterns of ideas and people forces the creative individual out of the cocoon too long associated with creative individuals. Certainly, there are examples of the creative genius who is antisocial. But, it is more likely that you will find the most creative among us to be individuals who are fully citizens of the world. The best designers by their very nature are storytellers. Early on in their explorations they storyboard ideas to represent the narrative that accompanies their ideas. These storyboards represent the images that are fully drawn to engage the client as a user and participant in the dream. When Walt Disney sought the financial support to build Disneyland, he brought with him a pencil drawing of a vision. His story connected with the potential lenders so strongly that the related risks were downplayed by the vision of an incredible individual. Today as we look at the work of individuals such as Frank Gehry, Renzo Piano, Charles and Ray Eames, Steve Jobs, and even Elon Musk, we are studying masters of the story. The story is supported by the necessity of utility but it is the basis upon which the play of the creative process begins.

Tania closes her text with a discussion of the moral dimensions of design. She incorporates gaming and crowdsourcing in her discourse, raising the questions of the ultimate intention of the design process as a toll for the empowerment of the individual. No stronger case can be made for a design education. Her description of a course syllabus framed on the experiences of Hurricane Maria including: understanding what happened, thinking about utopia, making in times of catharsis, and reflection and critique, describes perfectly the challenge of a designer to think expansively and narrowly: broadly and deeply: generatively and selectively; and to operate both as insiders and outsiders. The sources and references that inform her position are a rich collection of opinions and perspective that only further emphasize the inclusive nature of her message.

For me, design is a way of structuring life. It is a manifestation of our best angels. This text is a guide for the journey to discover those angels.

Marvin J. Malecha, FAIA, DPACSA
President, NewSchool of Architecture and Design, San Diego, California
Dean Emeritus, College of Design, North Carolina State University
2009 American Institute of Architects National President
1989–1990 Association of Collegiate Schools of Architecture National President
AIA Topaz Laureate
Association of Collegiate Schools of Architecture Distinguished Professor
American Institute of Architects Fellow
American Institute of Architects, North Carolina Chapter, F. Carter Williams Gold Medalist

Preface

Before starting graduate school in 2008, I had never heard the term design thinking. I had been working with non-profits and cultural organizations in Boston and more and more had been wrestling with just how to tackle the large-scale problems that they faced with communicating their mission, and with turning interest into action. In my very first graduate studio with Meredith Davis, I read Nigel Cross's (2007) *Designerly Ways of Knowing* as part of a group project on explaining design thinking as a tool for innovative teaching and learning. The idea that designers had distinct ways of problem-solving, and that visualization and translation were critical components of dealing with complexity and ill-formed problems was a revolutionary insight. I went on to teach design thinking with Marvin J. Malecha and then on my own. And through that experience, I developed an approach and perspective to design thinking that emphasized criticality through research, observation, and testing. Many of the ideas in this book are gathered from lectures, assignments, and projects I have given inside and outside of the classroom, and also part of a larger interest in how design is at its core a social activity and has a social impact.

    I would like to thank all of the people who directly or indirectly have contributed to the ideas in this book. To Meredith Davis, Denise Crisp, and Scott Townsend who were pivotal guides in my graduate career and helped cultivate my interest in design research. To Marvin J. Malecha who was an unparalleled mentor, and supported me fully in my own interpretation and expansion of design thinking principles and methods to include more critical research. To all of my colleagues—especially Sara Queen, Kathleen Rieder, and Brooke Chornyak—who are constantly challenging me to think about my own work in a more critical way. And finally to my family; my father who as a scientist and historian is always balancing truth with meaning; and my mother who's creativity and support keep pushing me forward. To David and Larry (my other parents) who are always there offering welcoming words of guidance. And finally to my sister Carin and her family—Danny, Anna, and Evan—who always, always make me laugh.

References

Cross, Nigel. *Designerly Ways of Knowing*. Basel: Birkhäuser Architecture, 2007.

Piano, Renzo. "Blueprints Before High Tide: An Architect Explains The Perfect Sandcastle." Interview with NPR Staff. August 1, 2015. www.npr.org/2015/08/01/428088284/blueprints-before-high-tide-an-architect-explains-the-perfect-sandcastle. Accessed March 28, 2019.

1 Introduction
Defining the drivers of design theory and practice

This book is both a celebration of design and a challenge to think about it differently. We are in a moment where design is center stage. Magazines are challenging us to "think like a designer" and championing design and innovation as the savior of our troubles. From a technological perspective, this is an exciting time to be a designer because we have the ability to speculate, knowing that our speculations will be a reality—not in 100 years, but in ten. Our wildest, craziest inventions are possible—it's just a matter of time. But there is also immense pressure on design to solve many of the problems that have been created in the last 100 years—everything from better infrastructural strategies to handle our ever-increasing city populations to how to better manage the personal debt that affects individuals and economies. Design is championed for being able to get us out of the mess that we are in environmentally, technically, and economically by developing products and environments that are cleaner, easier to manufacture and affordable for a wider range of users. This is a lot for the field to support, especially if we want to do it conscientiously. It is especially difficult considering design as a field is relatively young. Our history of self-reflection is short and we are still in the midst of defining a comprehensive and succinct set of theories and methods that drive it.

The strength of design thinking is that it forces designers to think expansively and narrowly; broadly and deeply; generatively and selectively; and to operate as both insiders and outsiders. One of the main attributes of any good designer is the ability to understand first-hand what potential users might need, and identify problems within a current situation. Designers operate as insiders by using strategies that invoke empathy. By simultaneously operating as outsiders, designers keep their minds open to new ideas from the world around them, while also identifying patterns of behavior that design can respond to. As a teacher of design thinking myself, I see the potential and the excitement that it has for helping students make connections and prompt insights that would not have emerged without it and to make proposals for those insights that move the idea beyond a philosophy and into a realm that is action and change oriented. The literature on design thinking is vast, from Bryan Lawson's *How Designers Think* (1991) and Nigel Cross's *Designerly Ways of Knowing* (2007), to Tom Kelley's *The Art of Innovation* (2001), Tim Brown's *Change by Design* (2009), and more recently Marc Stickdorn and Jakob Schneider's *This Is Service*

Design Thinking: Basics, Tools, Cases (2012). The books are but a sliver of the mountain of literature that promises design thinking will transform businesses, strategies, and products to be innovative, and highly sought after. Missing from these promises is a larger connection and critical consideration of how, when, and why to innovate. Considerations that, if entertained, might be answered with the decision not to design at all. Rather than ask, "How can we design the next best ballpoint pen?" this book hopes to get designers and students to ask, "Do we need another ballpoint pen? Where is the writing device that I design today going to be in ten years? How does the act of writing improve communication? What are future ways to capture, record, and access information?"

These questions necessitate a look at design that spans disciplinary boundaries and attempts to find commonalities. As the world becomes more integrated, so too does design. We cannot design an apartment building without considering how people will get there and the changes to traffic that might occur as a result. The design of a fitness app must wrangle with the different platforms that people will use to access it. The design of a water bottle cannot ignore what will differentiate its brand from other water bottle brands. Part of the reason this is true is that design is, and must be, of a moment. In other words, design will always be context-specific—responding to the needs and wants of a population, situation, or geography that is current and contemporary. In his 2008 article *Towards Relational Design* Andrew Blauvelt, curator at the Walker Art Center in Minneapolis, argued "I believe we are in the third major phase of modern design history: an era of relationally-based, contextually-specific design." If this is true (and I believe that it is) then a more integrative and cross-disciplinary look at what is driving all aspects of design is necessary.

Design as a rhetorical activity

The phase of design focused on relationships and context that Blauvelt proposes also hints at another important context for design—that it is a rhetorical device. The way that designers operate and the ultimate goal of design is to improve a given situation. This could be as simple as improving a drinking experience or as complex as helping users be in charge of their own healthcare. But in both of these cases, the behavior of the user changes, because they are able to travel with their beverage, or become experts and agents of their own healthcare agenda. This behavior, in turn, changes the way that they think about their world and their life—in both minuscule and pivotal ways. If designers understand and acknowledge this perspective, how might that affect the way that they approach design research, theory, and practice? That is a key question this book seeks to approach. It suggests a paradigm shift that John Thackara (2005) argues is critical to designing in a complex world and which focuses on a shift away from substitution and towards reduction.

We could easily transition from an acknowledgment of the rhetorical power of design to how this power might save the world. There are a lot of people who claim that if we just design better and differently, we can get ourselves out of all of the messes we are currently facing. I do not argue that design can't or shouldn't address current and pressing problems in our world. I also do not argue that designers aren't in a unique position to see a problem and come up with viable and innovative solutions to those problems. The issue is more that the literature and practice of "design for good" re-focuses energy away from root causes and towards band-aid solutions. In the same way that much of the debate in medicine centers on whether to treat the symptom or the disease, so too I would argue are the potential issues that arise when design is focused in a similar manner. For instance, the design of a straw with a built-in filter that would allow people in Sub-Saharan Africa to drink from local water sources (like a river) that might be otherwise undrinkable, fills an immediate need for people to get clean water. The danger lies when these types of solutions mask or numb us to underlying root issues, such as infrastructural, economic, and developmental inequality.

The concepts introduced in this book showcase a particular theoretical perspective. Primarily, that design should emphasize relationships, systems, and experiences over artifacts, objects, and consumption. But it also acknowledges a diversity of perspectives and counter-perspectives that ask the designer reading it to be critical, and rethink what is presented in a way that is situation-specific. Even though there are many methods within the pages of this book, methods situated within one section are not meant to only be applied to that section. It is meant to provoke critical and creative thinking, but not dictate a single way to approach a design problem. In writing this book, it became clearer to me how much crossover there are between the different theories as there are distinctions among them. In some ways, this book is suggesting a malleable taxonomy. One that sets up a system of classification in which the drivers become organizing principles, but the theories in practice might ultimately be evidence of multiple paradigms and perspectives.

I would argue these commonalities are driven (or should be) by a perspective on design action that puts people and values at the center. These are ethical considerations—for designers and users. Critical consideration for how design might affect (and encourage) an understanding of the world and each other—and by extension how we treat each—should be predominant. A consideration of how design interventions might encourage a new type of perspective or behavior must be considered earlier on in the design process. We can no longer wait and see what happens. We cannot make assumptions that design will always improve a given situation. And we must make a distinction between improvement of a current situation that is equally balanced with a critical consideration of projections for future impact. That is the ultimate aim of this book—to expand the perspective of the designer through theories, methods, and case studies and to show examples from inside and outside of design that are driving the way that designers consider their roles and the scope of design projects. I hope that this book will challenge some of the main assumptions of design and designers—namely, that design must always produce something new.

Design as an integrative activity

This consideration of design practice and focus—how designers understand and respond to the "wicked problems" that are at the core of the design process—encourages a need for more and better theories that looks across disciplinary boundaries to see what is transferable and applicable. But many would agree that theory is commonly viewed as an antagonist to the activity and practice of design—and that it can serve as an obstacle to "getting things done" (Margolin and Buchanan, 1995, x). Written over 20 years ago, Victor Margolin and Richard Buchanan (1995) identified this issue as:

> One of the anomalies of twentieth-century culture, particularly academic culture . . . [is the] excessive separation between theory and practice, between the words and symbols used to understand important subjects and the concrete actions of individuals and groups who employ personal or formal knowledge to accomplish practical purposes.
>
> (1995, x)

The aim of this book is to identify theoretical perspectives that guide how designers approach practice—not separating theory from practice, but rather exploring and identifying how they are integrated. Design does not, and cannot, operate on philosophy and theory alone. Without the connection between the design concept, the artifact, and the user, design does not exist. So any book on theory must include strategies and methods for applying that theory to a real-world design experience. There are many excellent books on design theory and practice in existence. In many cases, they focus on one theory with many examples of its practice, or on theory in general. What I hope this book will add to the discourse *and* to the practice is the ability for designers to begin to intrinsically link the theory (what) with tools and methods (how) to their overall practice (why). I also hope this book can serve as a type of toolkit to provoke new ways of defining design problems.

One of the ways that designers can challenge themselves to think about their work differently is to look outside of design to ways that other disciplines research, evaluate, and interpret their work. But much of the evaluation of design has been dictated by those outside of design practice—and in doing so, the focus has leaned to the artifacts that are a result of design practice, rather than the practice itself. In *The Idea of Design*, Buchanan and Margolin (1996) call for design to be recognized as a liberal art because of its integrative nature. They suggest an important need to broaden the discussion of design evaluation to include that which is focused on the human experience, but also to connect design philosophy and practice (x). This call is in part a response to the recognition of design's focus on "wicked" problems, and a necessary shift in motivation from what we (as designers) *can* do, to what we *should* do. As architectural practice dips into urbanism and visual communication; and as graphic design expands into strategies that involve spaces, places, and environments, the ability for designers to see across disciplines to find patterns and commonalities as well as differences is increasingly critical. By looking at design through its technology, usability, morality, sustainability, and cultural context and impacts, designers focus on how design shapes, and is shaped by, the human experience. But there is a larger motivation at play here, and that is in the building of design as a discipline. In *Time for Change: Building a Design Discipline*, design educator Sharon Poggenpohl (2009) argues "that design practice and education are changing, particularly in relation to . . . research and collaboration. If design is to develop as a discipline, it must necessarily develop further based on these themes" (1). At the center of this development, Poggenpohl continues, is the transformation of the tacit knowledge that designers traditionally employ, to explicit knowledge that is a core asset to cross-disciplinary communication and collaboration.

This is the shortcoming that makes design appear elusive, special, inarticulate, and even unknowable. As long as designers consider themselves to be first and foremost aesthetic finishers of ideas that are well advanced in the development process, they will be trapped by the tacit and unable to provide a clear explanation.

(5)

Since Poggenpohl's call, design discourse has been increasingly focused on building this explicit, critical knowledge. Designers are no longer comfortable or willing to be the "aesthetic finishers" that Poggenpohl aptly names. This book argues that we are at a critical moment in time, where the cross-disciplinary nature of design necessitates a common perspective on the main themes and drivers of design thinking and practice.

Challenging design paradigms

In his book, *The Sciences of the Artificial*, Herbert Simon (1996) defined design as "courses of action aimed at changing existing situations into preferred ones" (111). Through this book, I hope to challenge assumptions about those preferred conditions—what drives the paradigms that inform them, and how methodologies might shift the underlying assumptions. A common theme that will emerge is, how can we, as design students, academics, and practitioners, be rigorous in investigating, understanding, and responding to design problems. Acknowledging that the problems we face as designers are complex, "wicked," messy, and often without any singular solution, how we frame the problem for ourselves, and communicate that framing to our clients and other designers, has a profound effect on how we address them. This book is broken up into four sections that align with what I see as foundational components to design theory and practice: usability, technology, sustainability, and morality. I argue that these drivers, and the needs and contexts associated with them, provide a crucial foundation to examine how designers engage in current and future design practices across disciplines. These drivers also frame four distinct paradigms that designers operate under—from the operational, to the scientific, to the meaningful to the actionable. The sequence of chapters is meant to grow in alignment with these paradigms. Part 1, Design and usability: if a design falls in the forest . . . starts with an understanding of how the concepts and theories of usability contribute to the judgement and "expertise" of the designer. Part 2, Design and technology: not if, but when looks at how technology impacts what it is that designers create as well as how designers push technological boundaries, with specific focus on the impact of technological advancement on production and consumption. It then moves on to look at how usability studies can be expanded beyond the digital world where they are primarily located and utilized and adapted across design disciplines. Part 3, Design and sustainability: killing messengers takes a systematic look at how design understands and responds to issues of sustainability beyond the traditional concepts of environmental sustainability. Addressing such issues as planned obsolescence, this chapter will reconsider the role of design in making the "new." Part 4, Design and morality: do the right thing starts to unpack how design impacts moral judgments on the part of the user and the designer—and what designers can do to understand and evaluate and respond to those outcomes. The organization of the book loosely follows the evolution of design research and insight—from the human scale and need, to what is feasible from a technological position to how specific design solutions might impact the world—both environmental and on a human scale. Each section follows a similar structure—how these topics are theoretically considered in design; how design research methods can help provoke insights; how design processes can be utilized to more effectively address the problems brought forth; and specific examples of design theories in practice which showcase real-world examples of design projects that are engaging critical theories in the work they are doing. However, it is not intended that these theories, practices, and methods be seen as only developed as a result of that particular driver. For instance, systems thinking is valuable for understanding usability, as well as technology, sustainability, and morality in design. By organizing them according to what I see as large-scale drivers of design theory and practice, the intention is to provide a context through which to explain and exemplify these ideas. Hopefully, it will give a clearer picture of what these ideas mean, and for designers to practice and experiment with.

Gandhi was quoted as saying, "Your beliefs become your thoughts, your thoughts become your words, your words become your actions, your actions become your habits, your habits become your values, your values become your destiny." This book focuses on how our beliefs about design affect not only designers' thoughts, words, etc. but also how they affect the thoughts, beliefs, actions, habits, and values of the people who use them.

References

Blauvelt, Andrew. "Towards Relational Design." *Design Observer*, 2008. Retrieved from: https://designobserver.com/feature/towards-relational-design/7557. Accessed September 12, 2018.

Brown, Tim. *Change By Design*. New York: Harper Business, 2009.

Buchanan, Richard and Margolin, Victor, editors. *Discovering Design: Explorations in Design Studies*. Chicago, IL: University of Chicago Press, 1995.

Buchanan, Richard and Margolin, Victor, editors. *The Idea of Design*. Cambridge, MA: MIT Press, 1996.

Cross, Nigel. *Designerly Ways of Knowing*. Basel: Birkhäuser Architecture, 2007.

Kelley, Tom. *The Art of Innovation*. New York: Currency, 2001.

Lawson, Bryan. *How Designers Think: The Design Process Demystified, 4th edition*. Oxford: Architectural Press, 1991.

Norman, Donald. *The Design of Everyday Things*. New York: Basic Books, 2013.

Poggenpohl, Sharon Helmer. "Time for Change: Building a Design Discipline." *Design Integrations: Research and Collaboration*. Bristol: Intellect Books, 2009.

Poggenpohl, Sharon Helmer and Keichi Sato, editors. *Design Integrations: Research and Collaboration*. Bristol: Intellect Books, 2009.

Simon, Herbert. *The Sciences of the Artificial*. Cambridge, MA: MIT Press, 1996.

Stickdorn, Marc and Jakob Schneider. *This Is Service Design Thinking: Basics, Tools, Cases*. Hoboken, NJ: Wiley, 2012.

Thackara, John. *In the Bubble: Designing in a Complex World*. Cambridge, MA: MIT Press, 2005.

Part 1

Design and usability
If a design falls in the forest . . .

2 Design and usability
From universal to individual experiences

In the introduction to *Design Integrations*, Sharon Poggenpohl (2009) makes a call for the importance of design and designers moving beyond the heritage of craft and towards a more disciplinary perspective. The activity of reflection, Poggenpohl argues, urges the designer to improve not just on the making of things, but also on the impact of that thing on a larger context which could be audience, environmental, material or socio-cultural in nature. It forces the designer to contemplate more than how the object looks and towards how it might be experienced. As we move beyond design as a merely material activity and towards design as an experiential one, the increased focus on the people for whom we are designing is critical. But how we do this is also as critical. The perspective that we take, as designers—whether to lump all people into a single category, or to try to identify the particularities and patterns between individuals experiences—has profound effects on the design solutions that come about. One main assumption driving this chapter is to consider design not as an end goal—something static that a "user" will use (and hopefully love) but to think of it more as an organic set of conditions that human beings will manipulate, change, and transform. In reframing design in such a way, we can start to think of it as truly human centered. Brian Burns, in the book *People Want Toast Not Toasters* (2012) brings up a central point to how we must start thinking about usability. By reframing the experience not as a set of procedures that are understandable, but rather the successfulness of the outcome from that experience, we open up a host of alternative ways to design. To use Burns's example we can think about the design of a toaster as a series of steps that users have to go through to achieve their goal OR we can think about the experience of the goal itself and work backwards from that.

    This chapter on usability is one part champion of it, and one part examination of how we might do it better. As we lose more control over the outcome of our design actions, we must adapt and think about usability not as a way to control the user (and make sure they do what we want them to do) but rather think of it as an activity equally as focused on discovering opportunities for new design possibility. What does this mean? It means that rather than thinking of usability and user experience as a way to test the validity of a design, we might learn more, and create better designs if we are focused on the user as extending and manipulating our designs in new and interesting ways. But design has a long legacy of seeing the user as a generalized being—not focusing on the particulars of people, but rather reducing behaviors to lowest common denominator. During the Bauhaus, a driving force was standardization and the idea that design can, and even must, be applied similarly to all humans. In a way, this was meant to bring people together through design and to elevate design to a higher level through mass dissemination. Designers such as Charles and Ray Eames focused on high-production, low-cost design. They were part of a larger movement—in design, urban planning, and US culture at large, that was enjoying the fruits of the post-World War II boom and taking full advantage of that. The move from industrialization to a service economy that started also meant that people were moving into office environments which had a more nuanced impact on productivity.

Early user experience focused on developing practices that were scientific in nature—about how people behaved and responded to design, not as much how they interpreted or understood it as part of a larger system. In his seminal book, *The Sciences of the Artificial*, Herbert Simon (1996) made a case for the artificial world as a natural science: "The world we live in is much more man-made, or artificial, world than it is a natural world" (2). Simon expands his notion of the "artificial" to include the artificial temperature that we keep our homes at, the language that we have devised to communicate with one another. And in many ways, he's accurate. These are all elements of our experience that are intentionally devised by us. Sometimes, they are intentional, and other times not. Another is the invention of the computer. Early usability studies focused on the behaviors associated with certain actions or processes. Rather than asking why did the user make that decision, they focused on the decision that was made and how the interface could have acted differently. It's hard to believe (or imagine) that the origins of Western design did not (at least initially) think of design as adaptable.

Theories of usability: design as experience

In many ways, the evolution of user-experience and usability can be thought of in three distinct categories or timelines:

Usability as physical experience: human factors

The beginning of human-centered design focused on usability as a physical study, including ergonomics and human factors design. With roots in product development and industrial design, early user experience focused on the shape, form, size of objects and how they were able to be used in a physical sense. Henry Dreyfuss, the industrial and product designers, is given credit for developing the inception of this perspective in his book *Designing for People* (1955). Rather than people conforming to the design standard, Dreyfuss advocated for returning to the human body as the basis for product design decisions. In many ways, this was a return to historical, such as ancient Greek and Roman precedent which used the human body as measurements. In her book, *Beautiful Users*, Ellen Lupton (2014) provides a comprehensive historical account of early user experience concepts and theories—including Dreyfuss along with some of his contemporaries. As Lupton describes it, the trajectory of this early user experience included Dreyfuss's coining of the terms human factors and human engineerings, which used military examples of the human body to typify and standardize the dimensions of the human body. One of Dreyfuss's contemporaries, Niels Diffrient who worked in his office, took on this standardization in his toolkit, *Humanscale* (1974), which sought to further investigate the different human sizes that might be addressed as part of this new ergonomic investigation. As Lupton explains, Diffrient's book attempted to capitalize on the universal design movement of the 1960s and '70s, begun at North Carolina State University by Ronald Mace as a set of standards to be more inclusive to people of all abilities in the design process. "The authors of *Humanscale* acknowledged that the diagrams account for variations in height but not weight . . . The limb dimensions are averages; actual measurements vary from individual to individual. The goal in creating a standard system of measure—even an inclusive one like *Humanscale*—constantly comes up against human particularity" (2014, 26). More recently, industrial design companies like IDEO have advocated for the focus on "extreme users" as important study participants for user-experience design, which from a physical sense could include varying levels of ability or disability, size, or age, designers can accommodate for those at the mainstream, sometimes in more effective ways than simply looking at the averages. A particularly good, though at this point possibly overused, example of this concept is the OXO potato peeler, designed by Sam Farber, which was originally created for his arthritic wife who struggled with traditional kitchen utensils. With the over-accentuated, soft handle, the peeler was a great commercial appeal, both because of the design, but also because it was more comfortable for people with all levels of ability. The physical experience of design is still of paramount importance in user experience, but we must also look beyond the standards or averages and towards what is idiosyncratic to find useful, exciting solutions.

Usability as cognitive experience: knowledge, affordances, and schemas

In the 1980s, the introduction of user experience into human-centered design also introduced usability as cognitive study. As digital computers, and graphical user interfaces (GUIs) became more and more prevalent in the workplace, design become more concerned with how people understood design cues or features. Most give Donald Norman, the author of *The Design of Everyday Things* (2013), credit with breaking down the components of user experience in order to more fully study the impact of design products on human beings ability to successfully navigate through a design system. At the center of this is what Norman characterizes as the connection between the *Gulf of Knowledge* and the *Gulf of Execution*. As Norman argues, the Gulf of Knowledge is a mixture between knowledge that is "in the head," meaning knowledge that a person brings to a situation and knowledge that is "in the world," meaning information that a person can receive and interpret from things around him. A simple example of this might be a computer keyboard. Knowledge that a person brings to their interaction with it might be being able to recognize letters. So, for instance, a small child who doesn't know how to read, or someone who doesn't recognize letters (literacy, familiarity with the language, etc.)

would not be able to make meaning of the use of a certain type of keyboard because they wouldn't have that knowledge. Some of this necessary pre-knowledge is more nuanced. For instance, any given keyboard has symbols across it—some more interpretable (like the sound icon) and others less so (like the squares next to the F4 key on a Macintosh laptop). It is through the integration and interaction between the knowledge in the world and the head that user experience is key. Norman argues that it is imperative, and a primary responsibility, for the designer to make sure she is understanding the connection between these two things, and giving explicit visual cues where necessary to help users bridge the gap that might exist. It is through the interactions between these two things that affordances are uncovered—another key theory advanced by Norman. A term originally coined by J.J. Gibson in 1979 in the book *The Ecological Approach to Visual Perception* (2015), affordances characterize what is possible for a user to do with any given design. An important distinction between Gibson and Norman's definitions to the ability for users to perceive these potential uses. Norman emphasizes the importance of perception as key to usability, because if a user cannot perceive the affordance of a given object, then from a design perspective, it doesn't matter whether or not that ability exists as all. For instance, my coffee mug lid might have the affordance of being able to be opened and closed, but if I can't see how that is possible, or if I can't get it to open and close, it doesn't matter whether or not that affordance exists.

There are multiple types of affordances that are at the heart of any discussion of usability and user experience. In addition to perceived affordances, there are hidden affordances, anti-affordances, and false affordances. Respective to the distinction between Gibson and Norman's definitions of affordances, hidden affordances are the actions that are not perceived by the user. So, while they might exist, the user does not know that they do, and so they are not acted upon. There are myriad and exhaustive example of hidden affordances. Maybe recently you have turned on the TV and wanted to watch a show with subtitles and have struggled to find the setting to turn that feature on or off. Or maybe you have gotten a new phone or gotten an update to your existing phone, and then subsequently struggled to change the ringtone, or switch it to airplane mode. Each time the user struggles to locate a setting, or figure out a way to do something, they are running into an aspect of hidden affordances. An even more dramatic example of a hidden affordance is when the user doesn't even know that the affordance exists at all. Recently, I was struggling to figure out when a particularly text message had been sent. The time stamp only seemed to originate at the beginning of a thread and on a single day. I was lamenting this fact to a friend, when she told me that all I had to do was swipe to the left to reveal the specific time stamp. Never would I have guessed this, as it was completely hidden.

Anti-affordances are those affordances that are designed to intentionally prevent a user from acting in a certain way. Speed bumps are an example of this type of affordance as they serve to stop a driver from driving too fast. The screen that pops up when you are closing a file without saving it can be seen as a type of anti-affordance (Norman also calls these lock-outs). Other examples of anti-affordances might be the outcome of an affordance intentionally designed into the product or system, like the handrails on a public bench, which have the affordance of stabilizing a person as they get up, but also prevent people from lying down on the bench itself. More aggressive and controversial measures can be seen in the spikes and bumps that prevent homeless people from sleeping in public spaces, or the knobs on many stairs or benches designed to prevent skaters from using them. There's even a name for this type of measure: *defensive* or *hostile* architecture. In a 2015 *Guardian* article, Alex Andreou—who had once been homeless himself—described the range of these interventions.

> From ubiquitous protrusions on window ledges to bus-shelter seats that pivot forward, from water sprinklers and loud muzak to hard tubular rests, from metal park benches with solid dividers to forests of pointed cement bollards under bridges, urban spaces are aggressively rejecting soft, human bodies.
>
> (Andreou, 2015)

Andreou's article specifically asked the question if homelessness was getting lower, or if cities were just getting better at hiding it through the defensive measures outlined above. In reaction to a London apartment complex that put spikes outside its front doors to dissuade the homeless from taking refuge there, loud and angry public outcry placed a great deal of pressure on the company, who removed them just a few days after installation. As designers, the important and critical question to ask in this circumstances is how the usability of design can be open and inclusive.

False affordances give the perception of an affordance without really doing anything. Often known as placebo buttons in interaction design, these affordances give the illusion of action, without the user's action really having an effect on the outcome. Many people have

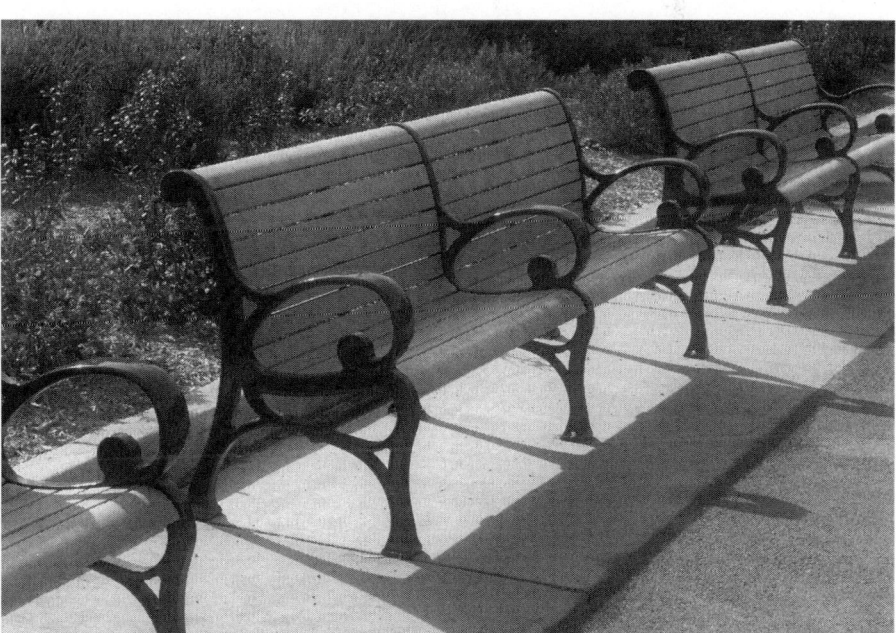

Figure 2.1

Example of anti-affordance intentionally or unintentionally designed into a city bench

Design and usability

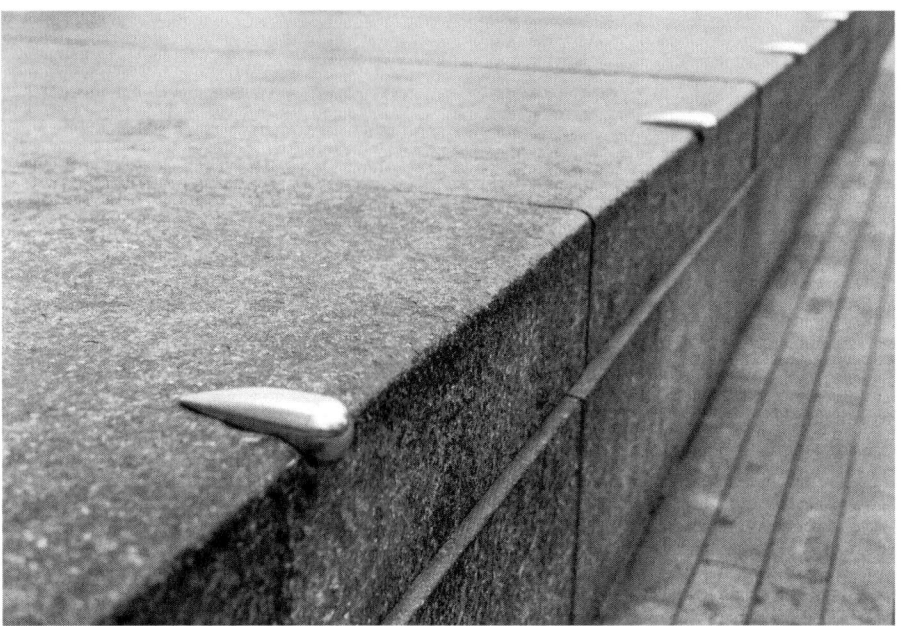

Figure 2.2

Defensive architecture, anti-skateboarding markers

argued that the button on a walk sign is actually a false affordance, and that pushing that button does nothing to actually trigger the signal to change, but only gives the illusion that the button will change the light. A slightly different definition of a false affordance would include the perception of action that is not able to be accomplished, such as stairs that lead to a brick wall, or a wheelchair ramp that ends at stairs.

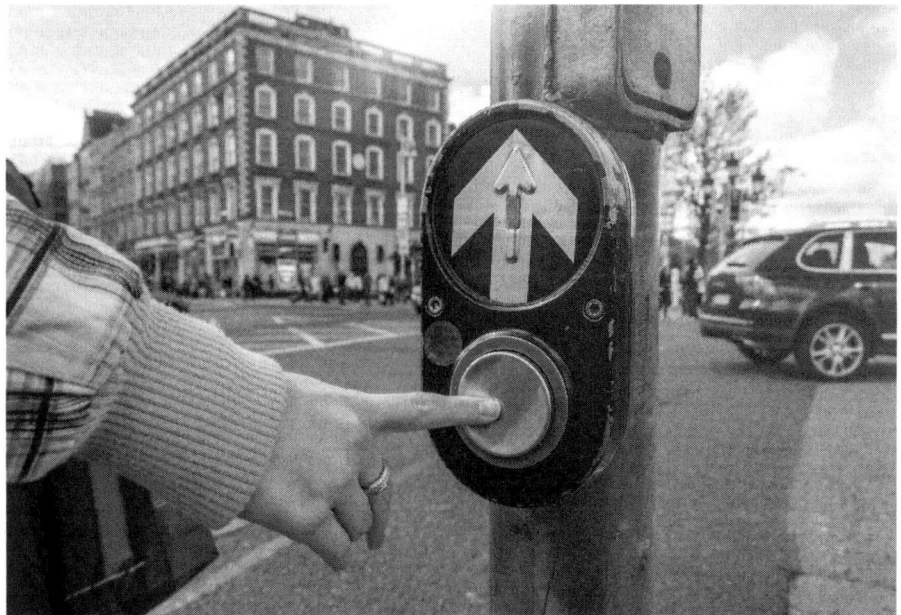

Figure 2.3

The walk signal button is often argued to be a false affordance

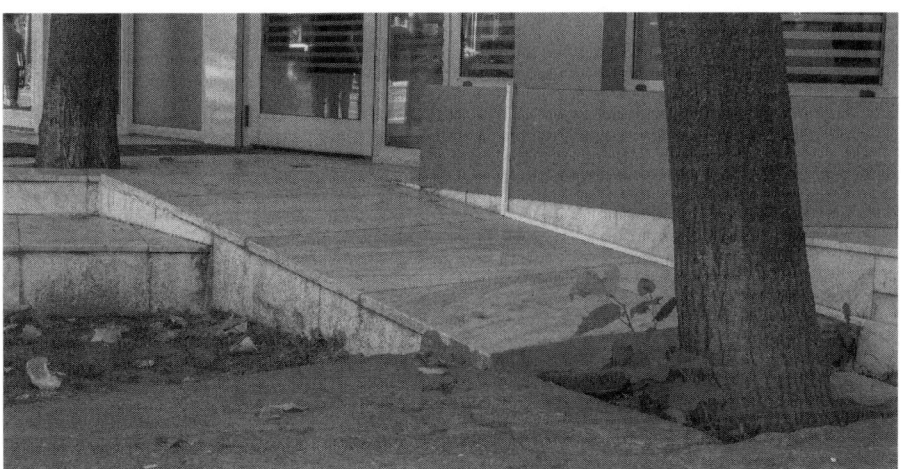

Figure 2.4
Wheelchair ramp that has no way to access it

Affordances are heavily reliant on the user's ability to detect their existence, which is also heavily dependent on the knowledge that a user brings to any given interaction with a design product. We use the example of a pair of scissors to highlight an intuitive object with perceptible affordances built right into them, but if a user has never seen a tool like that, the perception of the affordances necessary to operate it might still be hidden to them. Both the example of the scissors, and earlier with the laptop keyboard rely heavily on a fuzzier version of knowledge in the head, which is a general understanding of how a computer operates and a general set of procedures that are modeled in the user's mind that relate to writing in general. These sets of constructs are called schemas and are "mediated by learned or innate mental structures that organize related pieces of our knowledge" (Strauss and Quinn, 1997, 49). In other words, they are a set of mental constructs that are developed through experiences, cultural attitudes, values, and beliefs. Schemas allow people to apply previous knowledge about a situation to a new, unknown situation. Schemas can be generalized or specific. A good example of this is the classroom—it's a situation that is new to us every semester or year while we are in school, yet we are being introduced to it again and again. When you enter a classroom with a professor for the first time, you are applying the knowledge of previous classroom experiences to guide and inform the way that you act and interact in that new setting. So, if your previous experiences in a classroom dictated that you be silent, raise your hand before talking, and focus on a single right answer, then your behavior in the new classroom would reflect that experience, even if the new professor wanted to encourage a more free-flowing discussion. You would have a general schema related to your behavior in the class that might involve whether or not to talk at all, and then a more specific schema about how to talk—raise your hand. If you only had female teachers in the past, you might have some specific schemas about the way that female teachers instruct, and have a general schema about male teachers that is not informed by direct experience, but maybe by TV shows you have seen, or a book that you have read. And in fact, one of the biggest complaints that college professors have of their new students is that they are constantly wanting to know "what the professor wants" rather than discovering for themselves. But, performing to the standards of the teacher draws on the schema that most students have been encouraged towards in their pre-college education and reinforced through the standardized testing that most students in the US are evaluated upon. These types of expectations become more profound when doing cross-cultural comparisons among students from different countries.

Schemas can be very hard to dislodge, if that is the intent of the design. And often that is why new innovations draw on existing schemas of how something should operate in their early inception, such as when graphical user interfaces (GUI) were first being developed for the desktop computer. While the metaphor of the desktop was first introduced by Xerox PARC in the later 1960s, it was the first Apple Macintosh introduction of files, folders with icons that represented the physical counterparts that brought this metaphor to life. This effectively used the schemas that people had about what a folder or file was for. Users could then apply that previous knowledge to this entirely new environment to decrease the learning curve.

Usability as cultural experience: signs, symbols, and codes

Concepts and theories of usability and user experience increasingly acknowledge *usability as a cultural experience*, and focus on the cultural contexts that might be driving users' wants, needs, and expectations—even discussing the need to "decolonize" design practice (Tunstall, 2013). Clifford Geertz, one of the fathers of modern day anthropological study and methods, explained that:

> man is an animal suspended in webs of significance he himself has spun, I take culture to be those webs, and the analysis of it to be therefore not an experimental science in search of law but an interpretive one in search of meaning.
> (Geertz and Darnton, 1973, 5)

And it is precisely this significance that is driving new forms of design practice, especially as we seek to include people more and more in the design process. In recent years, design anthropology has emerged as an integration between these two distinct fields that seeks to better understand the particularities of cultural attitudes that affect how people understand design in the first place. In their book, *Design Anthropology* (2013), authors Wendy Gunn, Ton Otto, and Rachel Charlotte Smith argue that design and culture are "deeply entangled, complex, and often messy formations and transformations of meanings, spaces, and interactions between people, objects, and histories . . . by designing objects, technologies, and systems, we are in fact designing cultures of the future" (13). Adopting methods from anthropology might help designers navigate some of the messiness of wicked problems in new and interesting ways. Especially as design and collaborations become more global in nature, the schemas held by both designers and users become more complex. To that end, the goal of developing cultural understandings for design and usability is not to group or generalize to such a degree that only the superficial and stereotypical are emphasized, but to look to the distinctiveness of individuals to learn how design can be adaptive to a great many differences in use. The methods used to understand these distinctions will be discussed more later in this section, but the alignment of design and anthropology opens up a parallel conversation about how each have developed under an attitude of superiority and expertise that has to be challenged for mutual learning to truly exist. As outsiders looking in, designing usability with a sensitivity to or focus on culture as a core part of it,

> foster[s] sensitivity to the cultural and socioeconomic contexts and values of local populations to create sustainable and morally justifiable change and to avoid recasting users as natives and replicating forms of colonialism that anthropology was a part of during the twentieth century.
>
> (Gunn, Otto, and Smith, 2013, 13)

In fact, the design anthropologist Elizabeth Tunstall (2013) argues that design as a whole must recast the vision of its own role and relationship with the people who use our products. Building on arguments of Bruce Nussbaum and others, Tunstall questions the motivation of designers that are not dissimilar to those European colonial mindsets driving expansion in the late 19th and early 20th century. Quoting Nussbaum, she questions whether doing "design for good" is not just another form of value-imposition and cultural oppression, especially when designers feel morally supported in the engagement. Design can continue to learn from anthropology in this vein as well. The criticism of the essentially colonial mindset that colored early anthropology and ethnographic research has influenced contemporary methods, especially in way researchers observe and record. As a part of the documentation process, ethnographic researchers include their own reflection of how their participation in the situation, or their recording of the context, might have influenced the outcomes. Not unlike the "reflection in action" that Donald Schön introduced in *The Reflective Practitioner* (1983), this reflection on how the individual designer is interpreting a particular situation is critical for truly understanding and interpreting cultural attitudes in a meaningful way.

References

Andreou, Alex. "Anti-Homeless Spikes: 'Sleeping Rough Opened My Eyes to the City's Barbed Cruelty'." *The Guardian*. February 18, 2015. Retrieved from www.theguardian.com/society/2015/feb/18/defensive-architecture-keeps-poverty-undeen-and-makes-us-more-hostile. Accessed November 30, 2018.
Burns, Brian. *People Want Toast Not Toasters*. Ottawa: BuschekBooks, 2012.
Diffrient, Niels, Tilley, Alvin R., and Bardagly, Joan C. *Humanscale*. New York: Henry Dreyfuss Associates, 1974.
Dreyfuss, Henry. *Designing for People*. New York: Simon & Schuster, 1955.
Geertz, Clifford and Darnton, Robert. *The Interpretation of Cultures*. New York: Basic Books, 1973.
Gibson, James J. *The Ecological Approach to Visual Perception*. Abingdon, UK: Taylor & Francis, 2015. Classic Edition.

Gunn, Wendy, Otto, Ton, and Smith, Rachel C., editors. *Design Anthropology: Theory and Practice*. London: Bloomsbury, 2013.

Lupton, Ellen. *Beautiful Users: Designing for People*. New York: Princeton Architectural Press, 2014.

Norman, Donald. *The Design of Everyday Things*. New York: Basic Books, 2013.

Poggenpohl, S.H. "Time for Change: Building a Design Discipline." *Design Integrations: Research and Collaboration*. Bristol, UK: Intellect Books, 2009.

Schön, Donald. *The Reflective Practitioner: How Professionals Think in Action*. New York: Basic Books, 1983.

Simon, Herbert. *The Sciences of the Artificial*. Cambridge, MA: MIT Press, 1996.

Strauss, Claudia and Quinn, Naomi. *A Cognitive Theory of Cultural Meaning*. Cambridge: Cambridge University Press, 1997.

Tunstall, Elizabeth. "Decolonizing Design Innovation: Design Anthropology, Critical Anthropology, and Indigenous Knowledge." In Wendy Gunn, Ton Otto, and Rachel C. Smith, editors. *Design Anthropology: Theory and Practice*. London: Bloomsbury, 2013.

3 Experiential and adaptive design thinking

As an interweaving between the physical, cognitive, and cultural, the complexity of user experience necessitates an equally deliberate strategy of design thinking that aims to gather a more complete understanding of the dimensions driving behavior. Traditionally, usability and user experience focused on the visible manifestations of culture and cognitive influences, rather than the root causes of those behaviors.

Research methods for usability and user experience seek to look at the user experience from a number of different perspectives as a comparative study. They also seek out a more participatory interaction with the users, where not only can the designer observe how a person behaves under certain circumstances (or just in everyday life) but also how they are thinking, processing, and feeling during that same situation. And possibly more importantly, they can reframe how we are designing in the first place, by giving the user more agency and involvement in the design and development process. In their book *How Users Matter*, Nelly Oudshoorn and Trevor Pinch (2003) argue that the role of users has moved past that of passive recipient of technology and towards a more active participant in its creation (9). We could make the same argument of design in general, although as argued in Part 2 of this book, design and technology are inextricably and reciprocally linked. One simple thing that we might do in the research process is a simple renaming of the user as a reader or interpreter, which emphasizes the interpretive nature of design interactions.

Since so much of the examination of usability and user experience is derived from behaviors and use—which have complex and multifaceted reasons driving them, both the research and ideation inherent in designing for usability needs to take a mixed-methods approach. As designers, we are ultimately seeking to understand why a person finds satisfaction or joy in using a product, but these reasons have many dimensions which means that we always need to look at it from different angles. The research methods below are diverse in their process and methods, but the hope is that through the critical use of mixed methods, the designer can gain a more holistic, diverse, and comparative understanding of the factors driving how and why people interact with design experiences in the way that they do.

Design research methods: mixed methods research

Mixed methods research is a particularly strong method for usability-based research because of the complexity of the research being conducted. It is a way to validate the research findings through the triangulation of the data collected. Triangulation can strengthen research findings by collecting and interpreting data from multiple perspectives and sources (Crouch and Pearce, 2012). It is also particularly relevant because some of the data collected can be scientific in nature. For instance, eye tracking software and data collection can be useful as part of a study trying to understand where people look in a room or on a screen. It won't tell you why on its own, and so being able to further understand that dimension through surveys or interviews deepens the research study and gives more "fruit" for designers to work with in the design implementation phase. Mixed methods have historically been focused on different methods of qualitative research, but combining methods from quantitative and qualitative research can yield even richer results because of the diversity of outcomes for comparison. As Crouch and Pearce (2012) further argue "This mixing of data can occur at all stages of the research: by combining quantitative and qualitative approaches to data collection . . . and by using quantitative and qualitative tools for analysis or presenting research" (130). Below are some of the methods that you might choose from in a mixed-methods approach to usability.

Experimental and quasi-experimental research

After making such a case for bringing more qualitative perspectives into the examination and understanding of usability, to start off the research methods portion with an explanation of experimental research might seem contradictory. But especially as a first foray into research and involving people in the research process—and in considering the trajectory of usability studies, it might start to make sense. In the article, "Design Discipline vs. Design Science," Nigel Cross (2001) states that "A desire to 'scientise' design can be traced back to ideas in the twentieth century modern movement of design" (49). Considering the roots of this, the potential for design to gain credibility through more scientific studies is not surprising. The idea of the sciences as searching for "truth" is attractive to the fields of study—both for the undisputed nature of the goal, but also because of the difficulty with arguing against findings that have been deemed as such. But even when acknowledging that in dealing with wicked problems, there is no single truth, experimental and quasi-experimental research can still be valuable as a research method and paradigm for design research. As a quantitative method, experimental research can be valuable when "you need to generate research data that can lead to conclusions that are generalizable across a large population" (Crouch and Pearce, 2012, 69). In experimental research, a great deal of time is spent upfront in the design of the test, and in trying to control the variables, in order to isolate the cause of the problem. When engaging in true experimental research, researchers will use random sampling—picking from a random group of people who all might share a specific quality (a level of familiarity with the environment you are testing, for example) in order to validate the outcomes of the test and avoid skewing the results. For example, usability tests in the technology sector have often tried to isolate what is clear and confusing about an interface by giving a sample population the same test and seeing where mistakes are made, such as confusing one button for another one, or not understanding the purpose of a particular feature. In this test, participants might be given the same task or goal, or even the same set of procedures. The specificity of the test directly aligns with what the researcher is trying to discover. Experimental research can be particularly valuable in looking at the functionality of technological solutions and in adding and removing variables that might change the outcome of the test results. It can be a way to get to some truth in terms of technological systems.

Ethnographic research

Ethnographic research is a fundamental part of anthropology and seeks to understand the particularities and meanings behind the behaviors that are exhibited in a culture, situation, or environment. One of the main outcomes of ethnographic research is what is termed the thick description—a term popularized by Clifford Geertz (1977) and borrowed from the British philosopher Gilbert Ryle and referencing a detailed account of the research that then can be coded and examined to draw larger conclusions about the people involved. As Geertz also noted, the thick description is meant to help the researcher interpret (or avoid misinterpretation) of certain cultural phenomena she is observing throughout the research. Building further on Ryle's example of the wink, Geertz states that:

> the difference, however un-photographable, between a twitch and a wink is vast; as anyone unfortunate enough to have had the first taken for the second knows. The winker is communicating, and indeed communicating in a quite precise and special way: (1) deliberately, (2) to someone in particular, (3) to impart a particular message, (4) according to a socially established code, and (5) without cognizance of the rest of the company.
>
> (6)

In other words, the action of winking can be interpreted in a myriad of ways, just as a mistake in selecting the correct button, or going to the wrong floor in a building, and so it is up to the ethnographic researcher to try to understand the internal and external conditions that might be contributing to the misinterpretations of the user. Ethnographic research is an holistic approach, in that it is focused on gaining a comprehensive understanding of a situation. It is also explicitly "committed to uncovering and depicting indigenous meanings. The object of participation is ultimately to get close to those studied as a way of understanding what their experiences and activities mean to them" (Emerson et al., 2011, x). Through ethnographic research, conclusions are always gathered from direct evidence. But at the same time, ethnographic research also accepts and integrates the perspective of the researcher as fundamental to the conclusions that are drawn. A key part of this research is the creation and collection of field notes. These field notes—a result of observations and interviews, are key components of the ethnographic process. As Emerson explains in *Writing Ethnographic Fieldnotes* (2011), the very activity of note-taking—a core method in ethnographic research—puts the researcher directly in the middle of the research process because of the decisions to include, exclude information, write down their own interpretations of the actions and activities in the observed environment or situation.

Because of its fundamental attempt to gain a holistic understanding of a community, culture, or phenomena, ethnographic research combines different methods of observation, interviews, and participation towards that goal. Through a method called participant-observation, ethnographic research is based on a prolonged engagement with the group or environment being studied. This combination of methods, or fieldwork, can often take years to build up the trust and relationships necessary to engage in meaningful interactions. In most practical application of this method—design in particular—that timeline needs adjustment, but the basic perspectives can stay in place. The comparison of observation in tandem with interviews can provide a richer understanding of the motivating forces driving the needs and wants of user groups. Through participant-observation, the researcher is operating as both insider and outsider. At times, the researcher is simply observing a situation, and recording, interpreting and trying to making meaning of it. At other times, the researcher is a part of the situation, and might be fully immersed in the workings of the group, making notes and doing the interpretation at a later date. As mentioned earlier, a key to the way that the researcher observes and records is in the acknowledgement of how they are affecting the situation, by their presence and interaction with the subjects.

Conducting field visits

When conducting participant-observations, it's important that you are able to visit the site multiple times, at different times of the day, days of the week, situations. This will depend on what you are trying to observe.

1. Choose a sequence of days and times that you think will help you gain insight into the series of field visits. Depending on what you are studying, it might be helpful to pick the same day/time over a number of weeks OR a different day but the same time OR a series of different situations that are somehow connected. The main purpose is to be able to compare different situations for patterns and anomalies.
2. Choose a good location (or two): Where is there a lot of activity? Where can you comfortably sit for a while and hear and see details? If you are trying to observe without intervening, where can you be somewhat inconspicuous? If you are engaging with subjects, where will both of you be comfortable and what seems natural?
3. Observe and record what is happening around you (1–2 hours). Take notes with as many details as possible (these are your jottings). Write down the

actual conversations that you hear as summaries or verbatim. If you are in a public space, or have the permission of the place you are doing the research and the participants, considering video and/or audio recording the scene. Refrain from using language that infers a judgement (i.e. "A strange looking woman walked up") in these jottings. The elements that you should include in these notes (somehow separating):

- Descriptive observations: These should only be what you can see, smell, taste, hear.
- Initial interpretations/analysis: What do you think this means? Why? Make sure that you are connecting directly to what you are observing. These can also include questions and thoughts about how you might verify your initial assumption of meaning. These should be included in the margins of your notes and clearly separate from the recordings.
- Reflective questions/notes for yourself in moving forward (what is working well about your location? What might you need to change?) How do you think your presence in the space possibly changed how people behaved?

4. Consider a way to participate/interact. If you are doing this observation in a public space, you might need to approach people more casually, if this is a structured observation, consider how you want to start your interview and/or "break the ice." What might you want to understand better from a vendor, a customer, or someone else? Write down a few questions that you might want to get at (but you won't necessarily ask them directly)—how might you get at the answers in an indirect way?

5. Have at least one or two casual conversations (30+ minutes). Use the same format as you did for your observational note-taking (description, interpretation, and reflection) to record your experience here. Try to be natural in starting the conversation. If a vendor, maybe you ask about some of the products—if another customer, you might do the same. Don't be discouraged if you are not successful at first, just try again and learn from that experience (and that experience itself might be telling.) After each conversation, take a moment to write down as much specific detail from the interaction (specific words/language that stood out, etc.) as possible. Include some of the environmental details and what was going on while you were interacting. Record how long you talked and anything else that seems relevant.

6. Write a descriptive narrative of the observation. This should follow the same structure as your jottings and should happen shortly after the observation so that your initial experience is still "fresh." Make sure any analysis is supported by your observations and should include questions/ideas for further validation. Include a reflection on how you conducted the research, how you may have influenced the situation, and what you might do differently next time.

Observational research

In user experience research, observing is a fundamental and core concept to the process of usability testing, and can be equally as valuable as part of a controlled, experimental research project or a more open-ended ethnographic process. Observational research is as it sounds—conducting observations of perceived phenomena throughout the research process. At its best, observational research can highlight patterns of behavior or idiosyncrasies that would normally be overlooked. But if not done intentionally and with purpose, observational research can also use a small, individual observation and generalize without the necessary background to back it up. Jeff Sauro and James Lewis, authors of *Quantifying the User Experience: Practical Statistics for User Research* (2012) argue that there are four types of observational research with varying levels of participation on the part of the research. The first is complete observation, whereby the researcher attempts to minimize her impact on the activities of those being observed by being as inconspicuous as possible. The second is the observer as participant, where the researcher starts to interact with those being observed, whilst still retaining the role of research and researched. The third calls on the researcher to become more involved, acting in a more immersive capacity with those being observed. And the fourth and final is a complete participant where there is no distinction between the observer and the observed. Each of these levels of participation in the observation process should be considered in light of the type of information that you are trying to gather and the value of those roles in the ability to gain true and authentic insight. Sometimes, being a complete participant can hinder your ability to observe objectively. For instance, if you work at the place where you are conducting the observations, it might be difficult to truly remove yourself from the role of the employee and gain the necessary insight to draw objective conclusions.

Sampling observed phenomena

Sampling can be an interesting component of observational research and a way to quantify and elicit patterns from what oftentimes can be broad observations of behaviors. As Jeanne Altman, author of the article "Observational Study of Behavior" (1974) indicates, sampling occurs, or should occur, "whenever a student of social behavior cannot continuously observe and record all of the behavior of all of the member of the social group" (229). In sampling, a specific type of data is collected from the observed study. Altman further distinguishes between types of behaviors that might be recorded as events or states. Events are behaviors that happen in a moment, while states are behaviors that are more static (231). For example, the activity of sitting is an event because it happens in an instant, but being seated is a state in that it happens for a duration of time. Both of these types of information can be recorded during the sampling activity, but need to be tied directly to the question trying to be answered. For instance, if a researcher is trying to sample the types of monetary transactions happening at a local flea market, then the event of the card being swiped might be less important than the state of the customer using a credit card to pay. On the other hand, if the researcher is trying to better understand why certain vendors have more success encouraging customers to purchase more than one item at their stand, she might record a series of events such as each time the vendor suggests another item to add to the customer's order, rather than the number of items each customer buys. There are two distinct types of sampling: time-sampling and event-sampling. Time-sampling refers to the recording of any number of events or states over a certain period of time. So, a researcher at a flea market might sit in one place for ten or 15 minutes (or longer) and record one or more behaviors (events or states) that happen within that time period. Time-sampling is particularly useful when trying to better understand how a behavior might be linked to certain periods of time, times of the day, length of time it takes to accomplish a task or behavior or some other time-related phenomena. Event-sampling refers to the tracking of a single or series of events (or states) over a prolonged period of time or space. For example, traveling throughout the flea market and recording each vendor that takes credits cards, or the types of behaviors that are happening at a single stand throughout the course of the day. Again, the type of sampling should be dictated by the type of information that the researcher is trying to gather.

Surveys and interviews

The core of participant-observation is the integration of the observation in conjunction with interacting with and talking to the people who are being studied. Surveys and interviews are ways to interact with these participants, and to compare what is being observed with participants' own interpretation of that same behavior—not just what they do, but possibly why they do it, what values they hold and what is significant to them about the behavior itself. From casual conversations to more formal interviews, engaging users directly is critical to the design research process—especially around issues of usability. Most ethnographic researchers suggest the importance of building trust with people by engaging first in casual conversations to find common ground, and for the researcher to focus on better understanding the "language" of the people whom they will be engaging more deeply. Semi-structured discussions or interviews house a combination of pre-formed questions, but also allow for fluidity throughout the course of the discussion. In *The Design of Everyday Things* (2013), Don Norman introduces the Japanese strategy of the "Five Whys" as a semi-structured interview technique aimed at understanding the root cause of the design problem. By asking "why" in response to a series of questions, the interviewer gains a deeper understanding of the causes driving the behavior or problem. Norman's example of the investigation of a plane crash is as follows:

- Q1: Why did the plane crash? A1: Because it was in an uncontrollable dive.
- Q2: Why didn't the plane recover from the dive? A2: Because the pilot failed to initiative a timely recovery.

- Q3: Why was that? A3: Because he might have been unconscious.
- Q4: Why was that? A4: We don't know. We need to find out.

(166)

By continuing to ask why, Norman argues, the investigator moved beyond the simple explanation—one that usually involves stopping once human error is detected—and trying to identify what else might have been faulty about the situation. The Five Whys is equally as useful in situations where the problem is more behavioral in nature. Imagine asking the flea market vendor why she doesn't take credit cards. Her answer might be that they have never done it before. Asking why they have never done it before, or why never having done it before is the reason not to do it now, might elicit a deeper, more interesting response to the questions being answered. One of the most important aspects of these more organic conversations and interviews is to have an idea of the type of information you are hoping to get, but also being open to the conversation going in directions that you have not anticipated, but that might be equally as compelling and insightful. In *Doing Research in Design* (2012), Crouch and Pearce argue that a key component to effective interviewing is for the interviewer to minimize their influence over the conversation itself, and act more as listener than interrogator. "While interviews should be organized to enable a focus on issues that you want to explore, the questions can be little more than prompts or cues to open up opportunities for talk" (113). To achieve this goal, interviewers should refrain from talking a lot, or leading the interviewee. Their responses to questions should be encouraging and focus on drawing out elaborations from the interviewee, rather than steering the conversation in a preconceived direction.

More formal interviews take the form of surveys. Surveys are excellent tools for getting immediately quantifiable information and potentially doing a quick sample of attitudes or opinions on a situation and problem. Sometimes entire research projects are based on surveys, but for usability testing surveys are most valuable as a comparative tool mixed with observations and discussions. Surveys can have ask quantitative questions, such as "Overall, how would you rate your experience at the farmers' market?" and they can ask for more qualitative responses, such as "Describe your favorite thing about coming to the flea market." This is also known as asking closed (yes/no) and open-ended questions (explanation of something) as a way to gather different types of information. Surveys, or survey instruments, can not only ask people what they think about an issue, but can also embed in them an opportunity for participants to show you what they think about an issue. They can be imaginative, creative, and fun. For example, a survey could be designed to ask people to demonstrate how they would rearrange their office in the most ideal way—using small prototypes to do that. They could ask participants to include a memory on a map of a small city as a way to survey the public spaces that have personal meaning to people; or they could ask participants to paint a swatch of color according to their emotional state in different parts of a gym. Surveys can also be highly active and participatory. In one specific example conducted with the American Institute of Architects in Raleigh, North Carolina, participants were asked to map their daily routes according to the transportation method that they used daily (walking, bike riding,

Experiential and adaptive design thinking

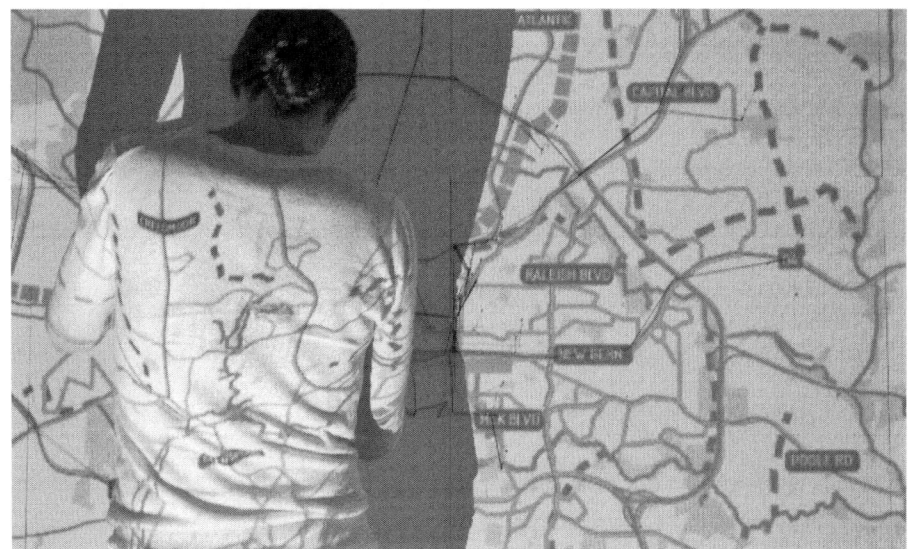

Figure 3.1
Participants map their daily routes

driving, taking public transportation, etc.) and the routes that they took. Using string, and pins, participants overlaid these routes over a projected image of the city. Through the accumulation of participants routes, patterns immediately emerged which showed how and where people were traveling on a daily basis. The projected map then shifted to include existing and proposed transportation plans for the city over the next five to ten years. These new maps then allowed the users to compare how their routes and methods

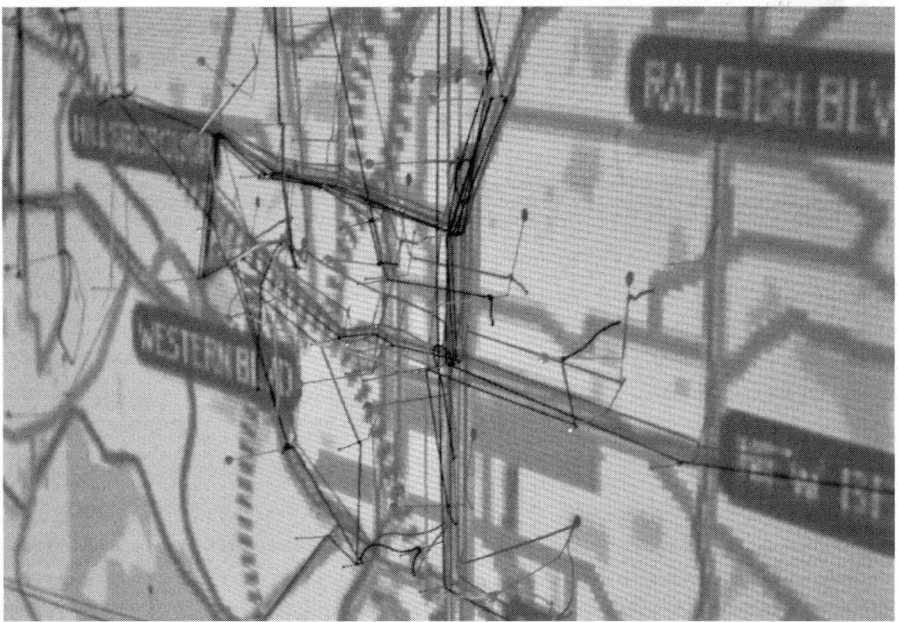

Figure 3.2
Detail of travel routes

Experiential and adaptive design thinking

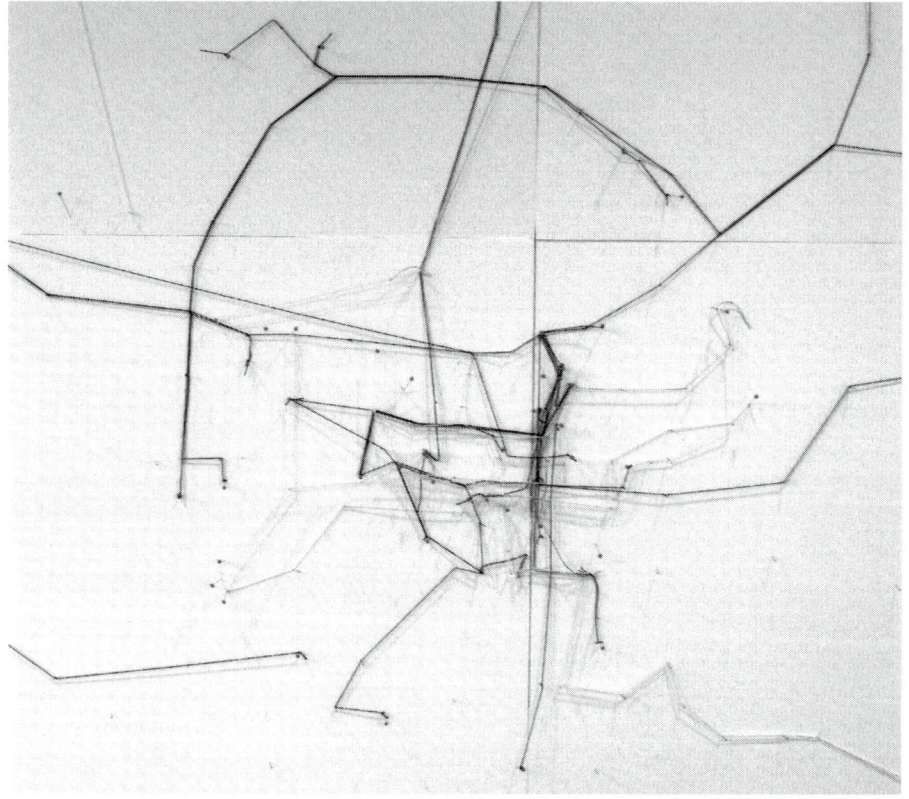

Figure 3.3
Accumulation of routes

aligned (or didn't align) with the plans the city was preparing to implement. In usability studies, surveys are an excellent way to compare the information that you are observing within the usability test to what people say they are thinking or feeling—in other words, to compare the visible with the invisible.

Designing a survey instrument

Surveys don't always have to take the form of asking how people feel about a design or a space. In fact, oftentimes having people demonstrate how they feel can put them at ease, and offer more unique and surprising insights into user behavior. The design of surveys can also serve as a creative activity to expand the ways that we gather information, and even be used to better understand how people might interact with the survey itself—what is confusing, what they are hesitant to answer or offer up information on, what makes them self-conscious—all information that may or may not be immediately relevant to the bigger project, but is vital information for making better and more effective information-gathering tools.

Below is an excerpt from an assignment given as a part of a First Year Design Thinking course at North Carolina State University. Students were first asked to observe human behavior surrounding a particular design experience, which included everything from dining experiences, to study experiences to retail experiences to health and exercise experiences. After identifying what were some wicked problems that arose from the observations, students then designed a survey instrument to compare and confirm the conclusions that they had drawn as a result of their observations.

In designing their survey instrument, students were instructed to engage in the following steps:

1. Do some additional research to test the conclusions you drew as a result of your observational exercise. These could include statistics (i.e. how many people ride their bikes in Raleigh, how much has the biking population grown over the past 2–3 years? How many people drive, vs. walk vs. ride the campus bus?); or more theoretical research such as human behavior, design theories, urban planning, etc. or collecting data on good solutions to the problem that you have identified (walkable cities, bike friendly cities, etc.).
2. Brainstorm a series of questions and issues related to this wicked problem and your additional research—things that you would like to know about the object and how people use it. How might you find out the answers that you didn't get through just observation and asking questions?
3. Brainstorm a number of different types of survey instruments and/or ways to gather the information that you have decided that you need to get. First and foremost, consider the type of experience you want the user to have and how that is aligned with the research topic you are gathering information on. Should the experience be fun? Serious? A learning experience (for the user)? Creative in nature? Consider how the experience is appropriate and relevant to your wicked problem?
4. Design a tool (or toolkit) that will help you further understand the problem. Consider the following:

    1. Do you want the users to know that they are giving your information or do you want them to just go about their business as they normally would?
    2. How are you capturing the information? Do people leave a "mark" on it? Does the tool automatically capture certain types of information?
    3. How engaging is the research tool? Do you want people to "play" with it? Pass it along to another person?

5. Pilot test your survey instrument on a minimum of five users. Record the results as both raw data (i.e. videotaping, image capture, etc.) and interpretive means (i.e. note-taking, diagramming, etc.).

Experiential and adaptive design thinking

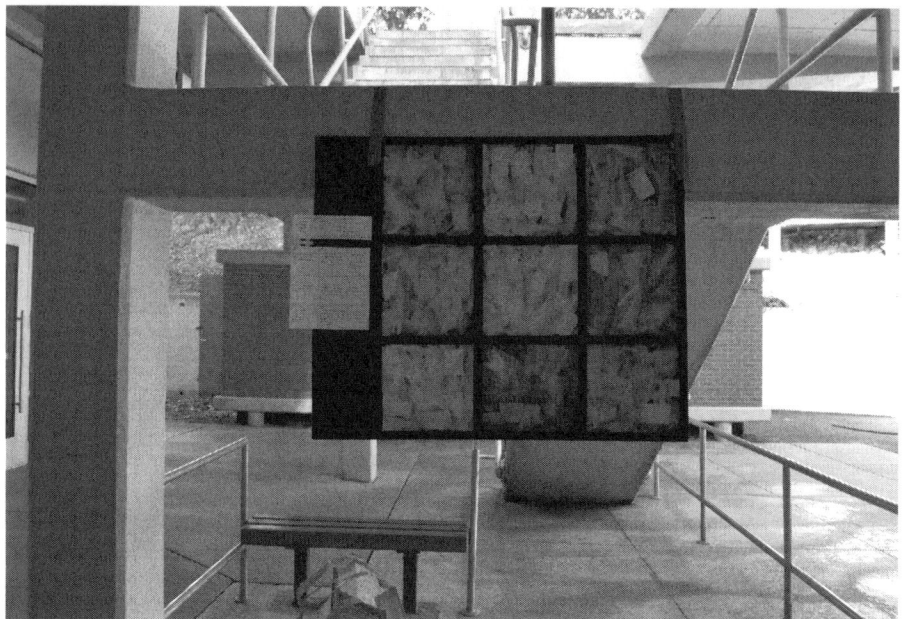

Figure 3.4

This paint swatch survey from Freshman design students Tara Lavrik and Jennifer Liu asked visitors to a gym to indicate their comfort level with certain areas of the gym using different intensities of color. The additive process provided a cumulative gauge on how people felt overall about certain zones. Image courtesy of Lavrik/Liu

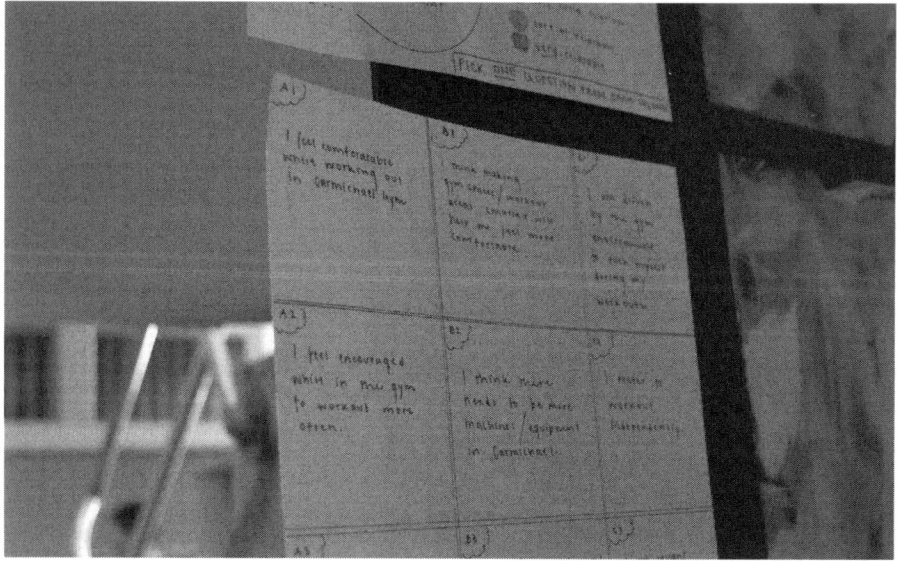

Figure 3.5

Detail of questions. Image courtesy of Lavrik/Liu

Experiential and adaptive design thinking

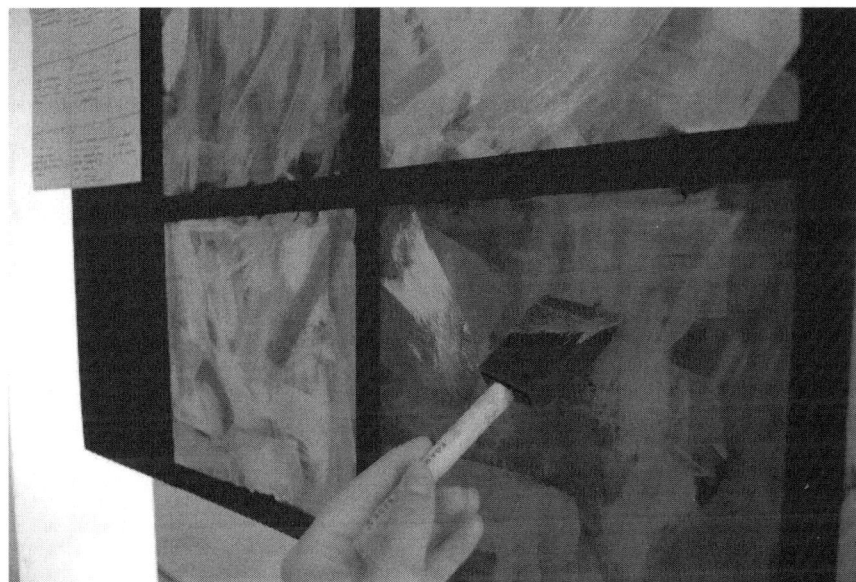

Figure 3.6
Participant contributing to the survey. Image courtesy of Lavrik/Liu

Conducting a usability pilot test

Usability tests are traditionally geared towards seeing how users interact with a design object—where they make mistakes, what is clear and unclear, etc. But they can also be used to see where people are confused, or need help and how they ask for that help, or what their emotional state is during the test itself.

The main focus of usability is in helping users accomplish goals. Don Norman (2013) describes the two main functions of usability as discoverability and understandability. The goal of a usability test might be to test theories of affordances (both perceived and unforeseen) as well as visual cues, procedures, emotional states, and many other instances of that experience.

While usability tests have traditionally been focused on digital and virtual environments, the principles are equally as valuable for more tangible design experiences (using a blender, for instance). If you are deciding what you want to study, select something that is complex enough to provide you a depth of study, but not so complex that your users need prior training just to understand what its even accomplishing (like GIS software, for instance.)

The specific steps in designing a good usability test are:

- Depending on what you want to learn, you may give the participants a specific task, or simply ask them to fiddle around (or browse around). Give

(continued)

> *(continued)*
>
> the participant a task of some sort. Provide enough structure so that they have some basic idea about what they are doing.
>
> - Clearly identifying what you want to learn from the study.
> - Clearly stating the task that your study participants will be doing.
>
> - Control your sample population. There needs to be intentional similarity or range of difference. Will they all be of the same general age? Will you do different ages? Will you identify a common demographic and use them for your sample?
> - Outline how information will be captured and recorded. You should be present at the study (though you can choose to be visible or invisible). Some options for recording are:
>
>   - Taking notes, images and pictures.
>   - Recording the event through video or audio.
>   - Have the participants talk out loud about what they are doing as they are doing it (this is a great way to identify stages of action, or what is perceptible and hidden, and what their emotional state is while they're doing the activity).
>   - It's good to use mixed methods here, so including a raw recording of the event as well as your own note-taking.

At the core of design research for usability is the concept of using a variety of methods (or mixed methods) to compare different aspects of the user experience. Specifically, to attempt to have people not only explain their behaviors or experiences, but also to demonstrate how their attitudes manifest into those observable behaviors.

Comparative design thinking methods and processes: including time and context to understand the complexity of user experience

User journey mapping and storyboarding

Journey mapping is a method often associated with user experience design and digital and web design. But journey mapping can be equally effective (and interesting) when used in the context of usability for physical environments and other design experiences. Journey mapping is often separated from experience mapping, but doesn't have to be. Experience mapping is one part of the user journey and so the integration of the two can be quite beneficial in creating a more holistic and comparative journey. Journey mapping is also reliant on the development of personas and scenarios that were discussed in Chapter 1 in order to encourage a concrete and specific experience. Because we have discussed the importance of thinking more holistically and comparatively about user experience in this chapter, journey mapping should necessarily be done for multiple user types as a way to evaluate the different ways that people currently or might interact the design experience.

In thinking about journey mapping in usability, a key part of the goal is to imagine, visualize, and anticipate user experiences through the design process based on the upfront usability research that was conducted. Journey mapping can be used in one of two ways: (1) as a way to examine the details of a current situation, such as how people currently navigate through a museum exhibit; or (2) as a way to articulate and speculate how someone might move through a proposed design environment or system, like how you might want visitors to navigate through a museum exhibit that you are designing. Journey mapping examines each step of a process or an experience. Journey maps are usually organized according to a sequence of steps through a process, but can be organized in any number of sequences. Most journey maps include actions, decisions, needs, wants, objectives, and emotional states. By pinpointing where a user must make a decisions (i.e. should I stop and read the introductory panel for this exhibit?) the designer can make better decisions about what to emphasize and how to encourage a certain sequence of steps. Conversely, it can also be used as a comparative tool to imagine many different paths and experiences through a single design environment. Megan Grocki, experience strategy director at Mad*Pow argues that journey mapping must have:

- Personas: the main characters that illustrate the needs, goals, thoughts, feelings, opinions, expectations, and pain points of the user;
- Timeline: a finite amount of time (e.g. one week or one year) or variable phases (e.g. awareness, decision-making, purchase, renewal);
- Emotion: peaks and valleys illustrating frustration, anxiety, happiness etc.;
- Touchpoints: customer actions and interactions with the organization. This is the WHAT the customer is doing; and
- Channels: where interaction takes place and the context of use (e.g. website, native app, call center, in-store). This is the WHERE they are interacting (2014).

In essence, there are any number of ways to create a user journey map, but the key aspects include what the user is doing and how they might be understanding or feeling about what they are doing. Using the example of the exhibit, this first high level behavior might include such activities as doing research about the museum exhibit, arriving at the museum, entering the exhibit, stopping at the various stations, leaving the exhibit, and sharing their experience with others. Expanding these high level behaviors beyond the immediate exhibit to include research and sharing their experience with others are opportunities for the designer to think about the larger system of what they are designing. What might we do to promote the exhibit, how do we want visitors to share their experience with others? What channels or opportunities might we give them to share their experience or to capture what is shared? The next part of journey mapping is to outline all of the touchpoints that a person would encounter throughout the experience. So, the website they might come across in their research, buying tickets for the exhibit, the introductory panel wall, where they might sit, etc. Another important component is to align these behaviors and touchpoint with the goals that the visitor or user might have. Why are they there? What do they want to get out of the exhibit? How does this align with the touchpoints? And finally, consider the emotions that your users might be experiencing as they move through these states and touchpoints. Are there places where what they will be encountering will be difficult or complex? How might the design address these issues of complexity?

Often, the next step of journey mapping is storyboarding. Storyboarding is a more specific type of journey mapping, in that it looks at the specific activities of the user with a designed object. So, in the museum setting, the storyboard would be more attached to the design of the exhibit itself, with potential content, spaces of interaction, etc. In a project (like the exhibit) that has multiple dimensions, a storyboard would be used for each specific type of interaction. Storyboards are especially helpful for interactions design, and when a variety of paths and interactions are possible. They can help manage all of the different variables and give some concrete performance. Much of the literature on storyboarding comes from the animation and film world as the method was originally developed as a sort of visual outline of the underlying story. In *About Face 3: The Essentials of Interaction Design*, authors Alan Cooper, Robert Reimann, and David Cronin (2007) argue that:

> Interaction design narratives are quite similar to the comic-book-like sequences called storyboards that are used in the motion picture industry. They share two significant characteristics: plot and brevity. Just as storyboards breathe life into a movie script, design solutions should be created and rendered to follow a plot—a story.
>
> (103)

And because all design—from buildings to parks to websites—are essentially interactive (as in, people use them and interact with them in some way) it is applicable to think about these tools being used to envision all types of design experiences. It is in these stories that the designer can imagine a variety and diversity of contexts that the design might exist with, or be used by. In architectural design, the format of the storyboard might expand beyond the traditional user experience storyboard to include more of the physical context in which the design will exist. Because of the importance of time and the natural environment, using storyboards in architectural design might well include more evaluation of the impact of time, environment (weather, light, temperature) on the physical structure and how that might impact the use of the space by people as a result.

In the Department of Architecture at the Universitas Indonesia, two professors brought storyboarding into the architecture studio as a way to reconcile the way that students were capturing and interpreting the urban environment. In the Urban Walk Project, students:

> are expected to learn how to communicate events and human activities unfold in space and time through different kinds of creative representations of the architectural setting. They also asked them to demonstrate appropriate ability in documenting, gathering, and filtering information from urban spaces.
>
> (2)

Specifically, students use the storyboard as a formative tool to help organize and plan their experience to a local market. "Treating a storyboard as visual plan could give

Experiential and adaptive design thinking

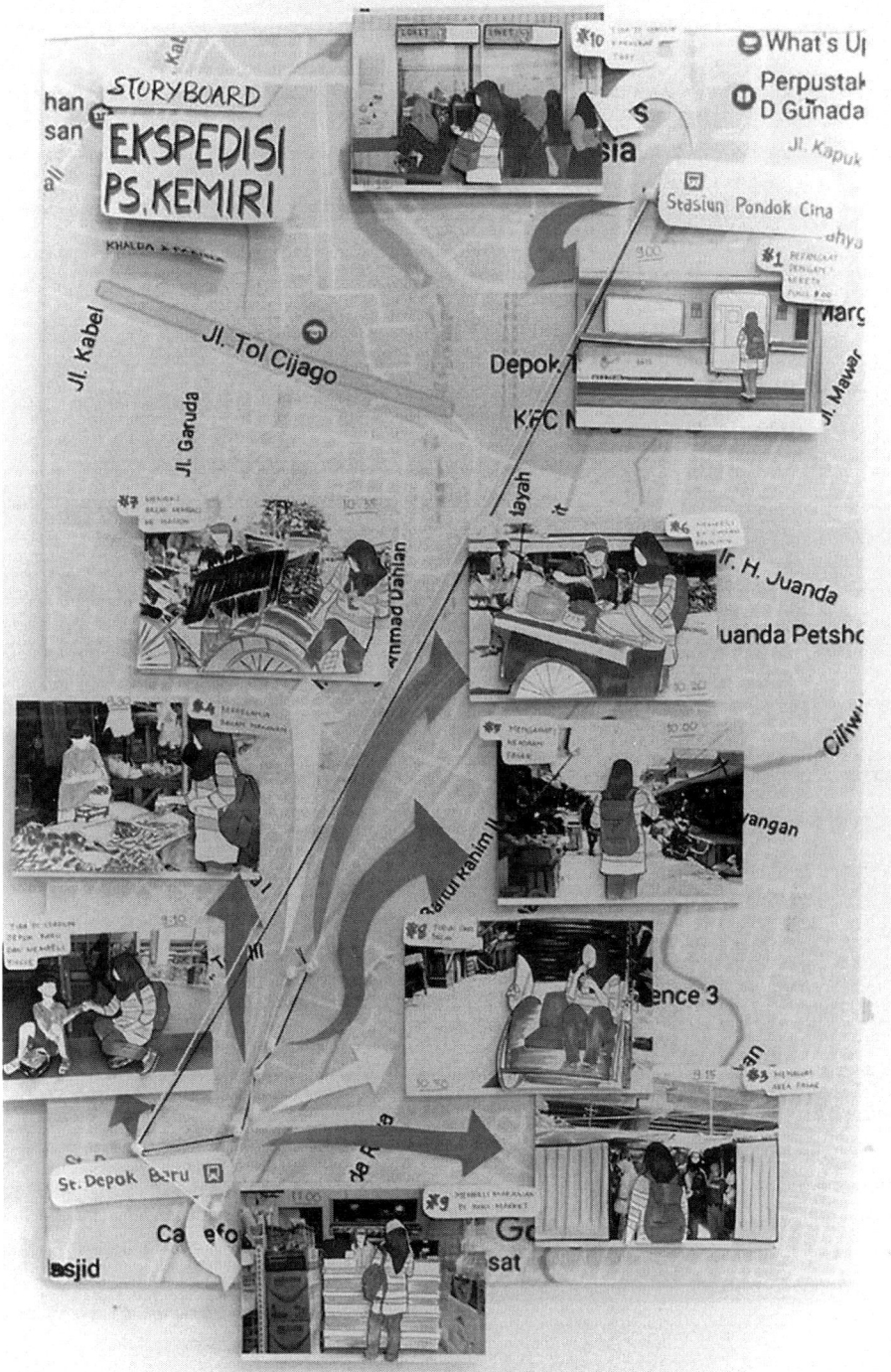

Figures 3.7–3.8

Examples of student storyboards of their observations of a market in Indonesia. Image courtesy of Arif Wahid and Paramita Atmodiwirjo

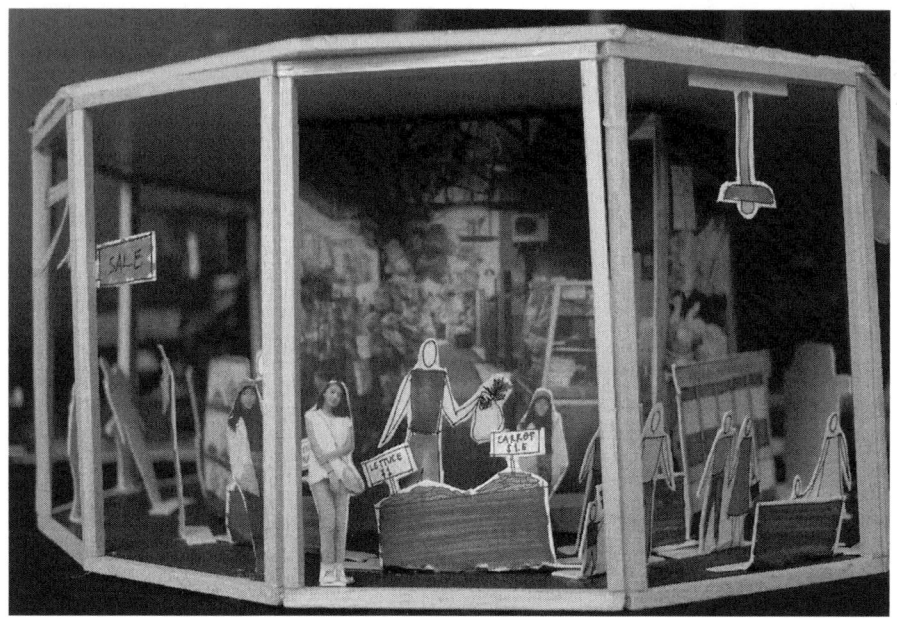

an adequate direction on what to do or what kind of escapade is there going to be experienced while giving the character enough room for improvisation in the upcoming events" (3). Students created both two and three-dimensional storyboards and were confronted through the experience with how space and time interrelate within the build environment. The storyboard annunciated that tension by encouraging the students to capture a single moment in time, but also to think about how each frame led into or related to the next. As a dynamic experience, the project also encouraged students to capture and process their field observations in more nuanced ways.

Prototyping

Prototyping can be a key way for designers to encourage users to interact with their designs in low-stakes environments that designers can learn from, and develop better design solutions as a result. Chris Meers of *The UX Review* argues for the benefits of prototyping to:

> [h]elp identify usability issues before going to code; Get early user feedback; Observe how users want to interact with your design; To work out complex functionality or screen flows; To help begin to define the interaction design; Faster to create than fully coded solutions (front and back end).
>
> (2013)

Prototypes can be full-scale or miniaturized version of the existing. Industrial designers might make an actual physical representation of the design object, interaction designers might make a paper prototype of an interface that they are creating, and architects and landscape architects might create a model. Each of these forms has slightly different outcomes in terms of what the design is attempting to achieve and how a user might interact or respond to it. The architectural model is a form of prototype, with the goal of better understanding the physical, tactical, and material impacts of the design. It's particularly interesting to consider how the model might be used as a way for users to gain a better understanding of the design from a first person perspective, and as a sort of user survey tool. Rapid prototyping uses everyday materials to create simple, rough prototypes that users can start to interact with to better understand the way a design will look, feel, or operate. The industrial design firm IDEO is well known for these types of prototypes and used them early on in the process—even before sketches have been done—to get a feeling for how a design will work. Paper prototyping is another form of simple prototyping and like storyboarding and user mapping, the goal of the prototype is not to examine every detail of the design, but to look at key moments of interaction or user experience. They can also be used to test out variations or iterations of a design before getting to a finalized version of it.

Conclusions

While much of the research and processes driving usability research has historically focused on physical and cognitive sciences, embracing the diversity of user experience can yield richer innovations in this space. As the cultural anthropologist Clifford Geertz famously stated in his book *The Interpretation of Cultures*, "It may be in the cultural particularities of people—in their oddities—that some of the most instructive revelations of what it is to be generically human are to be found" (1973, 43). Through a comparative approach to design methods and processes, designers gain deeper and richer insight into how design performs, the ways that others might interpret or interact with it, and most importantly, the way it contributes to shaping the human experience.

References

Altmann, Jeanne "Observational Study of Behavior: Sampling Methods." *Behaviour*, 48, 1974, pp. 227–265.
Cooper, Alan, Reimann, Robert, and Cronin, David. *About Face 3: The Essentials of Interaction Design*. New York: Wiley & Sons, 2007.
Cross, Nigel. "Designerly Ways of Knowing: Design Discipline Versus Design Science." *Design Issues*, 17(3), 2001, pp. 49–55.
Crouch, Christopher and Pearce, Jane. *Doing Research in Design*. London: Bloomsbury, 2012.
Emerson, Robert M., Fretz, Rachel I., and Shaw, Linda L. *Writing Ethnographic Field Notes*. Chicago, IL: University of Chicago Press, 2nd Edition, 2011.
Geertz, Clifford. *The Interpretation of Cultures*. New York: Basic Books First Edition, 1973.
Grocki, Megan. "How to Create a Customer Journey Map." *UX Mastery*. September 16, 2014. Retrieved from https://uxmastery.com/how-to-create-a-customer-journey-map/. Accessed February 26, 2019.

Meers, Chris. "Prototypes – The Beginner's Guide." *The UX Review*. May 10, 2013. Retrieved from https://theuxreview.co.uk/prototypes-the-beginners-guide/. Accessed February 26, 2019.

Norman, Donald. *The Design of Everyday Things*. New York: Basic Books, 2013.

Oudshoorn, Nelly and Pinch, Trevor, editors. *How Users Matter: The Co-Construction of Users and Technology*. Cambridge, MA: The MIT Press, 2003.

Sauro, Jeff and Lewis, James. *Quantifying the User Experience: Practical Statistics for User Research*. Waltham, MA: Elsevier, 2012.

Wahid, Arif Rahman and Atmodiwirjo, Paramita. "Storyboard as a Representation of Urban Architectural Settings." *International Conference on Architectural Education in Asia*. SHS Web Conference (eduARCHsia 2017). Volume 41, 2018.

4 Design as dialogue
Case studies of experiential design thinking

The architect and designer Charles Eames is quoted as saying, "The role of the designer is that of a very good thoughtful host anticipating the needs of his guests" (Miller, n.d.). The challenge for designers today is to base that anticipation on nuances, and to look beyond the surface of behavior to better understand the root causes. And as the relationship between designer and user becomes more integrated and interactive, we have better and more sophisticated and more creative methods by which to engage in this relationship. Throughout this section, the argument about usability attempts to look beyond the surface behaviors of people to and seek out a deeper understanding of the motivations that drive these behaviors and to critically reflect on the impact that design has on how users interact with it, and might adapt and change, for better AND for worse. For designers, this means expanding the methods by which we are gathering information and interacting with existing and future users of our projects. It also means remaining nimble throughout the research and design process—not using research only as a means by which to confirm our assumptions, but being open to the discovery of new ideas that might contradict what we thought we knew about people, their beliefs, desires, and wants and needs.

Creating new affordances in usability research

Once designers start to look for patterns, they start noticing them everywhere. So, the goal of teaching students how to engage is design research is as much about verifying the validity of those patterns as it is about identifying them in the first place. At the Maine College of Art, a graphic design instructor Brooke Chornyak engaged her students in a different type of triangulation in their user-centered research. Using more traditional methods like surveys and interviews, Chornyak also used non-traditional methods like podcasts and blogs as resources for students to gain a richer understanding of a particular culture and community. The ultimate goal of the project was to create a new affordance for an existing platform (Twitter, for example) that responded to the research conducted with the user group they had identified, and helped users search and browse through content. Designed as a series of sprints with a larger final outcome, the first phase (research) aimed to develop a comprehensive knowledge of the human-centered design process through several in-class design sprints. In small groups of three, students listened to a podcast Chornyak assigned. These podcasts cast a wide net, and set up culturally related problems like relationship management, paying for school, bullying, etc. Students were not assigned any specific platform or problem but to consider what might be a larger problem that the podcast suggested to them. From the podcast, they identified a particular area for further study. The second part of the project asked them to engage with users that identified with the topic the students were studying and conduct user-focused interviews, surveys and even observational studies to expand their understanding of the user groups motivations for browsing, searching, or alternative behaviors.

Student research and projects took on a range of topics, from the more logistical issues of package tracking and ad-blocking, to professional issues like organizing portfolios. A particular student project took on more serious and timely study when looking at how social media, and Instagram in particular, might use crowdsourcing to identify what could be triggers on posts to the platform. Calling the add-on, "SafeBrowse" users were able to opt into the service. Since these platforms rely on user-generated content the student realized that they would also need to rely on those same users to tag images and messages that might be triggers to users who had traumatic experiences related to them. Many images on these platforms

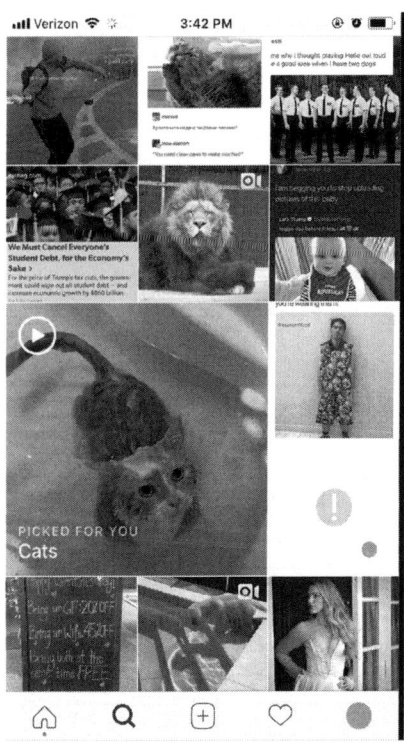

Figure 4.1

Screenshot from SafeBrowse. Instagram home screen which the SafeBrowse plug-in can be installed into. All images courtesy of Brooke Chornyak

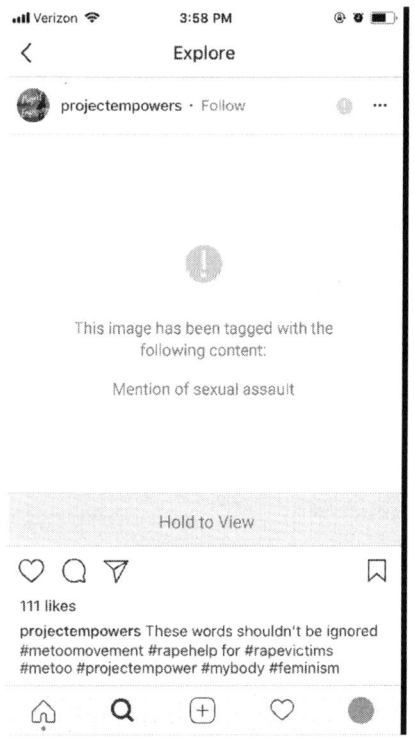

Figure 4.2

The SafeBrowse plug-in warns of a trigger the image might invoke

Design as dialogue

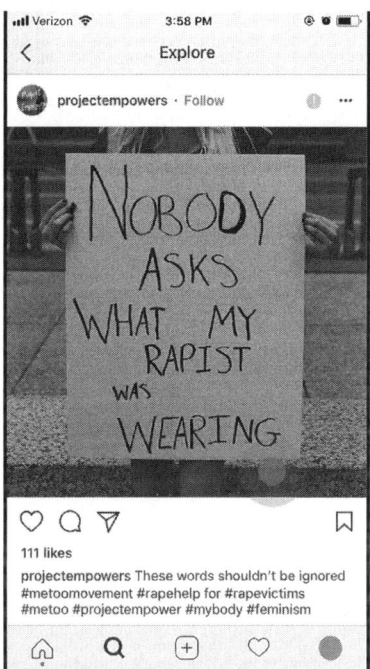

Figure 4.3
The original image after warning has been dismissed

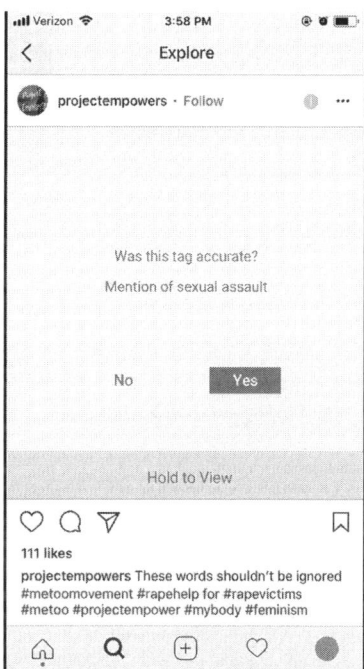

Figure 4.4
Crowdsourcing is used to validate and verify the tagging of the image as a potential trigger

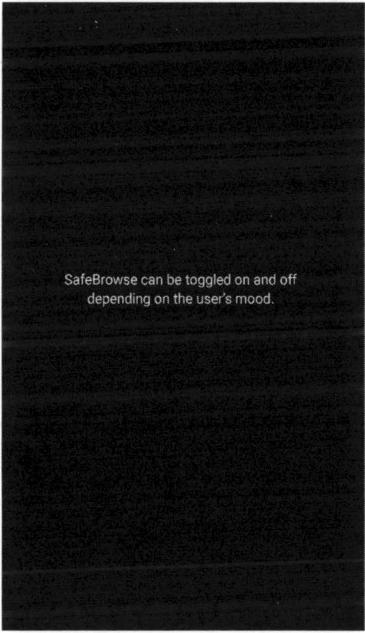

Figure 4.5
The SafeBrowse plug-in can be toggled on and off

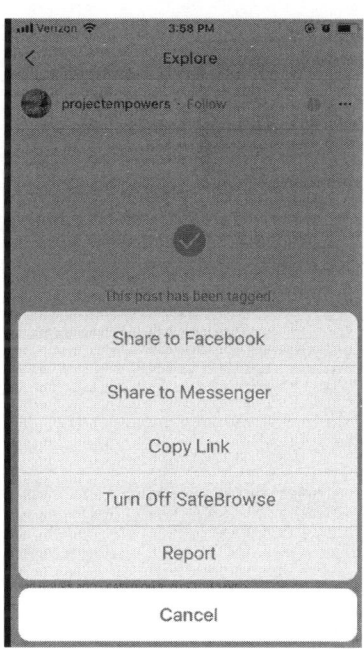

Figure 4.6
A crowdsourced survey helps teach developers of the plug-in whether or not the particular tag was helpful to the user

are posted to be provocative, but not necessarily understanding that they can be more painful to certain users than was necessarily intended in the provocation. The add-on would help the platform capture and tag what might be harmful images for some of the users, while also helping users be prepared for (or skip) those images that might be triggers for them.

Using Tinder as an existing platform, one student also examined the vetting process for connecting with people through this platform. While Tinder was originally conceived as a platform for users to connect with others for brief encounters, more recently it is being used as a more traditional dating platform. Through her research, the student identified the need for a more robust and participatory vetting process for users since this transition meant that users were deliberating more before agreeing to any sort of meet up. The outcome of this project varied in the final assessment by the other students. Since the rating process was quantified, students in the review had questions about what the criteria for the rating was. The categories the student assigned for rating, "presentable, engaging, polite and presentable," were questioned. How did the student know that these were the right categories? Could those evolve or be added on to if there were others that were more relevant or important to people? How did her research support the need for these categories? The student designer had also made the reviews inaccessible by the person who was being reviewed. Students replied that was unfair to the person, as they should have access to this information to be able to modify and change their behavior if it was being received negatively.

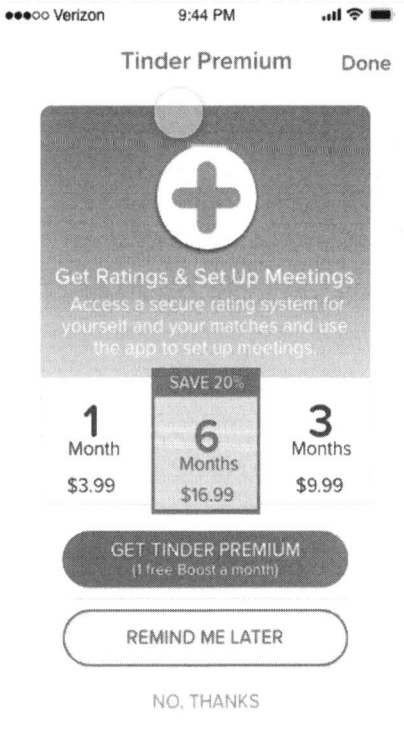

Figure 4.7

Screenshots from Tinder Premium install page. All images courtesy of Brooke Chornyak

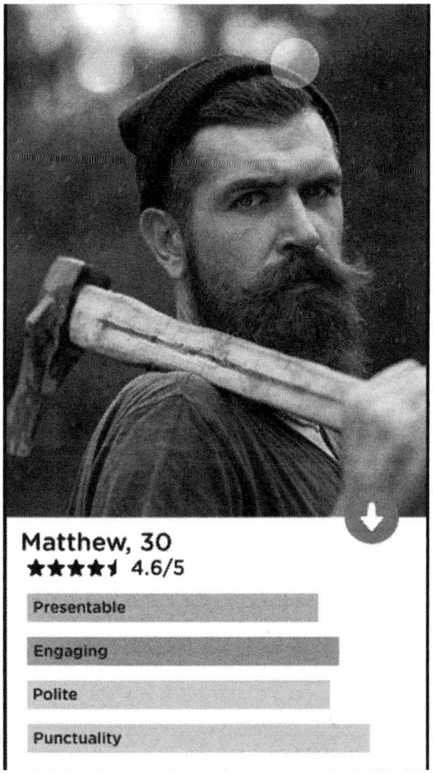

Figure 4.8

Example Tinder Premium features and rating system

Design as dialogue

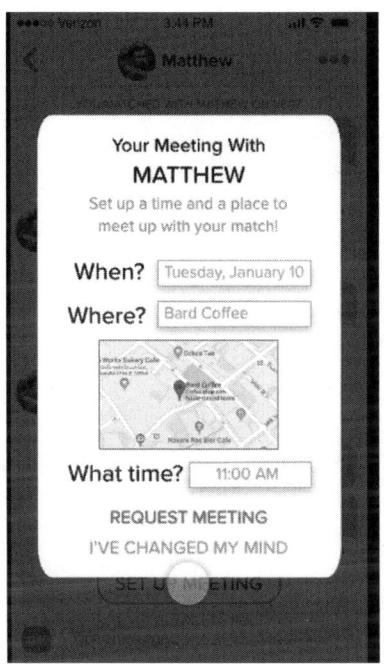

Figure 4.9
Scheduling a meeting with Tinder Premium

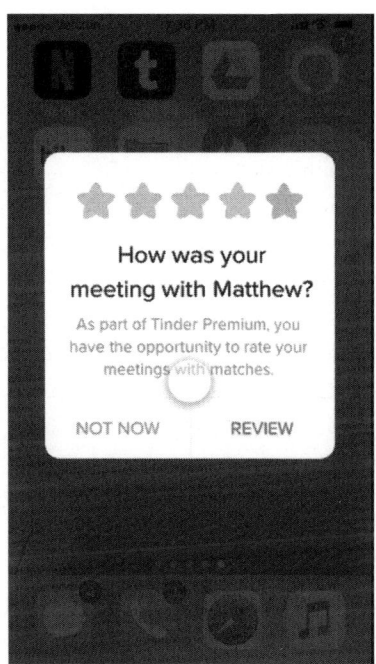

Figure 4.10
Ability to rate your meeting for other Tinder users to see

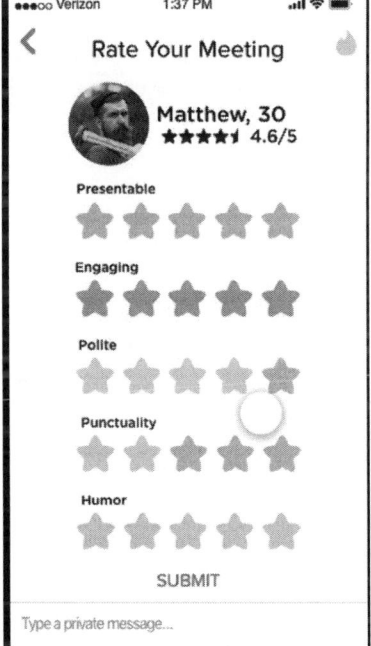

Figure 4.11
Rating detail

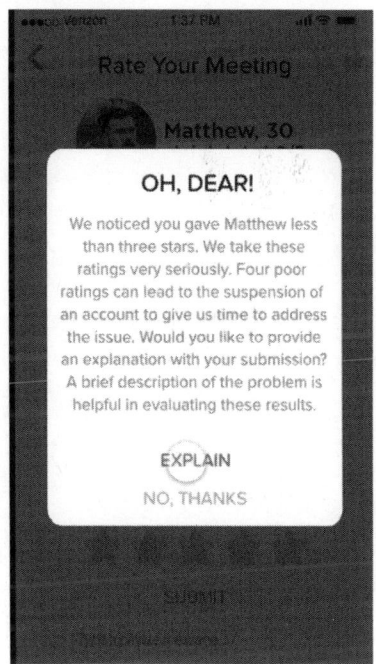

Figure 4.12
Prompt to explain a poor rating leads to accountability on the part of the user as well as the person being rated

Throughout the project, Chornyak used the review process to challenge the validity of the research and its connection to the final proposal as much, or more, than the particulars of the proposal itself. The questions that keep arising throughout the project, and that were prompted by the instructor, focused on how the research uncovered the underlying motivations that were driving the design decisions. How do you know that is true? How can we test our assumptions? What questions are still unanswered? These are the critical questions that need answering for usability research to be meaningful and impactful.

Usability and urban design: William H. Whyte, Google, and incremental user experience

When William Whyte conducted his New York City plaza study in 1970, he developed a systematic measurement and recording system to observe the way that New Yorkers used (or didn't) certain city plazas by using time-lapse photography to record people's behavior in those spaces. In *The Social Life of Small Urban Spaces* (2001), Whyte explained the trajectory of the study and what they were hoping to learn. During the time of Whyte's study, the city of New York had been giving incentives to developers building commercial buildings downtown. If the developers agreed to include public space on the exterior of the building, the city would allow them additional height on the building—something very lucrative to the developers. But what Whyte and others started to notice was that some of these spaces were being underutilized while others were heavily used. As part of a larger study which was looking at congestion in the city overall, Whyte used his study to convince of specific codes and rules that would force developers to create usable spaces for the public, not just a pass through. "For the millions of dollars of extra space it was handing out to builders, it had every right to demand much better plazas in return" (Whyte, 2001, 15). While Whyte would not necessarily claim that he was doing usability testing, he was. Whyte and his group used the type of comparative study reviewed earlier in this chapter, by using observation and interviews. As Whyte explained:

> We mounted time-lapse cameras overlooking the plazas and recorded daily patterns. We talked to people to find where they came from, where they worked, how frequently they used the place and what they thought of it. But, mostly, we watched people to see what they did.
>
> (16)

The group tried to understand who was using the space in terms of demographics—age, gender, type of work, distance traveled. They also tried to understand how they were using the space—as social spaces, in groups, and as meeting places. While the genesis of the study was around simple observation, the interviews and discussions led to a deeper understanding of the many reasons that people chose to use those plazas, or not. It gave insight to the city and by extension the developers to encourage the development of social spaces—spaces that are critical to contemporary city planning. The Project for Public Spaces which carries on

Design as dialogue

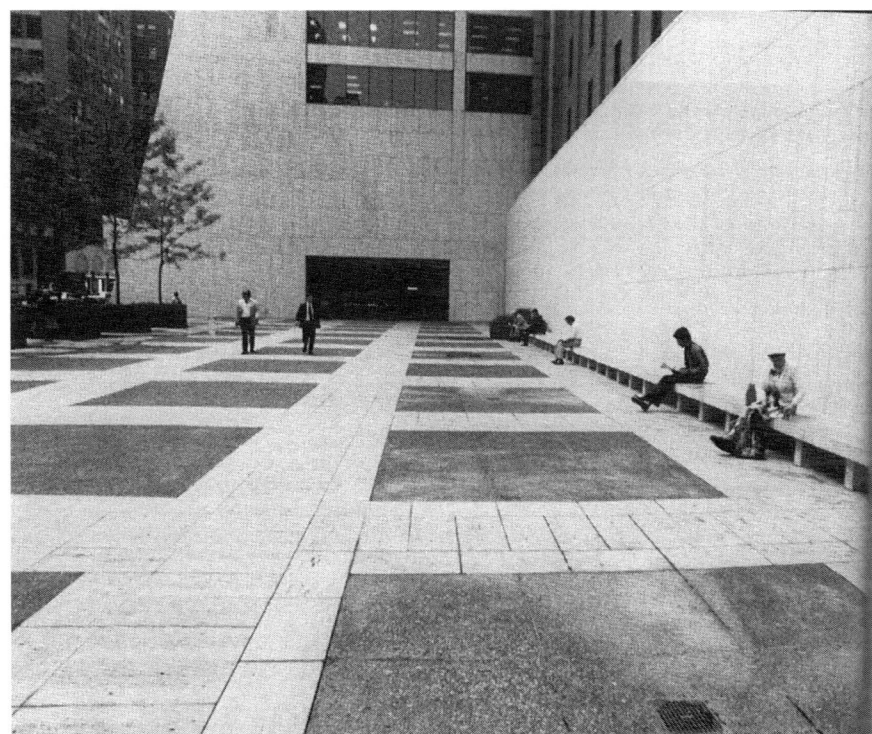

Figure 4.13

Still from The Social Life of Small Urban Spaces, reproduced with permission from Project for Public Spaces

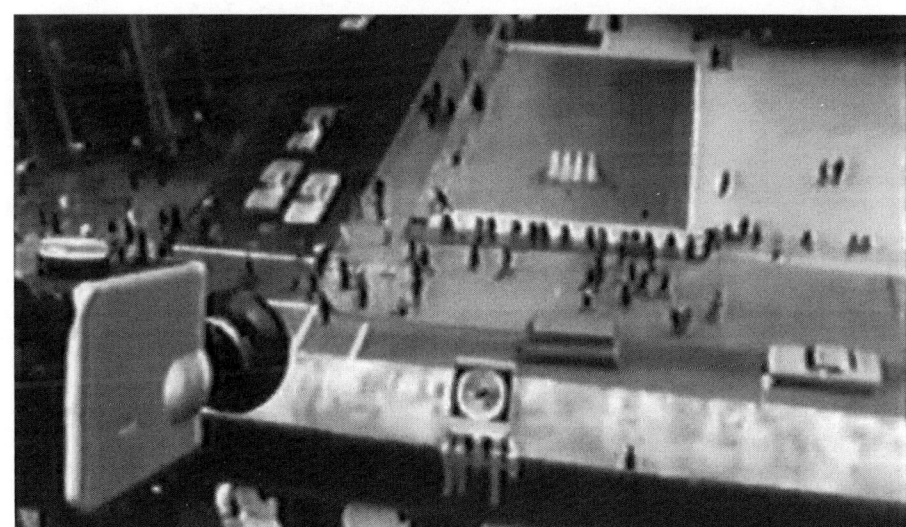

Figure 4.14

Still from The Social Life of Small Urban Spaces, reproduced with permission from Project for Public Spaces

Whyte's work, continues to implement these theories. Since 1998 they have used a concept called placemaking that engages citizens in activating public space. As they describe it, "[p]lacemaking inspires people to collectively reimagine and reinvent public spaces as

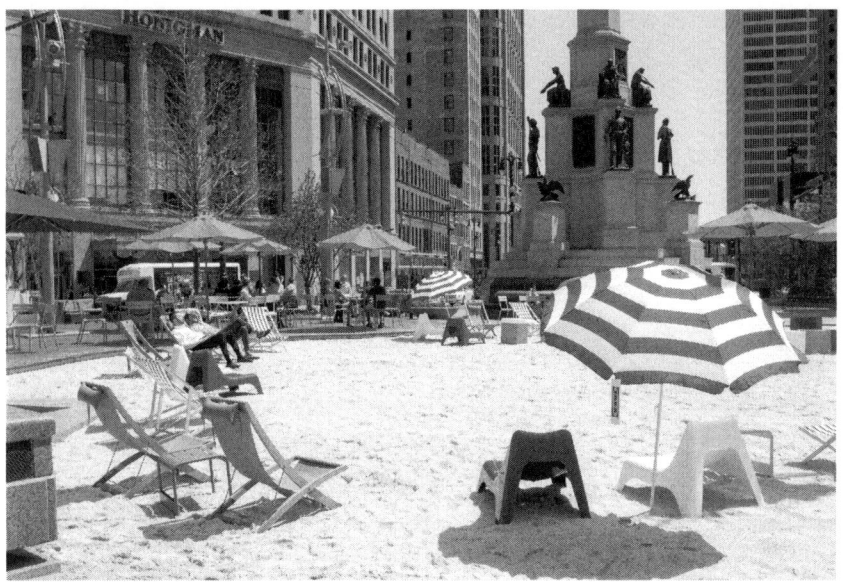

Figure 4.15

Project for Public Spaces Detroit Revitalization, reproduced with permission from Project for Public Spaces

the heart of every community" (Project for Public Spaces, "What is Placemaking?" n.d.) PPS has been involved in a long-term effort focused on revitalizing Detroit, a city in the U.S. that is a notorious victim of the decline in manufacturing. "Despite its challenges (or perhaps because of them), Detroit has become a proving ground for how Placemaking can be scaled up across an entire city" (Project for Public Spaces, "PPS Involvement in the Place-Led Regeneration of Detroit, MI", n.d.) Using traditional planning strategies in conjunction with participatory research and involvement with community organizations, the Project for Public Spaces has engaged in a large-scale collaborative and participatory effort to identify key opportunities and spaces that are ripest for development. In a city with a large population of citizens who are below the poverty line, sensitivity to issues like displacement and gentrification are key to the process. The Project for Public Spaces identified and made recommendations for activating a number of key areas, including a public market, parks, downtown, and a riverwalk. At the core of all of the efforts is an approach that invites key stakeholders into a dialogue about how to approach the revitalization effort in addition to how and what the strategies for revitalization should be.

William H. Whyte's seminal work can be seen in contemporary methods of urban planning like Sidewalk Toronto, a joint venture between Waterfront Toronto—a city planning organization—and Alphabet's Sidewalk Labs—an enterprise of the same parent company as Google. The project aims to develop a new type of urban planning that fully integrates technology into the planning process as a way to engage citizens in the planning process and rethink the way urban development takes place. Engaging in the specific goal of redeveloping Toronto's Eastern Waterfront district, Sidewalk Labs is particular focused on a new type of urban planning that engages citizens not only in the visioning process, but also as an incremental form of urban development. As Sidewalk Toronto claims, this new type of urban space:

will be a place that embraces adaptable buildings and new construction methods to make housing and retail space more affordable. A place where people-centred street designs and a range of transportation options make getting around more affordable, safe, and convenient than the private car. A place that encourages innovation around energy, waste, and other environmental challenges to protect the planet. A place where public spaces welcome families to enjoy the outdoors all day and all night and where community ties are strong. A place that's enhanced by digital technology and data, without giving up the privacy and security that everyone deserves.

(n.d.)

As a usability study, part of the interesting aspects of the Sidewalk Toronto project is the incremental approach that they are taking. Part of this incrementalism is what the CEO calls "radical flexibility." In a recent interview with the Project for Public Spaces, the Sidewalk Toronto team stated, "One of the ways that radical flexibility makes a difference in affordability is by creating the ability for spaces to adapt to new forms or new uses in a way that's faster and cheaper" (Peinhardt, 2017). As a case study of usability, Sidewalk Toronto is innovating in the way that they are using technology to engage citizens in the planning and design process. Using virtual reality as a tool for usability studies and testing, Sidewalk Toronto is hoping to engage citizens to interact with potential city plans through the VR environment. As the Sidewalk Lab's Chief Policy Officer, Rit Aggarwala stated:

> What we are working towards is using visualizations and modeling. Visualizations are always used in terms of renderings, but there's clearly an opportunity to use 3D imagery or virtual reality to give people a sense of what we imagine as being possible in Toronto. On modeling, planners always use these big, sophisticated, and often clunky models.
>
> (Peinhardt, 2017)

But Sidewalk Labs plans to continue to gather information on usability beyond the initial development stage by embedding technology into the very working of Quayside, the name it has given to the Eastern Waterfront district.

> Sidewalk Labs promises to embed all sorts of sensors everywhere possible, sucking up a constant stream of information about traffic flow, noise levels, air quality, energy usage, travel patterns, and waste output. Cameras will help the company nail down the more intangible: Are people enjoying this public furniture arrangement in that green space? Are residents using the popup clinic when flu season strikes? Is that corner the optimal spot for a grocery store? Are its shopper locals or people coming in from outside the neighborhood?
>
> (Marshall, 2017)

They will then evaluate all of this data to figure out what is working, and what's not and adjust accordingly. While this incremental approach to city planning has its roots in the work of Whyte and others it is an entirely new approach to the way that cities can potentially adapt to the way that people use them.

Design as dialogue

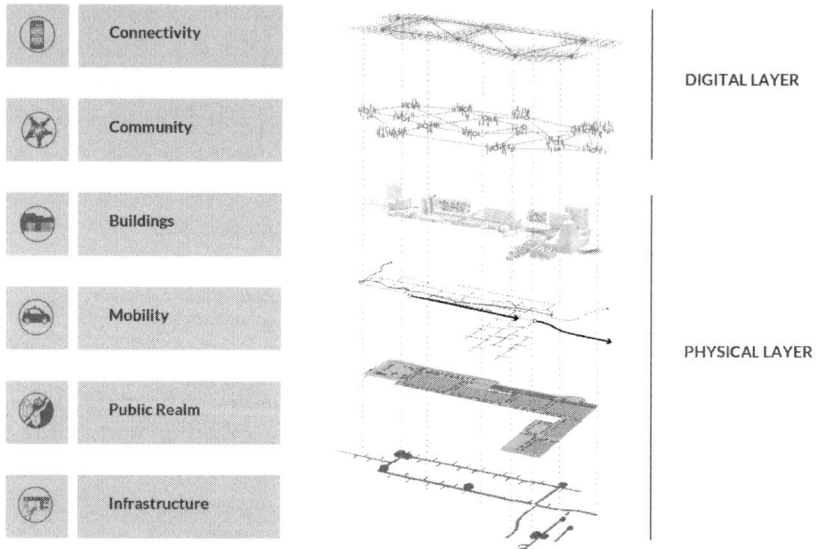

Figure 4.16

The city as platform. Courtesy of Sidewalk Labs

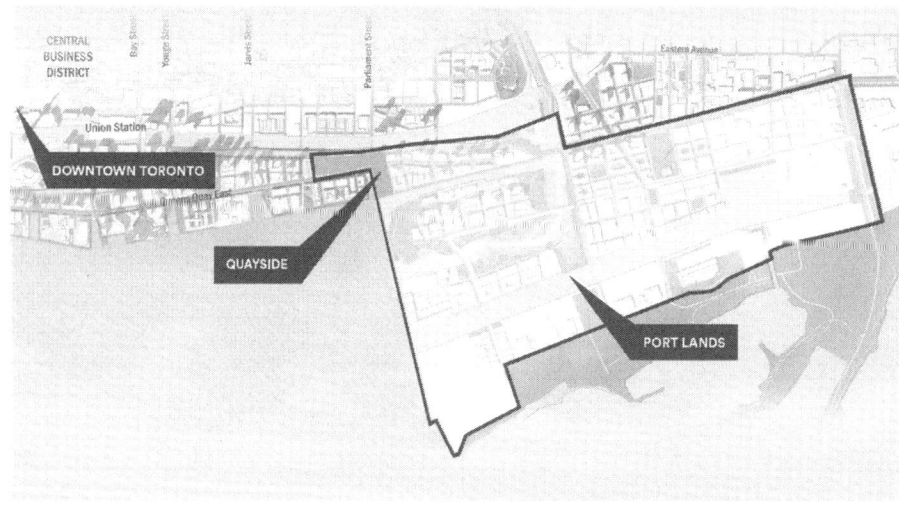

Figure 4.17

Three sites for the Sidewalk Toronto plan. Courtesy of Sidewalk Labs

In addition to the traditional structure that each city needs—such as buildings, public spaces, and public works' infrastructure, Sidewalk Labs adds another level of connectivity and digital infrastructure with the aim of building community and connectivity. Viewing the city as a platform, Sidewalk Labs envisions the network of physical and non-physical entities that make a city alive. Principles like affordability, mobility, sustainability, community, and city services and the integration of the public and private realm all see the city as a network that is alive, and always changing. This type of city necessarily relies on an incremental approach.

Design as dialogue

Much as participatory design and placemaking was a reaction to the lack of citizen involvement in the planning process, the history of incremental city design was a reaction to the utopian master plan that dictated whole scale redevelopment in favor of an incremental approach that gradually affected the status quo. As a theory of policymaking, incrementalism was first introduced by Charles Lindblom in the 1950s. According to Michael Hayes of the *Oxford Review*, "Significant policy change occurs, if at all, through a gradual accumulation of small changes, a process . . . called seriality" (2017). It has developed into a series of principles, or patterns that guide city planning in order to encourage commonality, but also engagement by a variety

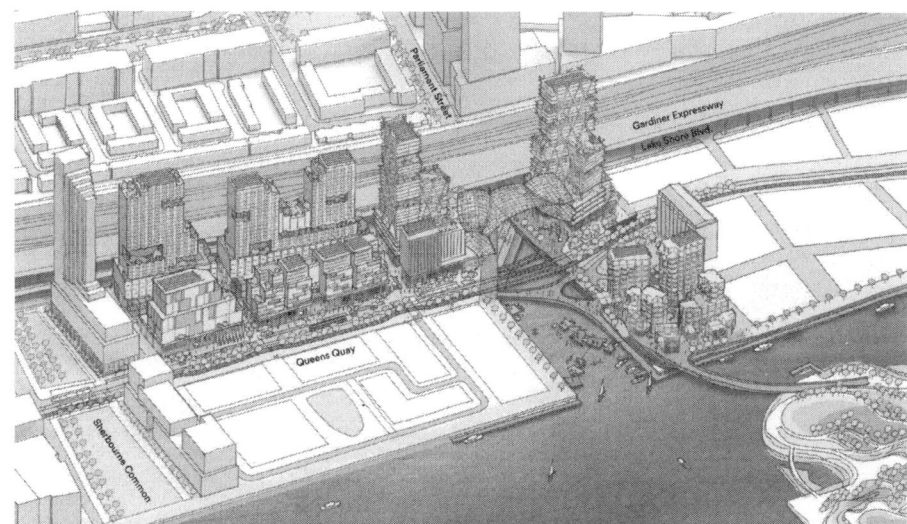

Figure 4.18

The Quayside plan. Courtesy of Sidewalk Labs

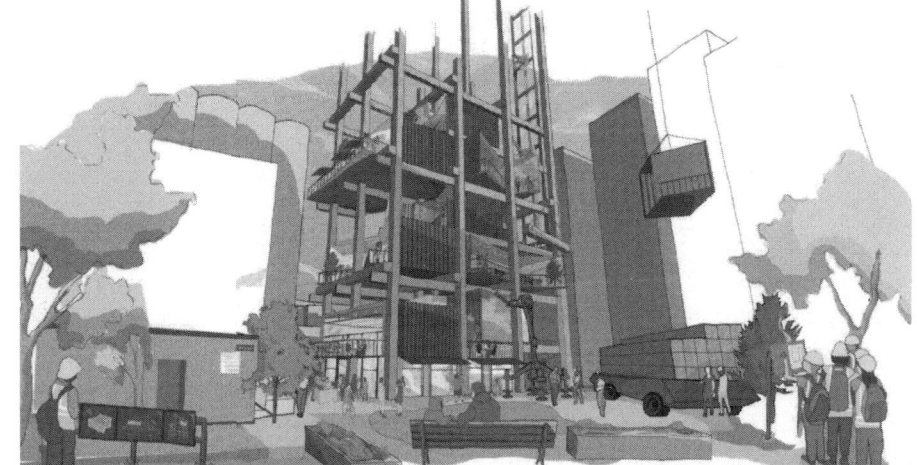

Figure 4.19–4.23

Slides from a community meeting presentation illustrating the principles of affordability, mobility, the public realm, sustainability, and community. Courtesy of Sidewalk Labs

Design as dialogue

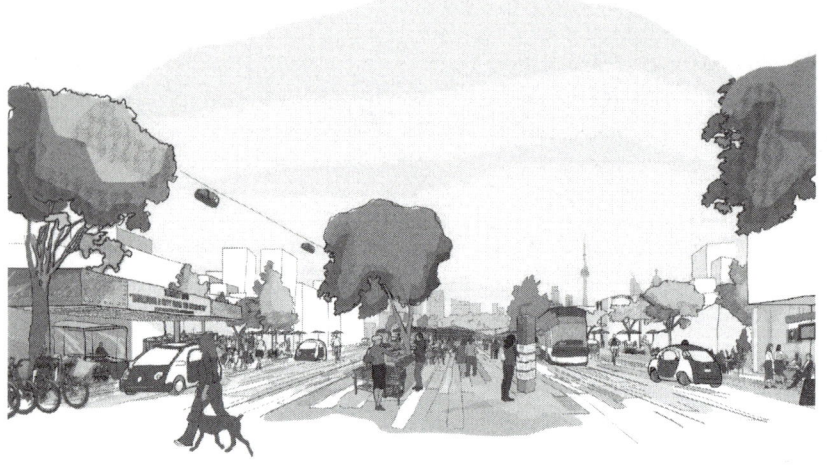

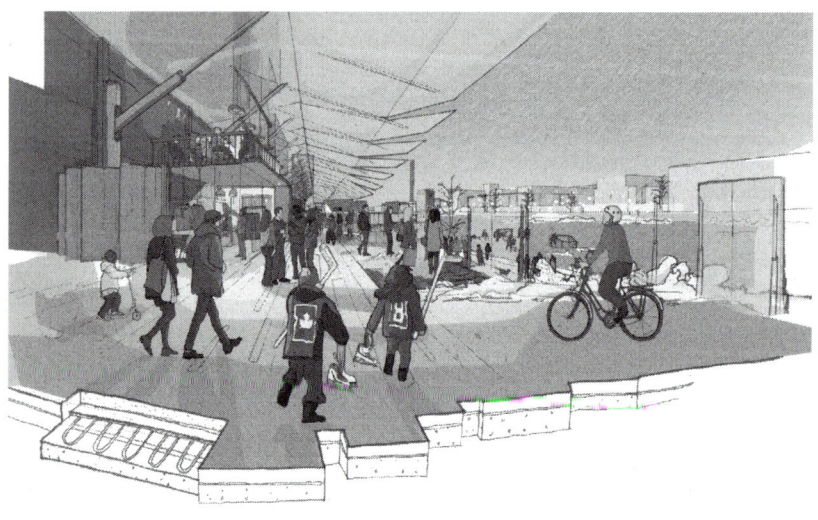

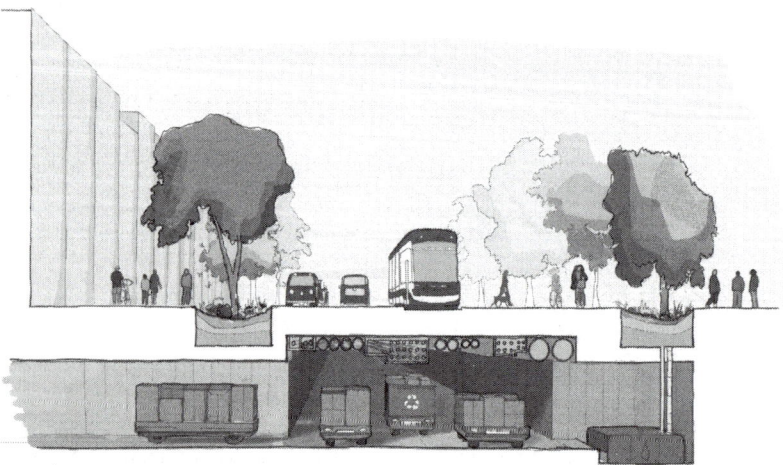

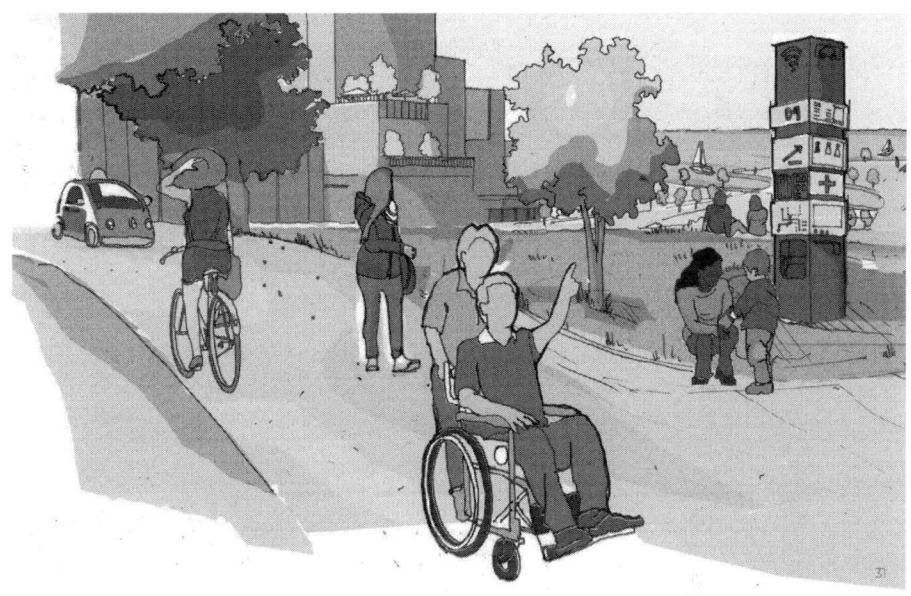

of people and channels. Rather that the whole-scale development or redevelopment of neighborhood, region, or town, incrementalism advocated for smaller-scale evolution of these public spaces that invited citizens and people to participate in its creation. Incrementalism in many ways rejected the idea of the urban planner as any sort of expert at all in the planning process. Rather, the people who lived in the spaces were the true experts, with master planners and urban architects becoming more a facilitator for what would be the citizens' wishes. But from a usability standpoint, this perspective can have its problems. In an online article entitled "Jane Jacobs and the Death and Life of American Planning" (2011), Thomas Campanella argues that this approach in many ways made the planning field impotent and that "In rejecting the muscular interventionism . . . planners in the 1960s identified instead with the victims of urban renewal. New mechanisms were devised to empower ordinary citizens to guide the planning process" (Campanella, 2011). These are much the same concerns that we wrestle with today in terms of usability studies. How do we balance the needs of the user with a bigger picture, holistic view of the plan in order to balance the multiplicity of constraints and needs that are driving the project—public or private? This is something that Sidewalk Toronto is wrestling with in new and interesting ways, through their integration of virtual reality and other measures of user experience, interaction, and participation.

Usability and accessibility

It must also be acknowledged that the case studies presented in this chapter discuss activating public space for certain groups of people. What is the responsibility of the designer to be inclusive in considering how people of many different means and abilities use and enjoy public spaces—whether they are physical or virtual? This can happen intentionally, like the anti-affordances mentioned in Chapter 2, but often they are unintentional, and a result of designers simply not thinking about the breadth of potential users that are out there, and the variety of abilities that they have. So a critical reflection that is necessary in all questions of usability is "for whom is this usable and for whom is it not?"

As part of a Master of Art and Design thesis project, Karen Jones (2017) addressed this very question when deciding to create a children's ebook for deaf children. The concept for the project was inspired by her own experience of having a deaf sister, and seeing the impact of that throughout her sister's life.

It is well-documented that reading in the early stages of life is critical to literacy and learning. In 2015 the American Pediatric Association issued a statement that recommended parent-child reading in the home "beginning at birth and continuing at least through kindergarten." Through listening to the words and then associating them with printed words, images, and other context clues children become familiar with and conformable with the reading process, and even learning overall. But for deaf children, this early childhood literacy is a great challenge. Despite evidence showing that there is no intellectual difference between deaf children and their hearing counterparts, by the time they leave high school, deaf students' academic achievement levels average six to seven years behind their hearing peers in the United States, with reading levels plateauing at about the fourth grade level (Hrastinski and Wilbur, 2016). Early sign language adoption by children is also linked to increased literacy rates, but few resources exist to help with this adoption in the earliest stages of childhood, and specifically related to reading. Additionally, 90% of deaf children are born to hearing parents which provides a further challenge as parents try to navigate finding resources for which they don't themselves have a language for. Using principles of universal design which include equitable use, flexibility in use, simple and intuitive use, perceptible information, tolerance for error, low physical effort and size and space for approach and use (Story, 2011), Jones developed a prototype application that would introduce young children to reading using the American Sign Language (ASL) system.

> With relatively recent advances in personal computers, mobile devices and internet access, there are more offerings for storytelling for ASL users, such as apps and videos. Widely adopted tablet technology provided me with a means for inclusive opportunities to share reading in ASL via a multimodal e-book that features an embedded animated character narrating the story in ASL.
>
> (Jones, 2017, 10)

Jones created the characters and five stories for her prototype application. Using a lemur as a main character—because of the variety of physical types of lemurs and the dexterity of their appendages which made them visually strong for signing—one of the major challenges of *Sign Me a Story* was in the communication of complex hand movements through animation. While the process of visualization increased the legibility by allowing Jones to emphasize and give visual hierarchy to important symbols, it was also challenging to create dexterity and clarity in the hand movements themselves. Jones's aim was to use storytelling to create a shared, common experience between parents and children. *Sign Me a Story* also aims to address deaf children's right to inclusion, while validating American Sign Language as a language worthy of original works. As Jones explained of the project:

> This journey began with an assessment of my core beliefs: that storytelling is the way we share common experience, that literacy is the foundation of autonomy, that purpose is found through service to others, and that personal fulfillment is gained in adding your voice to the chorus of greater good.
>
> (2017, 66)

Sign Me a Story capitalizes on the assets of an interactive application to allow children to replay or slow down the signing of a word or an idea. Because American Sign Language has a different structural order (Time-Subject-Verb-Object) than traditional verbal English language (Subject-Verb-Object-Time), the child also has the opportunity to click on any word in the text at any time and have the entire phrase or section of text highlighted to show the corresponding ASL translation. In addition to the educational components, features like this encourage agency and control that traditional books do not have. *Sign Me a Story* also has the ability to play sound, so that those who are hearing abled might also use the audio to help learn the associated signs along with the child. Throughout the entire project, one of Jones's main concerns was that of inclusivity, but she also admits to the difficulty, if not impossibility, that holds. One critique of *Sign Me a Story* is that it is not, in fact, inclusive of all because of the necessity of sight to trigger the stories. So, while sound can help a child enjoy the story, she does not gain the agency that other children do because she cannot interact with it. Still, *Sign Me a Story* is a critical step in considering how designers can use creative and critical design thinking to advance users of all abilities.

> Defining what it means to be accessible and inclusive means considering aspects of gender, mobility, age, cognition, education, cultural and socio-economic differences; in short, to attempt to encompass all aspects of human variation. This requires both inquiry and empathy. User experience is more than just how an individual interacts with an object, it is also how that interaction makes them feel; whether it is meaningful and valuable. The articulation of design choices leads to thoughtful, deliberate implementation and a way to justify and defend those choices. Through an innovative and thoughtful intersection of art and technology I hope to add to the body of work that supports and creates inclusive design.
>
> (67)

Design as dialogue

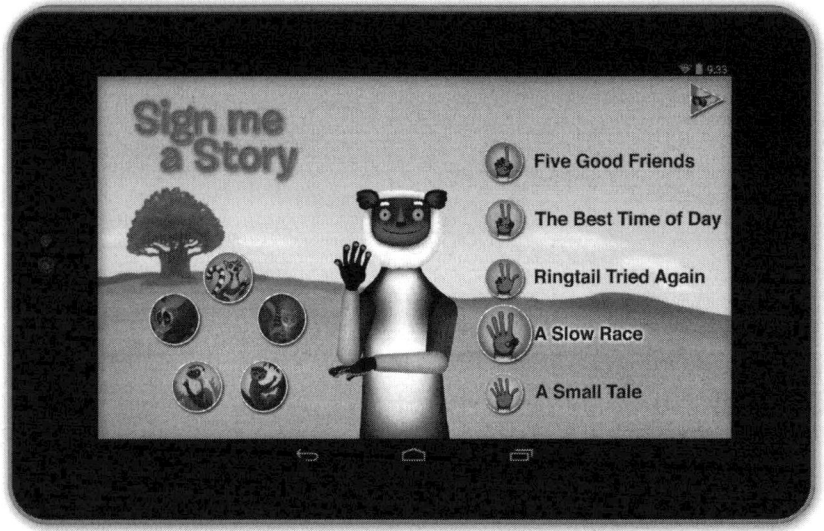

Figure 4.24

Opening screen from *Sign Me a Story*. Image courtesy of Karen Jones

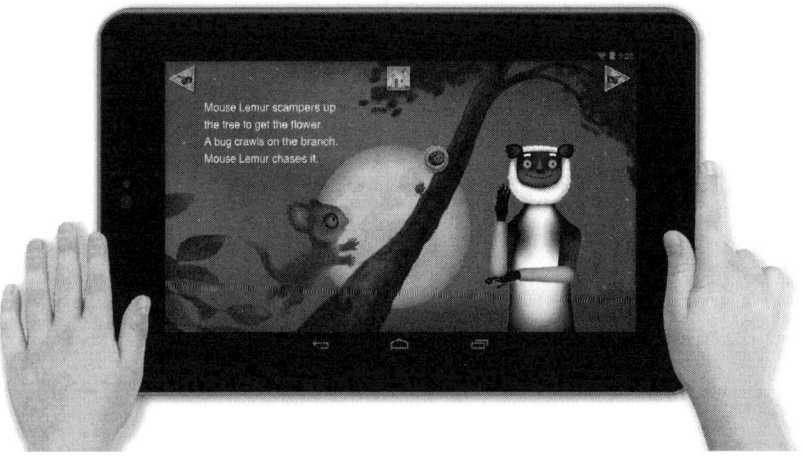

Figure 4.25

The lemur character signing a welcome. Image courtesy of Karen Jones

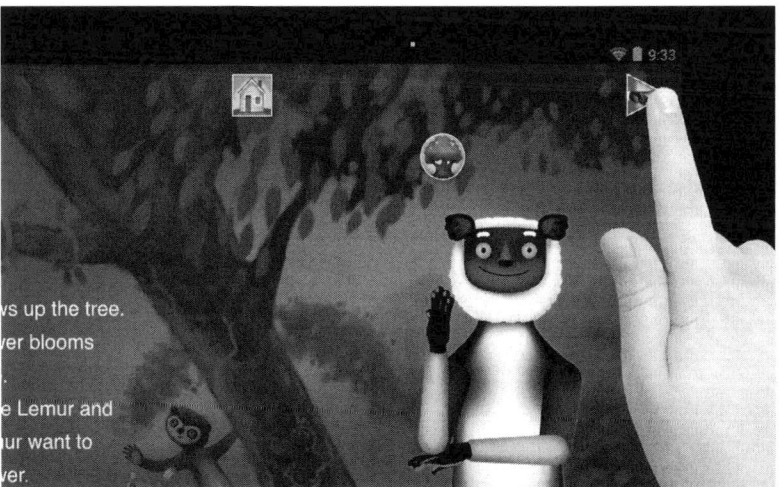

Figure 4.26

The five characters and narratives from *Sign Me a Story*. Image courtesy of Karen Jones

Design as dialogue

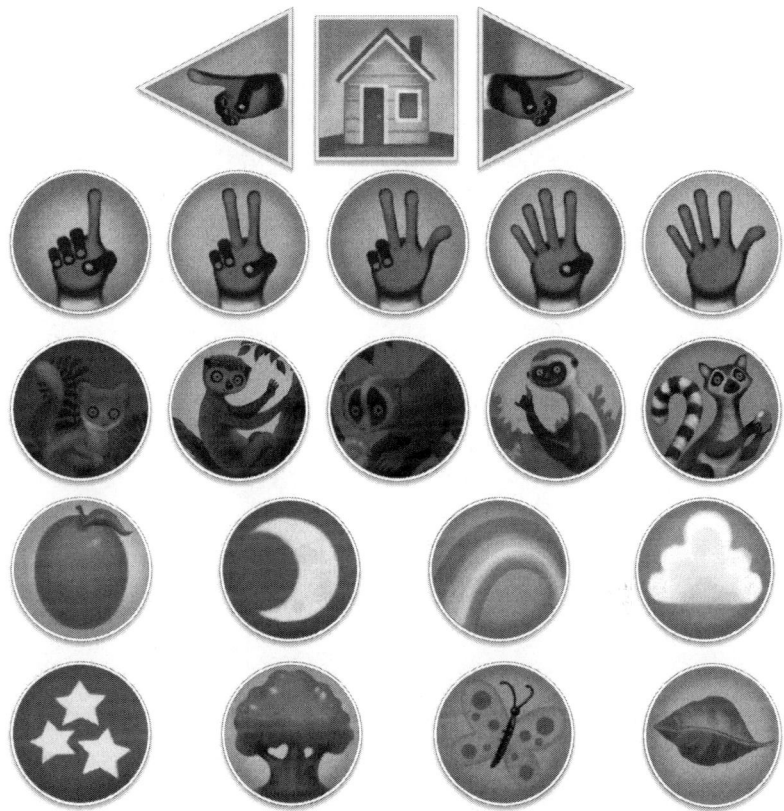

Figure 4.27

Icons to help guide the reader. Image courtesy of Karen Jones

References

American Pediatric Association. "Parent Child Reading and Story Time Promote Brain Development Prior to Kindergarten." August 3, 2015. Retrieved from www.aap.org/en-us/about-the-aap/aap-press-room/Pages/Parent-Child-Reading-and-Story-Time-Promote-Brain-Development-Prior-to-Kindergarten.aspx. Accessed March 28, 2019.

Campanella, Thomas. "Jane Jacobs and the Death and Life of American Planning." *Places Journal*. April 2011. Retrieved from https://placesjournal.org/article/jane-jacobs-and-the-death-and-life-of-american-planning/?cn-reloaded=1. Accessed September 21, 2018.

Hayes, Michael. "Incrementalism and Public Policy-Making." *Oxford Review*. April 2017. DOI: 10.1093/acrefore/9780190228637.013.1.

Herman Miller. "Our designers: Charles and Ray Eames." Retrieved from www.hermanmiller.com/designers/eames/. Accessed March 28, 2019.

Hrastinski, Iva and Wilbur, Ronnie B. "Academic Achievement of Deaf and Hard-of-Hearing Students in an ASL/English Bilingual Program." *Journal of Deaf Studies and Deaf Education*, 21(2), April 2016, pp. 156–170.

Jones, Karen. *Sign Me a Story: Shared Reading in American Sign Language With Interactive Animated Narration*. North Carolina State University Master's Thesis, 2017.

Marshall, Aarian. "Alphabet is Trying to Reinvent the City, Starting with Toronto." *Wired*, October 17, 2017. Retrieved from www.wired.com/story/google-sidewalk-labs-toronto-quayside/. Accessed February 26, 2019.

Peinhardt, Katherine. "Google's Urban Experiment in Toronto: A Q&A with Sidewalk Labs' Rit Aggarwala." Project for Public Spaces. November 30, 2017. Retrieved from www.pps.org/article/google-urban-experiment-toronto-sidewalk-labs-rit-aggarwala. Accessed September 21, 2018.

Project for Public Spaces. "What is Placemaking?" Project for Public Spaces, n.d. Retrieved from www.pps.org/article/what-is-placemaking. Accessed September 29, 2018.

Project for Public Spaces. "PPS Involvement in the Place-Led Regeneration of Detroit, MI." Project for Public Spaces, n.d. Retrieved from www.pps.org/projects/pps-involvement-in-the-place-led-regeneration-of-detroit. Accessed September 29, 2018.

Sidewalk Toronto. Retrieved from https://sidewalktoronto.ca/. Accessed March 28, 2019.

Story, Molly Follette. "The Principles of Universal Design." In Wolfgang F.E. Preiser and Elaine Ostroff, editors. *Universal Design Handbook*, Second edition. New York: McGraw-Hill, 4(1–6), 2011, pp. 4.3–4.11.

Whyte, W.H. *The Social Life of Small Urban Spaces*, Reprint edition. New York: Project for Public Spaces, 2001.

Part 2

Design and technology
Not if, but when

5 Reciprocity and impact

Design is fundamentally shaped by technology but we are also shaping it. Facebook cannot exist without the technology that is driving its platform but designers are also influencing the platforms that same environment exists within. From its inception, technology and technological innovation have had a huge impact on the world around us—both physically, socially, politically, and economically. In his book, *What Technology Wants* (2011), author Kevin Kelly (co-founder of *Wired* magazine) argues that with the creation of early forms of technology (i.e. tools) our early ancestors magnified their impact on the world exponentially, and in two key ways—through expansion and extinction. Early technological inventions contributed to population explosion by greatly increasing the amount of food early humans could attain. The increase in food also contributed to longer lifespans which had a profound effect on technological innovation by allowing the transfer of knowledge between generations. This transfer of knowledge exploded the pace at which humans could build upon previous tools and technologies—not unlike the open source culture we are seeing emerge today (but obviously nowhere near the contemporary pace or scale.) But this had another, more negative effect in that these technological advancements also created mass extinctions. As Kelly notes:

> Sapiens used innovations such as the bow and arrow, spear and cliff stampedes to kill off the last of the mastodons, mammoths . . . basically every large package of protein that walked on four legs. More than 80 percent of all large mammal genera on the plant were completely extinct by 10,000 years ago.
>
> (34)

This in turn, affected the environment and us: "We have significantly altered ourselves and at the same time altered the world" (37). Kelly calls this reciprocal phenomenon (or relationship) between technology and our world—the technium, which "extends beyond shiny hardware to include culture, art, social institutions, and intellectual creations of all types" (12). The technium is an ecosystem, bound and affected by the many forces that are surrounding it, it is everyone and influencing and influenced by everything.

We can look beyond digital technologies—although in contemporary life that is usually what we think of when we hear the word—and see evidence of the profound impacts technology has had on human culture and experience. In his book, *The Alchemy of Air* (2009), Thomas Hager tells the story of the Haber-Bosch machine—one of the most profoundly influential technologies developed in the 20th century, though many of us have never even heard of it. Developed by Fritz Haber (a scientist) and Carl Bosch (an industrialist), the Haber-Bosch machine was developed in the first part of the 20th century in order to mass produce artificial fertilizer to support the growing urban populations that resulted from the industrial revolution. Natural fertilizer is dependent on "nitrogen fixation"—the transformation of nitrogen into ammonia which acts as a fertilizer to plants and other living organisms. At the end of the 20th century, scientists realized (or surmised) that the natural nitrate deposits supporting the creation of natural fertilizer were unsustainable. This began a frantic search for a way to mass produce artificial fertilizer, which the Haber-Bosch process was successful at doing, and eventually at an industrial scale. But the outcomes of this innovation were not all positive. As Hager argues, "as a species, we long ago surpassed the natural ability of the planet to support us with food . . . only about 4 billion of us could live on what the earth and natural farming supply" (2009, 11). When Hager wrote the book, the human population was about 6 billion, and today it measures 7.5 and is still growing. So this growth in population fueled by our ability to grow more and more food also means more waste, more consumption, more development, and less natural resources to sustain the world that we live on. As Hager further argues, the discovery and industrialization of artificial fertilizer had other, more profound and dark connections, including the development of chemical warfare used by the Germans in World War I. The use of chemical weapons ultimately led to the tough sanctions imposed on Germany at the end of the war which many attribute to the rise of Hitler and the horror of World War II. Whether or not there is direct causation, there is no denying that the Haber-Bosch process directly contributed to the materials of modern warfare.

This story connects directly to the conundrum of our relationship with technology. It is unavoidable, and in a way, technology has always been ubiquitous. Since the invention of the tools that Kevin Kelly references, human life has been dominated by technology—agricultural technologies make possible our ability to walk into any store and buy bananas 365 days a year; manufacturing technologies make products faster to create and easier to afford; and of course digital technologies allow us to work closely with a group of people halfway around the world. This is not a novel idea. But many (including myself) would argue that the innovations associated with digital and networked technologies has exponentially increased the scale and speed of impact on our daily lives. So much so that we spend most of our time trying to keep up with them, allowing less and less time to make conscious decisions about how we are using them. Are the negative impacts associated with current technologies just exacerbating a phenomena that was already in play? Or are these technologies actually encouraging new types of social interactions and fundamentally changing the way that we operate in the world and the values that we place on quality of life and what it means to be human? As the writer and urbanist Adam Greenfield has argued in *Radical Technologies*:

[T]he most basic tasks we undertake in life now involve the participation of a fundamentally different set of actors than they did even 10 years ago. Beyond the gargantuan enterprises that manufacture our devices, and the startups that develop most of the apps we use, we've invited technical standards bodies, national- and supranational-level regulators, and shadowy hackers into the innermost precinct of our lives.

(2018, 13)

Holding positions for Nokia, Razorfish, and other technology companies that focus on networks at various scales, Greenfield's message points to a fundamental change in how we live our lives, and what we are willing to accept, including what we consider a "safe" environment. As these technologies become more pervasive and ubiquitous, they also become more invisible. We are not thinking about how our text messages get from our phone to our friends, or who might be there to intercept—the same is not as true of a paper letter sent through the mail.

But technology is not all bad. It also gives us access to worlds and people that we have never had before. The story of Wikipedia is a great example of the power of technology to bring out the best of our humanity. What is particularly interesting about Wikipedia is just how much thought and structure has gone into what is essentially an open-sourced encyclopedia. Many would think of Wikipedia simply as a resource to find out who a baseball player is, or to better understand an obscure term, but in actuality there is a complex system behind who and what is being created on this open platform. In the book, *Good Faith Collaboration: The Culture of Wikipedia* (2012), Joseph Reagle characterizes two main tenets of Wikipedia Culture (meaning, those people who are engaged in contributing to the product of knowledge that Wikipedia collects and disseminates), neutral point of view and good faith. Both of these tenets need to be agreed and operated upon for the structure of the open-sourced platform to be self-sustaining. "The neutrality stance permits collaboration between those who might otherwise fall into rancorous discord" (53) and the assumed good faith stance "is intended to counteract the common reflex to assume the worst of others" (60). While both of these foundations are simple, and might even seem obvious, their articulation as a part of the sharing culture of Wikipedia, creating a culture of mutual respect and building that allows the system to grow "WikiLove," "a general spirit of collegiality and mutual understanding" (63).

Technology is part of a larger system that is motivated by human wants and needs to make life easier. Nicholas Carr, the author of *The Glass Cage* (2015), looks deeply at technology through the lens of automation and paints a dire portrait of our decreasing ability to perform certain tasks. While early technology was focused on creating substitutions for manual jobs—washing clothes, vacuuming our house—today, that automation is taking over more and more of our cognitive and intellectual tasks. And these cognitive tasks are linked to other forms of abilities—such as wayfinding, communication, and problem-solving—that are decreasing as we become more and more reliant on our technological services. As technology becomes more ubiquitous and we become more and more reliant on it, we begin to believe what Carr calls the *substitution myth*. Namely, that our technology is a substitution for a discrete activity. In reality, Carr further argues, the technology is changing the very nature of the task. And our reliance on this technology to be able to accomplish these tasks leads to phenomena such as *automation bias* which "creeps in when people give undue weight to the information coming through their computers. Even when the information is wrong or misleading, they believe it" (Carr, 2015, 67). Simply understanding the persuasive quality of these technologies is a strong first step for designers, but even more critical is to transfer that understanding to users through the designed objects and experiences that are created.

Up until now, technology has been described as a tool for automating work, but a huge part of technology is also driving the way that we experience the world around us. A key element of automation is connected to the drive toward simulating reality in the form of activities, tasks, or experiences. One such example is computer-generated imagery (CGI) technologies which we see in many films today which has the primary aim of "authentically" simulating an environment or an actor without the viewer recognizing the simulation itself. In 1970, the Japanese roboticist Masahiro Mori suggested that as robots become more human-like—and as the simulation became more real—people would develop a more positive emotional response to them. But it hasn't proved to be that simple. Studies have found that there is a tipping point to this positive emotional response. As machines become more visually human-like, there is a point at which the authenticity has a negative effect on our emotional response. Otherwise known as the "uncanny valley," this uneasiness is described as "a characteristic dip in emotional response that happens when we encounter an entity that is almost, but not quite, human" (Lay, 2015). There is something unsettling about CGI technology that makes an actor look younger than the audience knows she really is, or to show an actor walking when we know he is paralyzed, as was the case in the 2009 Super Bowl commercial featuring Christopher Reeve. In this case, the illusion of reality is being directly confronted with what we know is true which in turn makes the viewer uncomfortable with the technology. This awareness of the simulation or technology is what Jay David Bolter and Richard Grusin (1999) characterize as hypermediacy. Along with immediacy and transparency, hypermediacy forms the core of remediation, which is the re-forming of older media into new environments and mediums. In many cases this remediation is implicitly (or explicitly) an act of progress to simulate a more "real" experience. So, animations or interactive films remediate traditional films which remediate photos, which remediate paintings or texts of other stories. Immediacy in new media technology attempts to fully

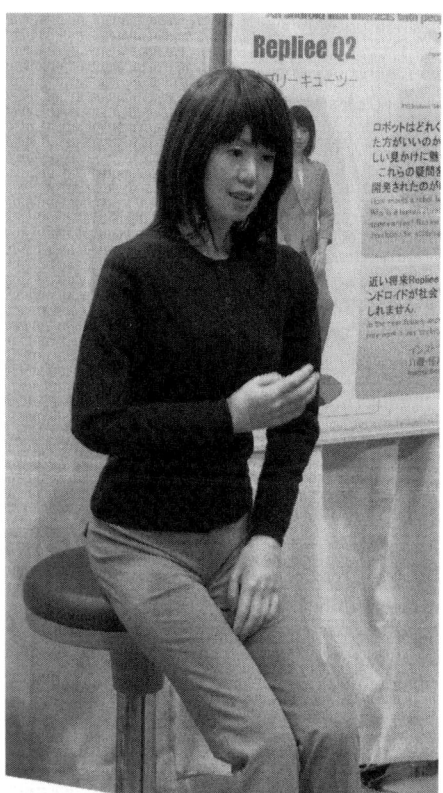

Figure 5.1

The Uncanny Valley seen in Repliee Q2. Taken at Index Osaka. Brad Beattie, Wikimedia Commons

Reciprocity and impact

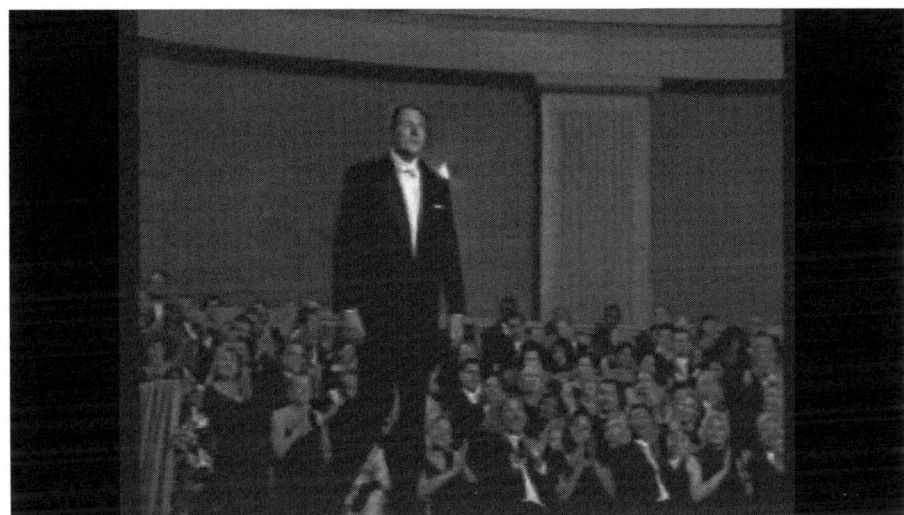

Figure 5.2
Screenshot of Christopher Reeve in Super Bowl commercial

immerse users in the experience, and to remove all traces of the act of mediation by the technology. Transparency is directly related to immediacy through the attempt to remove the interface and any trace of mediation. Hypermediacy, on the other hand, encourages the viewer to be hyper-aware of the medium or interface. Television (and particularly cable news shows) use these tactics with the number of screens and windows that are happening simultaneously, constantly calling the viewer to be aware of the medium itself. In their argument, hypermediacy is an intended outcome of the designer—the designer wants the user to be aware of the act of mediation, so they can click windows closed, make choices about how to navigate through a website, etc. Where the phenomenon of the uncanny valley becomes prominent is when that hypermediation is not intended.

As with most things, artists are particularly adept at questioning the validity of these experiences, and to call attention to phenomena that ordinary people might overlook, or take for granted. The artist Jenny Holzer (2004) is a provocative example of how hypermediated experiences can call attention not only to the impersonality of technology, but also the pervasiveness of messages that these channels feed us on a daily basis. One of Holzer's particularly powerful series involves LED screens, in which she programs "truisms"—messages such as "I cannot tell you I love you" or "All things are delicately connected." But where viewers encounter these messages is what makes the hypermediated experience profound. These messages might be on a movie billboard, or an LED screen in Times Square, or in the window of a corporate bank. It is precisely through this surprise encounter, and the tension between media and message where the work holds its power, and forces the viewer to confront the message and how it's being delivered—in many ways calling more attention to the message because of the cognitive dissonance it provokes.

As reality and simulation become more intertwined, it is interesting to consider how remediation is changing how we experience everyday life. Whereas previously much of the remediation was focused on entertainment, now we are seeing it integral to our everyday experiences—from work, to home life, to errands and domestic responsibilities—which indicates a further integration of technology into our lives, and part of a living network that is constantly shaping our lived experience.

Theories of technology and design: dynamic networks

Technology as a living network

In *What Technology Wants* (2011), Kevin Kelly also argues that technology is not so much a tool as it is an ecology—capable of growth, learning, and self-healing. In making this analogy, he paints a cautionary tale of how much technology (or the technium, as Kelly has coined it) can take over if we let it. But this is exactly the point he is trying to make. By understanding technology as an entity with the same motivations as other living beings, we—the ultimate creators of it—must recognize the self-propelling nature of it and consider that more fully when using and creating it. In one particularly powerful chapter, "The Unabomber was Right" Kelly recounts the many inventors who were convinced their invention would save the world. From the inventor of dynamite to that of the machine gun, new technological innovators almost always see their invention as contributing positively to the world:

> Most of the new problems in the world are problems created by previous technology. These technogenic problems are nearly invisible to us. Every year 1.2 million people die in automobile accidents. The dominant technological transportation system kills more people than cancer. Global warming, environmental toxins, obesity, nuclear terrorism, propaganda, species loss, and substance abuse are only a few of the many other serious technogenic problems.
>
> (193)

But rather than use this to argue against new technological innovations, Kelly's real argument is that we, as the creators of these systems, need to fully appreciate and understand the outcomes that can be a part of them. If we understand technology as an ecological system, we cease to see it as independent, and in need of (or being used by) operators with differing motivations, knowledge, needs, and wants. And maybe more importantly, we also start to understand it not as a static element, but as an evolving one.

Edward Tenner, the author of *Why Things Bite Back* (1997) calls this "The Real Frankenstein." As he explains it,

> Frankenstein's fateful error was to consider everything but the sum of the parts he had assembled. The "limbs were in proportion, and I had selected his features as beautiful." The hair was "of a lustrous black, and flowing; his teeth of pearly whiteness." But he had failed to understand the body as a system. Thus the "yellow skin scarcely covered the work of muscles and arteries beneath," and the watery eyes . . . seemed almost of the same color as the dun white sockets in which they were set . . . Mary Shelley was pointing to a dilemma of all science-based technology—at a time when science was only starting to influence technological practice. How can we understand a system before we try to change it? Disaster inspires so much of our understanding.
>
> (12)

Reciprocity and impact

As we start to think of technology not just as an element, but as a system, we can see how it might interact, which might also lead us to think more about the type of system that we want to create, or be a part of. And while we might think of most of the highly controlled systems evidence of early 20th-century manufacturing technology, closed systems are still very much in play today. As our relationship and use of technology becomes more pervasive, there is an understandable desire to want to manage and control their complexities. While our natural goal as designers and people might be to try to tighten and control the system, that can have disastrous effects if we ignore the need for people to be able to move around within the system. In 2016, one of the worst mass shootings in the United States happened at an outdoor venue in Las Vegas, Nevada. As the gunman opened fire from the 32nd floor of a hotel onto a crowd at a music festival below, the images of the chaos show people trying to climb over the wall that was containing the venue. This trope is common in many outdoor venues—where one might assume that that dominant concern is in controlling how people are entering, more than how they might exit. So when chaos erupts, there is not a measure to exchange this closed network for an open one. As an alternative example, the Boston bombing in 2013 showed how an open network like the subway system (or "T") almost immediately shifted to a closed one. All of the lines were shut down, people evacuated and monitored to prevent movement through the network as they tried to track down the people responsible for the bombing. It could be argued that it's much easier to go from an open network to a closed one, but our challenge as designers is to think about both of these cases.

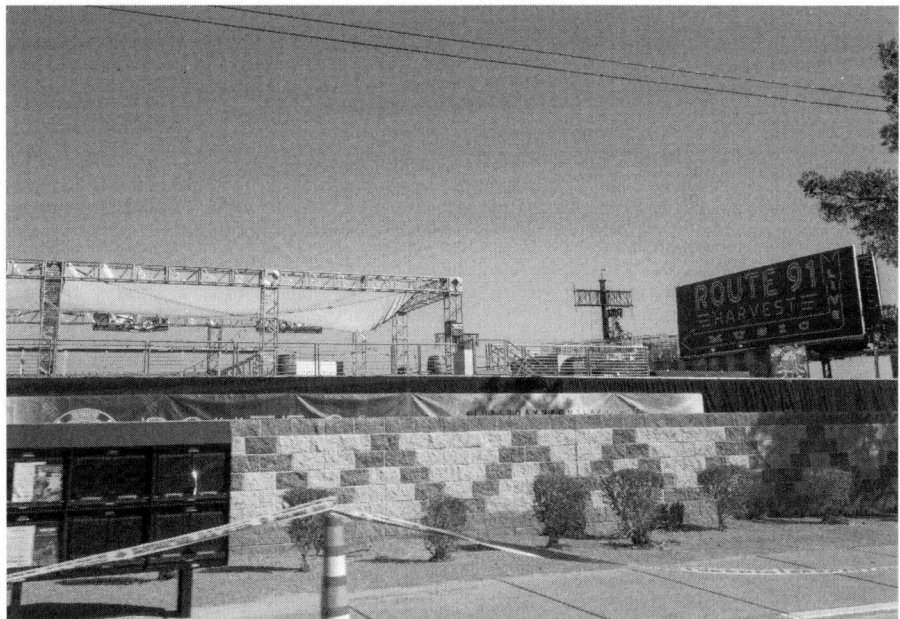

Figure 5.3
Outdoor music venue in Las Vegas

As we use our currently networked technology for more and more convenience, we necessarily make ourselves more vulnerable. We are intrinsically linked to a much larger system, which makes it that much more difficult to isolate and address or "fix" one node or component of it. Advocates for the increasingly networked experience argue that the

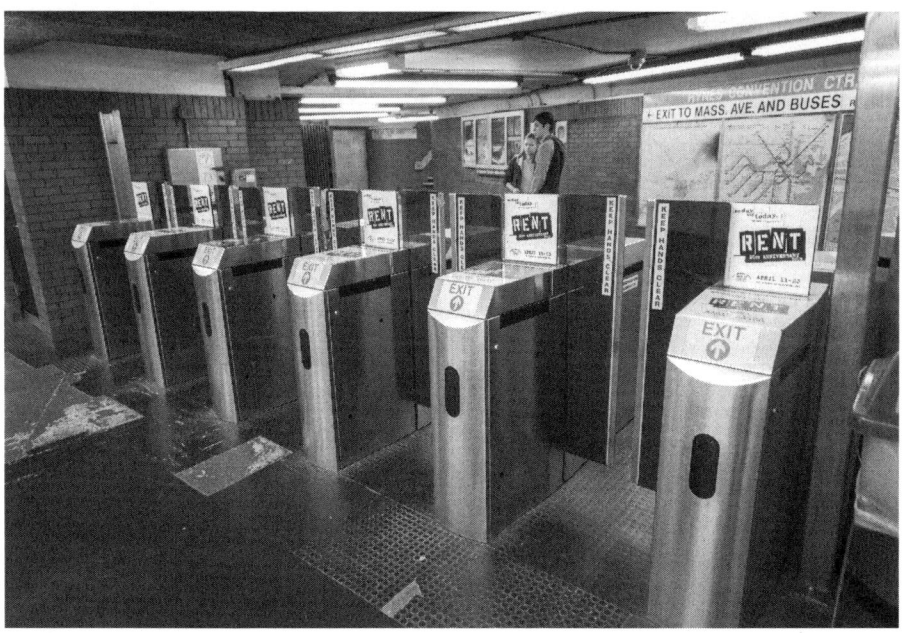

Figure 5.4
Boston Subway system

real power in new technologies lie in their ability to connect to one another and to us. So, we don't have to be present to turn off our alarm system, our refrigerator can tell us when we need milk, or our home can tell us when the temperature is too high or low. We can also get alerts when our child's test scores are posted, set limits to their screen time without physically taking the device away or monitor our own health and well-being through the devices that we are constantly connected to. David Rose, MIT Media Lab professor and inventor advocates for the potential of this "internet of things" to enchant us. In his book, *Enchanted Objects* (2015), Rose starts off with his nightmare, which just might be our reality today. In his nightmare:

> the cold, black slab has re-architected everything—our living and working spaces, our schools, airports, even bars and restaurants. We interact with screens 90% of our waking hours. The result is a colder, more isolated, less humane world. Perhaps it is more efficient, but we are less happy.
>
> (2)

Even in the few years since Rose wrote this book, our dependence on these "black slabs" has grown exponentially, and while maybe not to the extent that Rose projects, we are well on our way to making his nightmare a reality if we do not start asking ourselves some fundamental questions about what we want our human experience to be, and how design can contribute to it in a meaningful way. But as these networks grow, and as technology becomes more ubiquitous, it also becomes less transparent. It is harder to actually "see" what this network is doing and how it is connecting to all of us. It requires more trust from the user that the network is functioning, and that the intentions behind it are productive.

The transparency of technology networks

While the fact of technology being a ubiquitous medium (or part of human culture) might not be a new one, its increased invisibility certainly is. The move to wireless computing and internet might be the most obvious example, but you can also add smart technology to the transparency argument. As current technologies continue to learn more and more, what they are actually learning and responding to becomes less and less obvious to the user. In an effort to automate more and more processes, the user's ability to modify these processes become more and more difficult. We have all had the experience of searching for something on Amazon, only to have that item and about four or five different variations, start to show up in advertisements on other sites that we are visiting. Adam Greenfield, mentioned earlier in this chapter, authored another book looking at the ubiquity of technological networks in our everyday lives. In *Everyware: The Dawning Age of Ubiquitous Computing* (2006) he argues that "networked digital information technology has become the dominant mode through which we experience the everyday" (6) and quite possibly as a result of this, we seek to question it less and less. We don't doubt that our watch is telling us the wrong time, unless we are confronted with the fact of an error (like the sun is setting at what our watch tells us is 11pm and we're not in Alaska). But there are very real examples of disastrous results of not questing the accuracy of the technology. In their book, *Windows and Mirrors*, (2005) authors Jay David Bolter and Diane Gromala emphasize the importance of language in our idea of technological transparency, especially with regard to computer technology. Bolter and Gromala argue that "When interface designers chose window to describe the framed rectangles on the screen . . . they made a choice that had vast cultural significance" (42). As such, we think of the computer window as a transparent tool that is not mediating, interpreting, or translating what is behind it but simply providing a view into the background. A similar argument can be made about the form that the interface takes—with little pictures of folders and pages and trash cans. Those analogies are based in physical forms and so we associate the simplicity of the physical folder with that of the digital one. At best, we have faith in the interface that it is an accurate simplification of a more complex system behind it, and at worse, we don't even recognize the complexity at all. There are a host of man-made disasters that reinforce this concept. One of the most well-known is the Titanic, the "unsinkable" ocean liner that only had about half of the rescue boats to accommodate passengers and crew when it sank after hitting an iceberg in 1912. A less well-known counterpart to the sinking of the Titanic was the Chicago's Iroquois Theatre fire in 1903 in a building deemed "fireproof" and with no fire system installed. Bolter and Gromala catalog the near-meltdown of Three Mile Island in Pennsylvania as an example of this phenomena because of the lack of recognition of the malfunction of the monitoring device itself. Simple, less harmful examples might be the GPS navigation system that takes you down a dead end road. It's always a strange feeling when confronted with the fact that the interface is wrong. If you're like me, you keep checking it, because it so fundamentally contradicts our belief and faith in it.

Another aspect of transparency in our networked society relates to issues of trust and privacy. In the ubiquitous networked society that we are heading speedily towards, surveillance can be both our friend and our enemy. In his book, *Connected* (2003), Steven Shaviro argues that "If universal surveillance is unavoidable in the age of the network, then the next best thing might well be to make sure that the results of this surveillance are available to all" (39). If footage from video surveillance was not just made available to police and FBI, but also citizens, then the monitoring is more reciprocal. On the other hand, one of the main arguments against mandatory body cameras for law enforcement, and even in releasing the footage of those officers who already have this body cameras installed, is that they don't show the context of the entire situation. This connects back to the simplicity/complexity argument in the previous paragraphs, and the false assumption of completeness that much of our technology instills in our interactions with it.

Technology as a material and rhetorical network

In *Understanding Media*, Marshall McLuhan (1994) argues that "the 'message' of any medium or technology is the change of scale or pace or pattern that it introduces into human affairs" (20). His most famous example of this is the lightbulb, because it is seen as content-less. But McLuhan argues that is it by its very act of illumination creating the message that we, as viewers are focused on. Many of us would see this as the message, and overlook the very tool or system that is making that message visible. In McLuhan's argument, by understanding the medium as the message we are more attuned to studying its impact and place in the system. McLuhan goes on to explain that media is often seen as a "make happen" agent, but not a "make aware" agent (73): "We make our tools, and then our tools make us" (xxi). So the question becomes, how can technology be better understood for the agency that it has and gives? We change as a result of the tools that we use and embrace, and because of that, there is an agenda associated with it. Google Maps is devised as a crutch to help us navigate the world in an easier way, but by extension the same technology prevents us from understanding the world in a holistic way, or thinking critically about the route that we should take, or even from the route that might be most enjoyable. It privileges the shortest or the quickest route, and by extension our motivation changes (or solidifies) to focus on the destination rather than the journey. What are we missing along the way, and how does the tool change our perception and even our goals?

    One of the most popular and potentially promising uses of technology is the increased use of gaming for education purposes. Technological games have the power to give people ongoing access to learning far outside of the classroom. And advocates for the potential for the "gamification" of learning would argue that it lends itself well to lifelong learning through simulation and first person decision making. Ian Bogost, the author of *Persuasive Games: The Expressive Power of Videogames* (2010) has argued that the power of games as a persuasive and education tool lies in the procedures that are necessarily and inherently built into them. This concept is not limited to games, but can also be applied to any technological device that necessitates (or demands) a sort of operational procedure to interact with it. As Bogost explains it, procedural rhetoric:

is the practice of persuading through processes in general and computational processes in particular. Just as verbal rhetoric is useful for both the orator and the audience, and just as written rhetoric is useful for both the writer and the reader, so procedural rhetoric is useful for both the programmer and the user, the game designer and the player. Procedural rhetoric is a technique for making arguments with computational systems and for unpacking computational arguments others have created.

(3)

Procedures, Bogost argues, are often associated with rules and have many different implications for technological experience. From the procedures or rules that designers use to get a computer to respond or react, to the procedures that users must go through in interacting with a piece of technology, to those rules and procedures that users engage with when playing a game, or using a word processing program, the activities are changing what we believe we can accomplish, and what we do accomplish as a result. This idea of the procedure persuading the user of a particular "truth" about the technology or interface is particularly timely.

What does this mean for viewers and designers? In one sense, it means that the media that we consume is shaping our understanding of the world, and by extension the values and the biases that designers bring to the design process. In another sense, it means that designers' ideas are being shaped and formed through the tools used to create it.

References

Bogost, Ian. *Persuasive Games: The Expressive Power of Videogames.* Cambridge, MA: The MIT Press, 2010.

Bolter, Jay David and Gromala, Diane. *Windows and Mirrors: Interaction Design, Digital Art, and the Myth of Transparency.* Cambridge, MA: The MIT Press, 2005.

Bolter, Jay David and Grusin, Richard. *Remediation: Understanding New Media.* Cambridge, MA: The MIT Press, 1999.

Carr, Nicholas. *The Glass Cage: How Our Computers Are Changing Us.* New York: W.W. Norton & Company, 2015.

Greenfield, Adam. *Everyware: The Dawning Age of Ubiquitous Computing.* San Francisco, CA: New Riders Publishing, 2006.

Greenfield, Adam. *Radical Technologies: The Design of Everyday Life.* New York: Verso, Reprint edition, 2018.

Hager, Thomas. *The Alchemy of Air: A Jewish Genius, a Doomed Tycoon, and the Scientific Discovery that Fed the World but Fueled the Rise of Hitler.* New York: Broadway Books, 2009.

Holzer, Jenny. "Truisms, 1978–87." *The Museum of Modern Art, MoMA Highlights.* New York: The Museum of Modern Art, 2004.

Kelly, Kevin. *What Technology Wants.* New York: Penguin Books, 2011.

Lay, Stephanie. "Uncanny Valley: Why We Find Human-Like Robots and Dolls so Creepy." *The Guardian.* November 13, 2015.

McLuhan, Marshall. *Understanding Media: The Extension of Man.* Cambridge, MA: The MIT Press, Reprint edition, 1994.

Reagle, Joseph. *Good Faith Collaboration: The Culture of Wikipedia.* Cambridge, MA: The MIT Press, Reprint edition, 2012.

Rose, David. *Enchanted Objects: Innovation, Design, and the Future of Technology.* Scribner, Reprint edition, 2015.

Shaviro, Steven. *Connected or What It Means to Live in a Networked Society.* Minneapolis, MN: University of Minnesota Press, 2003.

Tenner, Edward. *Why Things Bite Back: Technology and the Revenge of Unintended Consequences.* New York: Vintage, Reprint edition, 1997.

6 Networked design thinking

While the previous chapter might make you think technology is our enemy, the point is really to more fully consider how we are using it in design and in our lives. We can look at the tools and technologies presented earlier and see positive and powerful impacts. The person who posts the racist comment can be met with an avalanche of public shaming which might end up costing him or her a job and friends. The home monitoring system can avert a burglary or a refrigerator full of spoiled food. One of the most important components to understanding the larger network that technology is a part of comes with the way that designers engage in problem-framing. Problem-framing involves the way that designers understand the scope of the problem being addressed. They are influenced by values and assumptions that are formed through previous experiences. Many of the design thinking principles introduced in this chapter aim to break apart some of these assumptions to encourage designers to see the complexity and depth of a problem and to find new territories where a design intervention might take place. For example, looking at a simple comparison of how to handle bicycle traffic in a large city reveals very different ways that the problem is framed, and as a result the experience of cycling. Bike lanes that are separated from traffic are often thought to be the safest solution to helping cyclists travel around the city. They provide a distinct separation between cars and bikes and often help cyclists feel safer through this separation. In this scenario, the problem of bicycle traffic is framed as one of needing to keep bikes *separate* from cars in order to keep them safe. This can be further dissected if we start to look at how buffers are constructed. In some cases, there is a buffer (usually simple painted lines) between the car and bike traffic. Sometimes, these are single lines, sometimes there are double or angled lines. In each of these small differences, the problem has been framed by the designer slightly differently, emphasizing the needs of the car over the cyclist or vice versa. Most of the time in the US, the bike lanes become a buffer between the sidewalk, parked cars, and moving cars. In many cities in Europe, that is not the case, and the parked cars become a buffer between the cyclist and moving traffic with both directions of bicycle traffic operating on one side of the street (or even in the middle of the street) to allow for a greater and safer separation. In yet another scenario, what is known as a "sharrow" is painted on the street, which reflects another way of framing the problem of the coexistence of bikes and cars sharing the same space. Sharrows are simple bike icons with a series of arrows that indicate that cars and bikes can both ride in the same section of road. Some argue that the sharrow is more dangerous to the bike lane because there is no buffer. Cyclists often feel less safe on a street where a sharrow exists. But sharrows might also be a better solution to the bike lane because they actively educate drivers about the rights of cyclists to be on the road (which is a law in most US cities). In many cases, bike lanes or sharrows are late additions to urban infrastructural design and so the approach is to retrofit the existing infrastructure which was built for cars, to "make space" for cyclists with the least amount of disruption. In doing so, the way problems are framed is not one of looking at the larger network but to look at just one piece of it (i.e. how to fit a bike onto a particular road). Technology is particularly adept at helping us think in pieces, because it is constantly changing and augmenting our lives. The digital bike lane light by Etopstech creates a "make your own bike lane" which on its surface seems to solve a lot of the problems that the traditional bike lane or sharrow can't address. But it also discourages a system of overall networked thinking to problem-framing, instead putting the onus on the cyclist to make sure they are safe, rather than putting some responsibility on the cars, streets, and other motorized vehicles to share communal space. This is where networked design thinking can place a critical role.

The goal of this chapter, however, is to encourage us as designers to shift our perspective of technology from a tool, or a component to part of a dynamic system that can and will evolve and change. So, when using or incorporating current technologies into our design proposals, designers must consider them dynamically and as part of a larger network. Networks can be static, but more often than not they are dynamic and operate much like a system with different elements moving into the network, affecting its operation and moving out of it.

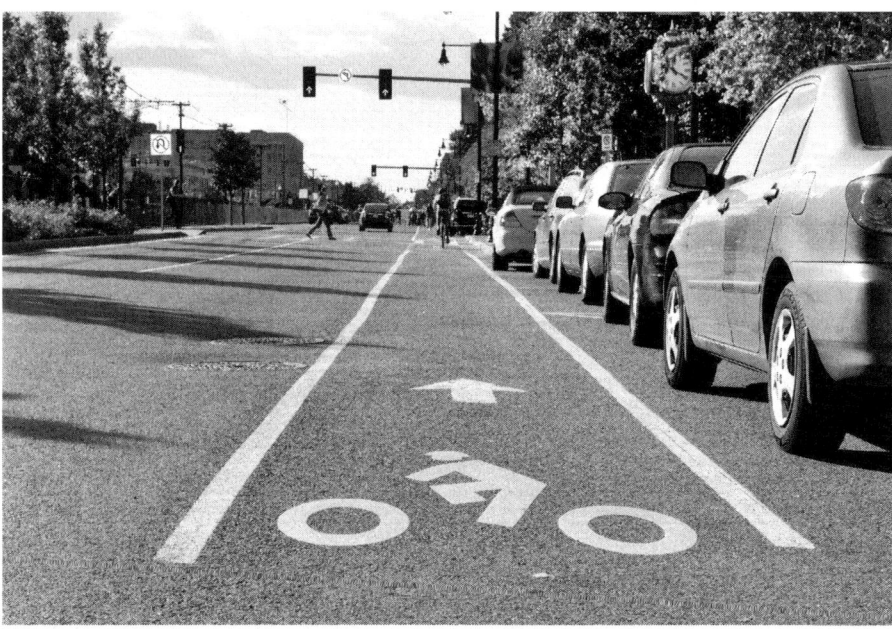

Figure 6.1

Bike lane with minimal buffer. Image courtesy of Shutterstock

Networked design thinking

Figure 6.2
Sharrow. Image courtesy of Shutterstock

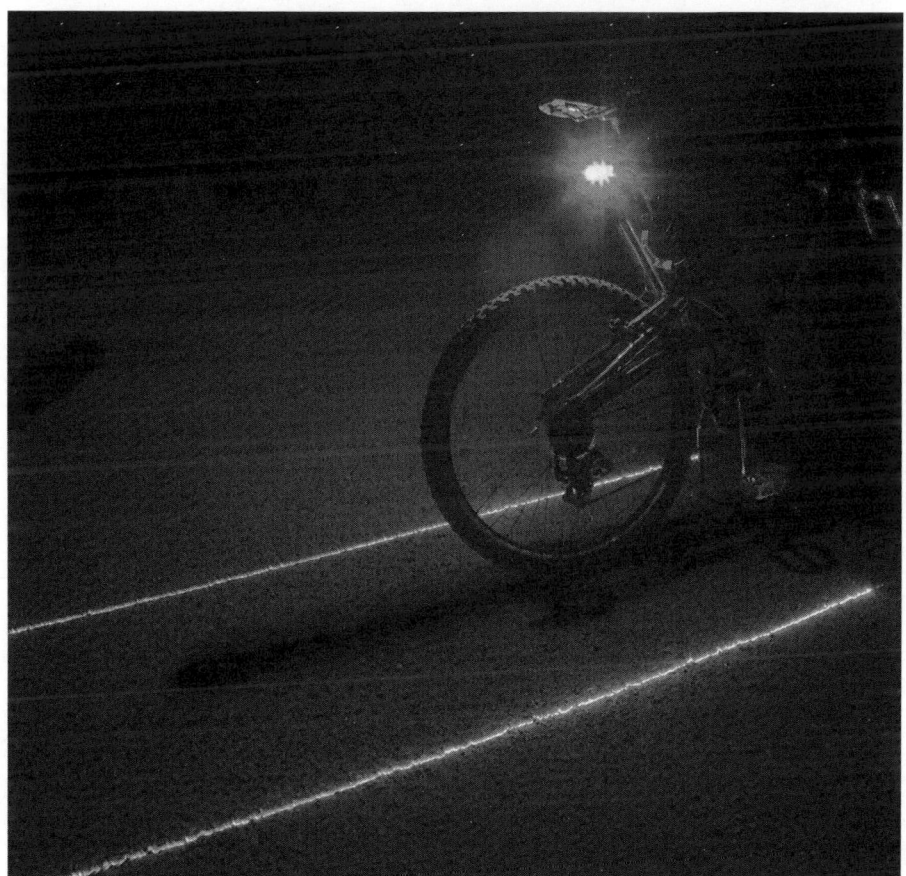

Figure 6.3
Digital light bike lane. Image courtesy of ETOPSTECH

In 2017, one of the most dangerous and longest-lasting wildfires raged in California. The result of a drought, unprecedented dry ground conditions, and uncontrolled (Santa Ana) winds, the wildfires destroyed over 1,000 homes, ravaged over 505,000 acres, and cost the state $10,000,000 (Yan, Simon, and Vercammen, 2018). In addition to these immediate effects, the wildfires also caused dramatic air pollution in major cities in California as the smoke and debris from the fires settle on the ground. They caused major power outages as infrastructure was damaged and generally taxed to redirect resources to fight the fires that moved as fast as 4 miles per hour, in some cases giving people only minutes to escape their homes before they were engulfed in flames. While it might be easy to chalk this dramatic event up to climate change, it is actually the confluence of a number of coexisting conditions—some that have built up over time and some that are of the moment. How these elements interact with one another form the basis of the network. They rely on one another, and one (or multiple) changes in that network can have profound effects, either positive or negative. Almost every year, California faces some sort of water crisis. Some scientists even claim that California is in a mega-drought, in part because of Silicon Valley and the agricultural economy that it has built up in a "semi-arid" climate. One technological advancement that has been proposed to deal with the water shortage is desalination technology, which essentially takes ocean water and uses a reverse osmosis process to remove the salt and turn it into fresh drinking water. In essence, finding a new way to increase the stock of water in the water system for California to replace the lack of rain. While proponents hail its potential, critics of the system question its effectiveness and safety. For example, the salt that is removed from the water is often filtered back into the ocean. While on a small scale this might have little to no effect on the salt levels, on a larger more industrial scale (like the plant opened in Israel in 2013) scientists worry that the salt levels will affect marine plant and animal life, which in turn can affect fishing, tourism, etc. Others worry that the process is so expensive, that it might limit who has access to the water, creating an economic and public health divide.

Because technology is often focused on addressing the symptoms of a problem (i.e. how can we give people access to their mail and phone calls and documents all in one portable device) rather than the root case (i.e. are we working too much and connecting with one another too little?) the history of technological innovation has focused in the wrong area. But, there are still many advantages and potentials for technology to enhance our world and lives in meaningful and exciting ways *if* we choose to focus on the larger picture and reciprocity between the human and human-made, technological world.

Design research methods: visualizing networks and patterns

Thinking about technology as part of a larger, dynamic network has the potential to fundamentally alter the way that we, as designers, choose to approach wicked problems and technological issues. Research methods that can encourage a better understanding of the networks and patterns underlying any design problem can help us as designers see the relationships between interconnected parts of a design problem. If the ultimate goal is to get at the root causes of any wicked problem, these methods can also help designers see not just what the current outcomes of the problem is, but also what might be contributing to them in the first place.

Critical cartography/critical mapping

With roots in geographic sciences, critical cartography has emerged as an examination of how maps are generated and used as a result—specifically because of the increased access to data. At the core of how we are defining and using critical mapping is the examination of the map as an artificial production—something that has agendas and is shaped by the motivations of the map creator. And since we know that design is not a neutral activity, it's equally as important to understand the research that is driving it as non-neutral. What the map offers is a critical use of elements like scale, orientation, organization, and framing to help us make meaning of abstract data, but also persuade us of a certain truth. And how might we use these tools to engage in a more critical dialogue surrounding the artifact of the map itself? Scale, orientation, organization, and framing provides a structure and specific tool we can use to compare and contrast data and findings. Mapping can also be used as a tool to pose questions, and encourage debate and deliberation in the design research process. Critical cartography in design research is most productive when reframed not as a finished product used only to prove or underscore the proposal that will result from it, but when utilized as an iterative, exploratory, and comparative tool. As a powerful analytic tool, the map also breaks complex issues or systems into smaller pieces to allow designers to extract, study, and question a single component or relationship in depth. As a synthetic research tool, mapping allows designers to take the diverse observations and data they have gathered surrounding a question and its contextual relationships to render new insights and relationships previously unseen. The patterns that the map uncovers provide a clear entry point for the researcher to ask critical questions that support or deconstruct preconceived ideas (Allen and Queen, 2015).

Correlational research

In thinking about systems, relationships are of paramount importance. In their book, *Architectural Research Methods* (2013), David Groat and Linda Wang illustrate two distinct types of correlational research that are critical in architectural/design research—relational and causal-comparative. As further explained:

> Although all correlational studies, by definition, seek to describe the relationship between or among key variables, the term relationship study is meant to distinguish those studies—or components of larger studies—that focus specifically on both the nature and the potentially predictive power of those relationships.
>
> (273)

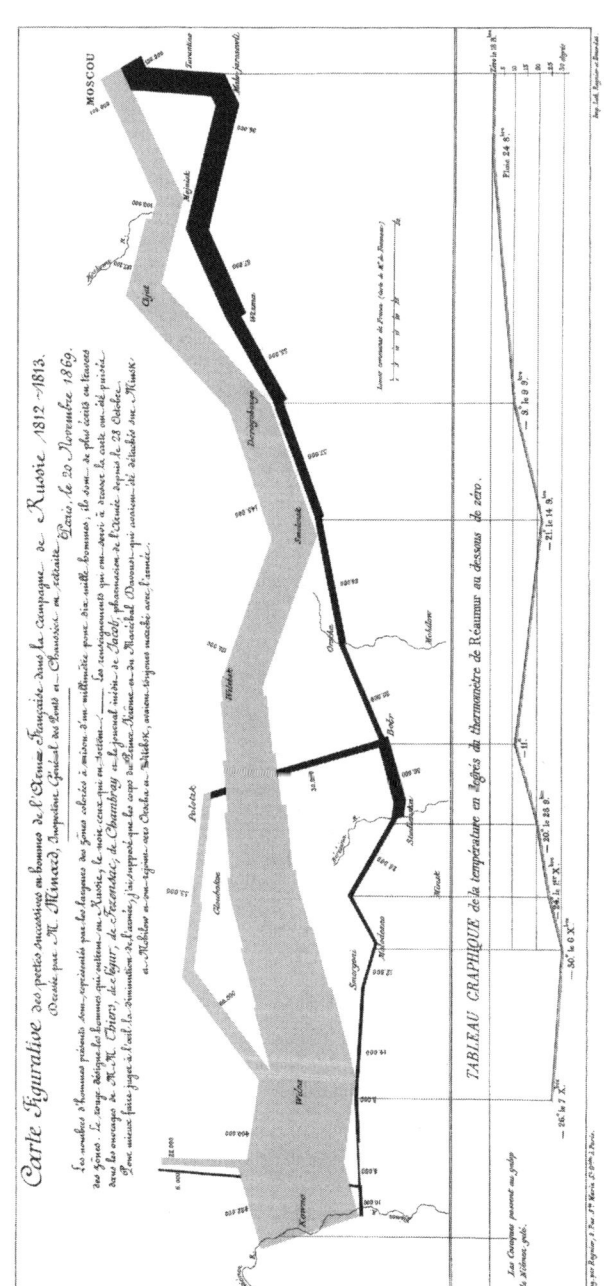

Figure 6.4

Charles Joseph Minard's map of Napoleon's March on Russia

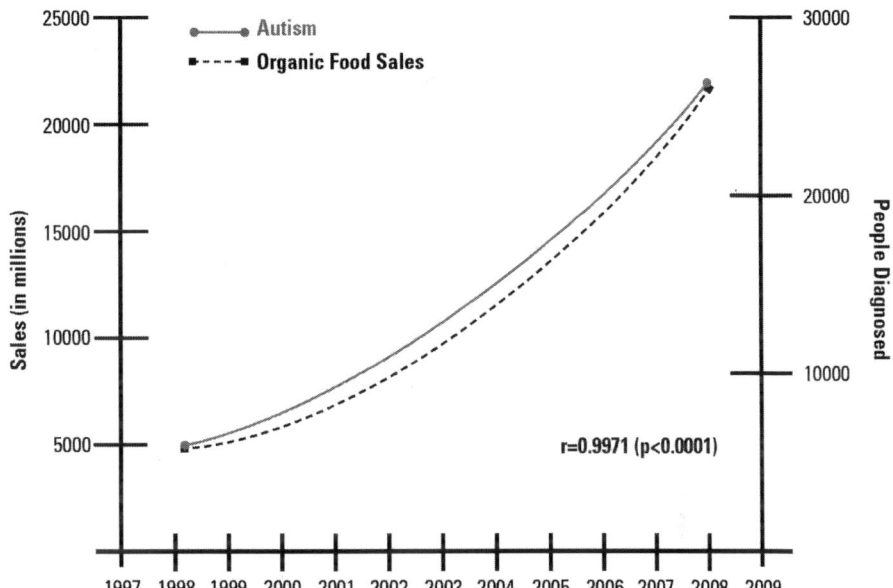

Figure 6.5
Autism and organic food chart

While correlational research does not indicate causation, it can be a first step to indicating what is causing a problem in the first place. A well-known example of this is the chart a Reddit user created to demonstrate the correlation between the rise in autism and the rise in organic food sales. If not understood that a simple relationship does not emphatically link two pieces of information the data can be misleading. This chart has been riffed on to make this point more evident.

But visualizations and information graphics are also great ways to reveal patterns of relationships that would otherwise be invisible. In a 2015 *New York Times* article, vaccination rates of kindergarteners in California showed patterns in geographic clusters of students who has much lower rate of measles vaccinations than the state average. As the authors indicated, "More than a quarter of schools in California have measles-immunization rates for kindergarteners that are below the 92 to 94 percent the CDC says is needed to maintain so-called herd immunity" (Bloch, Keller, and Park). One key pattern that emerged from the study showed that students in wealthier districts had lower rates of vaccination and much higher rates of the personal exemption the state had for personal beliefs. These visualizations are particularly powerful because, as a user, you can compare the rate of vaccination and toggle back and forth between the personal beliefs that support the exemption. The size of the school is indicated by the size of the point that marks it, which suggests smaller and larger populations of students, and the potential significance of these decisions not to vaccinate. Schools are further distinguished as public or charter, another suggestion of patterns but also suggesting a common system of values and wealth that might contribute to the decision not to vaccinate. All of these factors suggest patterns and connections but do not dictate them. Additional interviews with health experts point to deeper reasons for this lack of vaccination, including being lulled into a false sense of security and seeking out alternative forms of vaccination in some areas with older and wealthier residents. Through this interactivity, a deeper dimension relating to the potential causes of the lack of vaccination reveals key areas for further investigation. That is the key to correlational research, as a suggestion of causation and always requiring additional research to delve more deeply into the cause.

Networked design process and methods: exploring connections

Visual thinking

Visualization and visual thinking can be an important aspect of thinking about technology as a system because it allows the designer to simultaneously look at the "whole" of the system, but also the parts of the system. Robert McKim, the author of *Experiences in Visual Thinking* (1980), has characterized three distinct components of visual thinking. The most common (though not necessarily the most recognizable) is seeing. Seeing is really about recognizing—what is around that might offer an answer to a problem or design idea. Watson and Crick, the scientists famous for uncovering the DNA structure (or double helix) did so in part by constructing a large model of it. This construction helped them to see exactly what was going on in the structure, but maybe more importantly, it allowed others to see it too, thereby understanding the complexity of the system more easily. McKim's second element of visual thinking, imagining, is also a critical component to the construction of ideas and concepts. The final element of visual thinking is sketching. Concept mapping as a diagrammatic tool is one example of sketching that is often used in visual thinking because of its power to process information and also to show where there are gaps in learning and understanding. In their book, *Learning How to Learn*, Joseph Novak and Bob Gowin (1984) argue that the power of concept mapping "can . . . provide a kind of visual road map showing some of the pathways we might take to connects meanings of concepts' (15). This act of translation—from the abstract to the concrete—is a core to visual thinking and to considering the larger systems inherent in design problems. Concept maps can be particularly effective as a tool to help make meaning of projects or ideas that have many different components. They can be used to code and organize like entities and to help see patterns—both linear and non-linear.

Lateral thinking

The cognitive psychologist and consultant Edward de Bono coined the phrase lateral thinking to describe it as "closely related to creativity . . . concerned with the creation of new

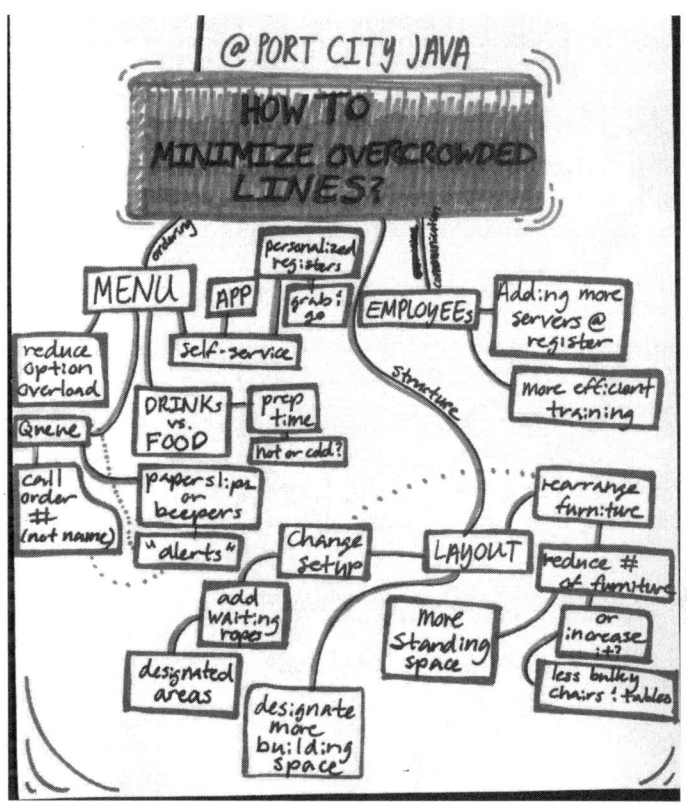

Figure 6.6

Concept map of issues and options reducing the wait in lines at a local coffee shop. Image courtesy of Annie Dang

ideas ... [and] concerned with breaking out of the concept prisons of old ideas" (6–7). Lateral thinking is also characterized as structured ideation. Whereas horizontal thinking is pure brainstorming without any criteria or prompt, lateral thinking is a process that provides constraints, prompts, and structure to the idea-generation process. Because our brains and memory are "hardwired for efficiency," and because our perceived investment into a specific idea can actually hinder the recognition or development of good ideas, de Bono argues that these structures are necessary to keep our creativity fresh. Technology can actually be a limitation to new and fresh ideas as well, as we have become so dependent on the tools necessary to visualize our ideas, we can allow them to dictate the production of ideas, rather than facilitating them.

Using analogies in lateral thinking

De Bono indicates a number of techniques that can be used to force new connections or associations within the idea-generation process. Idea-generating tools are designed to break current thinking patterns—routine patterns, the status quo; focus tools are designed to enhance where to search for new ideas; harvest tools are designed to ensure more value is received from idea-generating output; treatment tools are designed to consider real-world constraints, resources, and support. Analogy is one idea-generating tool that is particularly useful in the world of design for two important aspects. First, analogy can help us understand one thing in terms of another. The design of a computer desktop is a perfect example of this. The designers of the first graphical user interfaces (GUI) intentionally used the visual modes of a folder, paper, a trash can, an envelope (for email) because they knew that users would be familiar with those icons. In that way the transition would be easier and seamless for those users because they could use their previous knowledge of how those physical items work and transfer that into the digital world. But analogy can also be used to extend the understanding of how something might operate. Thinking about how a classroom might operate by comparing it to a beehive on the surface might give you images of buzzing around, lots of movement, students going out on a search and coming back with something that then all of the students use to make a collective project. But taking it one step further, you might discover that the drones in a beehive actually move from role to role throughout their lifetime, which could help you think more specifically about how the design of a classroom might help students occupy different roles, or take on different personas based on the content, or in the classroom could give new insight into how to design that space.

Using analogies for ideation

Use a random word selector (such as wordcounter.net/random-word-generator) or randomly choose a number of nouns or verbs, even by opening the dictionary and randomly pointing to a word! If you are a teacher, choose one to two words per student; if a student doing this for yourself, you can choose two to three to use with this exercise. They should not necessarily have a direct relationship to your project. Select one of the words and use it to do the following:

- Create a propositional statement/question like "How might the design of [a chair] be more like a beehive?"
- Write down as many qualities of how the word feels or behaves as you can think of. Avoid writing down how it looks (to avoid creating a design that just looks like a beehive . . .) Examples of qualities might be: busy, warm, satiating, productive. . . .
- For each of the words that you wrote down, create five sketches that incorporate that quality explicitly in the design. Don't be afraid to sketch down some wild ideas that you know will probably never be realized (some small part of them might!).
- See what you can do to combine multiple designs, or build off of them! Try to extend the understanding of how something might operate.

Using morphologies in lateral thinking

Morphologies are another technique that can inspire lateral thinking through an even more structured method. Originally formulated by Fritz Zwicky in the late 1960s, morphologies (or morphological matrixes) were meant to help deconstruct the complexities of an idea as a way to "the study of all relevant interrelations among objects, phenomena and concepts by means of methods which are based on the utmost detachment from prejudice and carefully refrain from all prevaluations" (1967, 273). As a problem-solving tool, morphologies can help designers break down a problem in order to scrutinize and evaluate each component of the problem individually. As a generative tool, morphologies can help isolate one component of the problem on which to build and then combine each individual component in new and interesting ways. As generative tools, morphologies also help us combine and recombine ideas. In design thinking, morphologies can be used in a number of key ways. They can help us identify user motivations and isolate a number of different reasons for why someone would use the design being worked on. Morphologies can also help ideate on key features that are based on the user motivations, the wicked problem, the context of use, or any number of other drivers. They can also help identify the context or setting where people might encounter or use the design, in order to extend the understanding of needs and wants, and even to consider problems that someone might encounter using the design or new technologies that might enhance the design experience. Maybe more traditionally, they can expand our considerations of formal characteristics of the design, to push us in new directions and consider new materials that might enhance the enjoyability of the design on the part of the user.

Creating a morphology

Morphologies can be used in a variety of ways. They can help designers think about the aesthetic features of a product or service, or they can help force new associations related to user motivations, behaviors, and goals. They can also be a combination of these criteria. Depending on the nature of the project, it might be worthwhile to create a number of different morphologies to explore a wide range of possibilities for accomplishing the goals of the design projects. Morphologies can also be as complex or simple as you choose. If you've never used this technique before, it is worthwhile to start off on a smaller scale to avoid fatigue with the process. As you become more experienced, and depending on the demands of the project, the scale and range of your matrix can grow.

To begin, create a 4 x 4 matrix. Along the top edge of the matrix write four criteria that the design needs to address. These criteria could be physical

(continued)

> *(continued)*
>
> or aesthetic features, user goals, or interactive elements. As an example, in the design of a new banking application four elements that might need to be addressed or incorporated are the need to deposit checks, check balance, project saving trends, and plan a budget.
>
> Along the left edge, write four types of experiences that you want your user to have with your product. These experiences should be derived from the goals of the project, and/or user demographics, needs, or motivations. They can also be a combination of these attributes. To continue the example of the banking app, brainstorming a list of experiences, you might write, "game, education, storybook, competition." In the box where the two intersect, create written or visual examples of how your design could encourage that behavior using the particular quality. Then, combine different ideas from different categories to create a richer and more complex idea.

The invisibility of much of the technology and its impacts require design methods and processes that reveal or make visible that which is invisible. And more specifically, to show the connections between and among how users engage with technology and how that engagement impacts other parts of larger networks that involve other people, environments, and situations. Recognizing the intrinsic need for technology to help designers create new experiences does not mean that we can't be equally as critical about how that technology is being used and adopted.

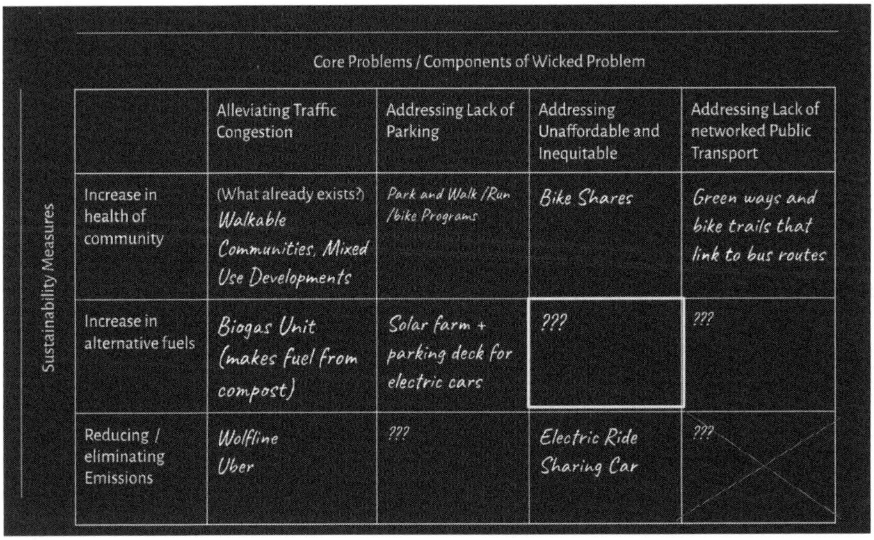

		Core Problems / Components of Wicked Problem			
		Alleviating Traffic Congestion	Addressing Lack of Parking	Addressing Unaffordable and Inequitable	Addressing Lack of networked Public Transport
Sustainability Measures	Increase in health of community	*(What already exists?)* Walkable Communities, Mixed Use Developments	Park and Walk /Run /bike Programs	Bike Shares	Green ways and bike trails that link to bus routes
	Increase in alternative fuels	Biogas Unit (makes fuel from compost)	Solar farm + parking deck for electric cars	???	???
	Reducing / eliminating Emissions	Wolfline Uber	???	Electric Ride Sharing Car	???

Figure 6.7

Example of a morphological matrix used to explore innovative solutions to waste reduction on a college campus. This morphology shows user-types and goals. Image courtesy of the author

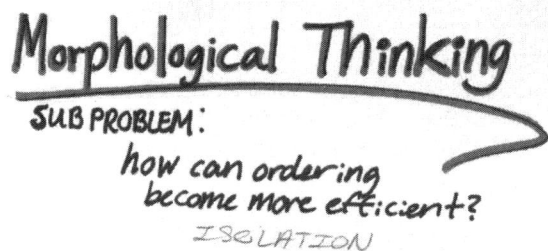

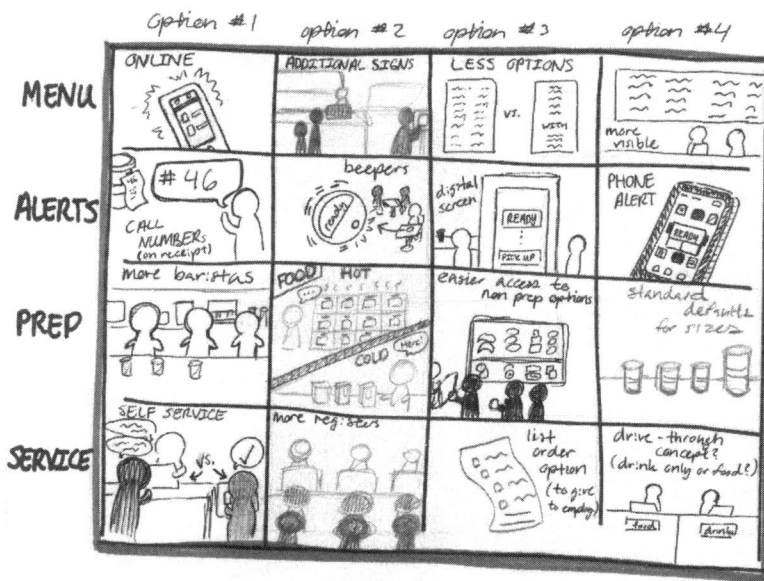

Figure 6.8

Example of a morphological matrix used to explore different options for reducing the wait in lines at a local coffee shop. Image courtesy of Annie Dang

References

Allen, Tania and Queen, Sara. "Beyond the Map: Unpacking Critical Cartography in the Digital Humanities." *Critical Making: Design and the Digital Humanities.* Special Issue of *Visible Language,* edited by Jessica Barnes and Amy Papaelias, December 2015, pp. 78–99.

Bloch, Matthew, Keller, Josh, and Park, Haeyoun. "Vaccination Rates for Every Kindergartener in California." *The New York Times.* February 6, 2015. Retrieved from www.nytimes.com/interactive/2015/02/06/us/california-measles-vaccines-map.html. Accessed September 22, 2018.

De Bono, Edward. *Lateral Thinking: Creativity Step by Step*. New York: Harper Colophon, Reissue edition, 2015.

Groat, Linda and Wang, David. *Architectural Research Methods*. Hoboken, NJ: Wiley, 2013.

McKim, Robert. *Experiences in Visual Thinking*. Boston, MA: Cengage Learning, 2nd edition, 1980.

Novak, Joseph D. and Gowin, D. Bob. *Learning How to Learn*. Cambridge: Cambridge University Press, 1984.

Yan, Holly, Simon, Darran, and Vercammen, Paul. "California Wildfires Have Destroyed 1,000 Structures . . . and Counting." cnn.com. December 12, 2017. Retrieved from www.cnn.com/2017/12/11/us/california-wildfires/index.html. Accessed September 22, 2018.

Zwicky, Fritz. "The Morphological Approach to Discovery, Invention, Research and Construction." In Fritz Zwicky and Albert Wilson, editors. *New Methods of Thought and Procedure: Contributions to the Symposium on Methodologies*. Berlin: Springer-Verlag, 1967.

7 Visualizing the invisible
Case studies of networked design thinking

The ubiquity of technology has had profound cultural impacts locally and globally. Thinking about technology as a network in and of itself, but also part of a larger network with nodes and connectors should encourage us to consider the reciprocal relationship that it has with users. Sometimes our designs simply need to acknowledge and address a current situation that has been caused by, or exacerbated by, the introduction of technology in a specific situation or to culture overall. Sometimes we might be trying to undo damage, but at the very least, we need to be examining the impact that technology has on us as designers (in the types of designs we are creating) and to users and how they are engaging with design and how it might be impacting their quality of life.

Discovering the root causes of inequality through mapping the social histories of urban development

Current access to open-source data, and access to platforms and software like ArcMap, SimplyMap, and Tableau have given designers new opportunities to examine and better understand the larger context of design action. If primed to do so, using these tools as part of the research process can also encourage students to look at the multilayered and multidimensional network of decisions that design is based on, and that impact the everyday lives of people who will interact with those decisions. When looking at something as expansive as urban development, we are not often looking for the underlying reasons and decisions that have contributed to the current status of a city. Especially in the United States, issues of gentrification have driven new considerations about how cities can grow without marginalizing certain populations. And often, the rich histories of certain communities are not elevated because of historical issues tied to race, power, and segregations. Through a graduate level cross-disciplinary research seminar course co-taught with my colleague, Sara Queen at North Carolina State University, we explored the ways that the map can function reciprocally as a tool to articulate research findings, as well as to challenge the assumptions that are driving the research process itself. We also wanted to encourage students to uncover some of the hidden histories that might make certain communities more vulnerable to erasure through urban development, and uncover how certain populations had been impacted by urban infrastructure throughout history, encouraging a view of urban development as a complex network of policies and decisions that were infrastructural, political, economic, social, and environmental in nature.

The map is a particularly powerful tool because of its ability to shape reality, even more so than to reflect it (Corner, 1999). The genesis for the seminar arose from the confluence of a number of different observations that we had regarding how students were conducting research, how they were engaging with new tools of research like GIS and open-source data platforms, and how they were making sense of and articulating that research both textually and visually. An important factor in engaging students in the research process is to encourage them to be more reflective and reflexive practitioners. As Christopher Crouch and Jane Pearce argue in *Doing Research in Design* (2015):

> if design is the result of the negotiation between the designer and the objective circumstances that shape the world that the designer works within, then it helps us to understand that research is similarly the result of the research attempting to resolve the inquiries about the world.
>
> (5)

Throughout the course, students engaged in case study and mixed methods research, with specific focus on historical, data-driven, and ethnographic methods. Through a focus on Raleigh's urban landscape, students considered the types of case study they might engage—whether broad or deep—with a focus on illuminating patterns and correlations between history and urban development.

Map Series 1:
The Nature of Urban History

Mapping Precedent:
Spatio-Temporal Maps

Research Method:
Archival

Critical Comparison:
Scale, Isolation

Data Sources:
GIS Shape files, Demographic and Quantitative Data, Historic Maps

Map Series 2:
Connecting Histories

Mapping Precedent:
Relational Maps

Research Method:
Case Study, Mixed Methods

Data Sources:
Qualitative Data, Archives, Individual Histories, Interviews

Critical Comparison:
Orientation, Hierarchy

Map Series 3:
Perceptions of Place

Mapping Precedent:
Image Maps

Research Method:
Observational and Ethnographic

Data Sources:
Personal Observations, Surveys, Data Collection

Critical Comparison:
Framing

Figure 7.1

Matrix of research methods and mapping typologies

The map as a vehicle for critical research holds rich possibilities for discovering previously unrevealed power structures and impacts. The inherent qualities of the map are particularly rich for helping see connections between different types of information because it isolates and foregrounds certain information (such as roads, and buildings) and helps the researcher see how those one or two pieces of information relate to one another. Another important quality, framing, helps to focus the area of research (city boundaries, for instance) so that the researcher is making intentional decisions about the scope of the map, and by extension the research itself, in a really tangible way.

The map also has two important roles in the research process: 1. It helps students translate complex research into a visual form that was accessible but also rich and complex; and 2. It forces students to confront their own biases about the narrative that they were constructing as a result of the research itself. Students also used the map to

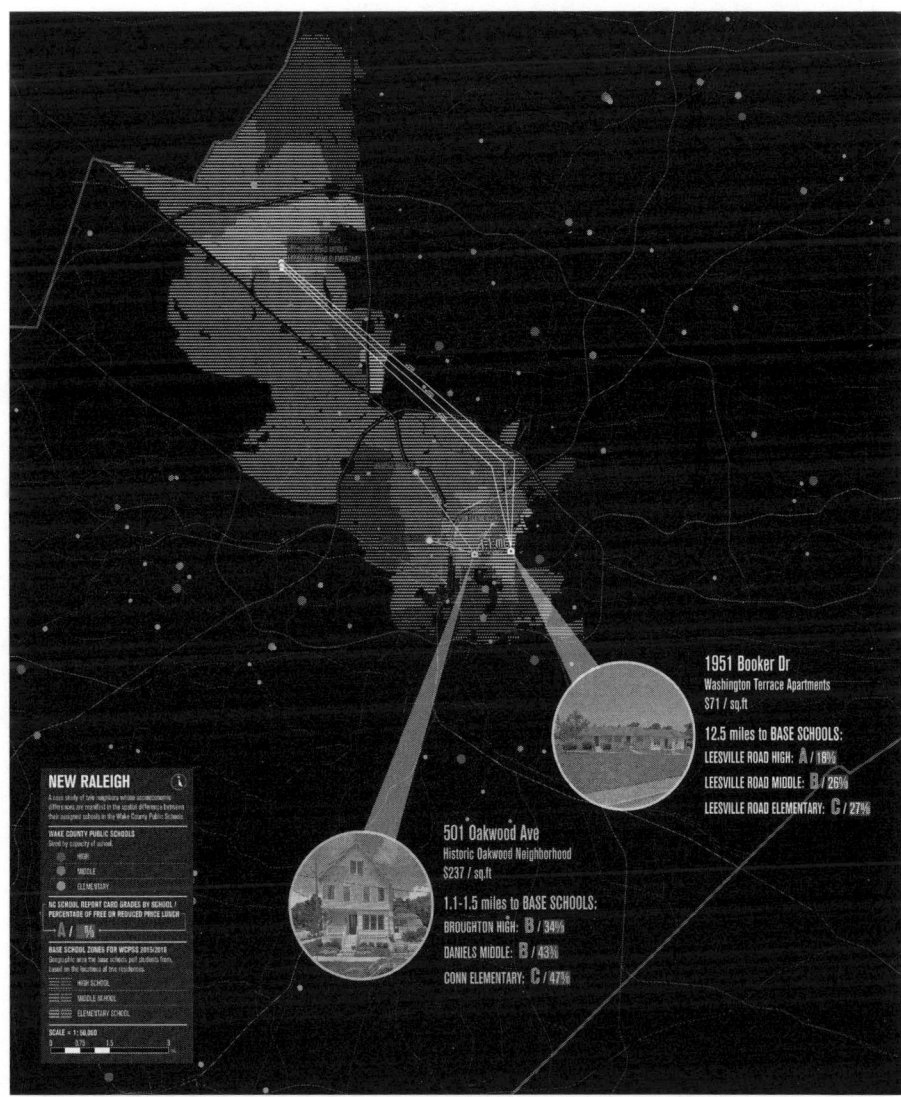

Figure 7.2

GIS data map of education and urban development. Image courtesy of Rebecca Ryan

Visualizing the invisible

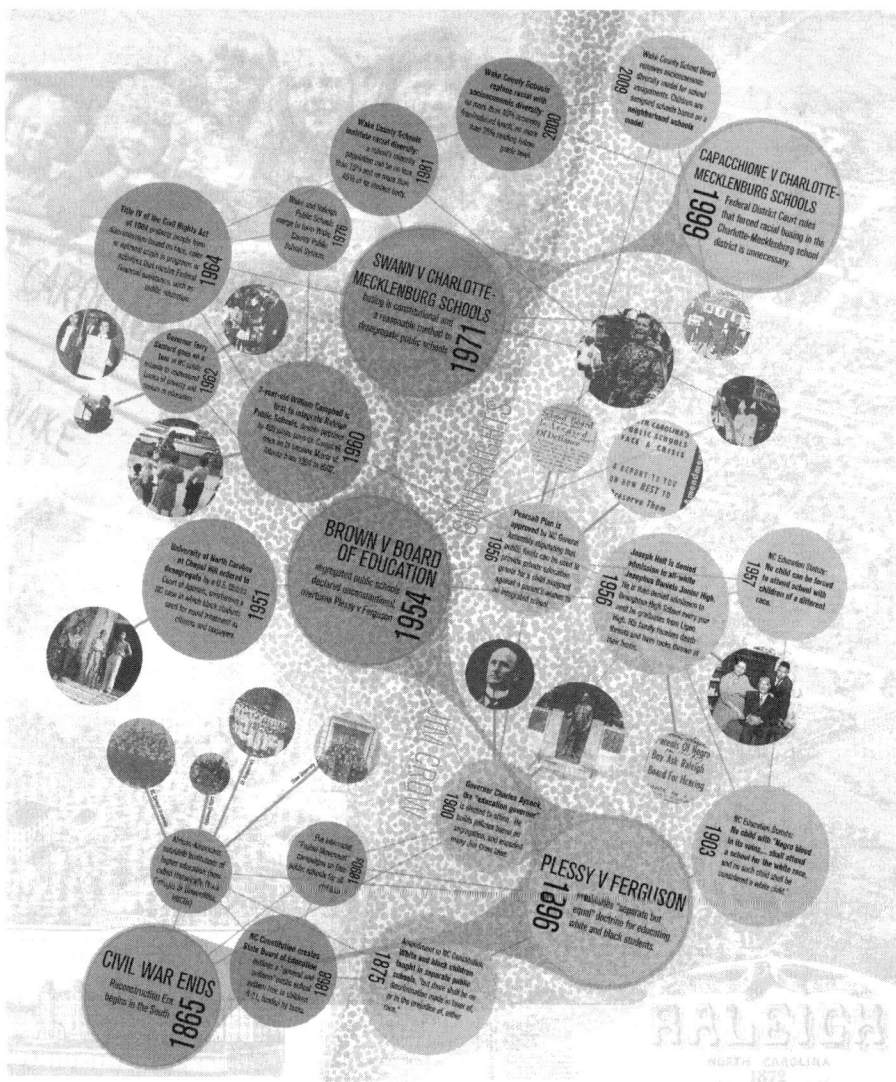

Figure 7.3

Looking at the history of education access and equality in Raleigh, NC. Image courtesy of Rebecca Ryan

engage in a number of different research methods, namely archival and historical research, case study and mixed methods and even observational and ethnographic research. All of the research methods and the maps themselves were used as comparative tools to gauge and judge the validity of research findings and to engage in critical discussions about the impact of infrastructural and urban development on the people living with the city. Students researched topics ranging from educational access, to railroad and town development, to crime and civil disobedience.

Students did a series of three maps, each of which looked at a specific topic of urban development. These lenses—social, economic, political, environmental, or infrastructural—used non-traditional methods to frame their research into urban development.

Visualizing the invisible

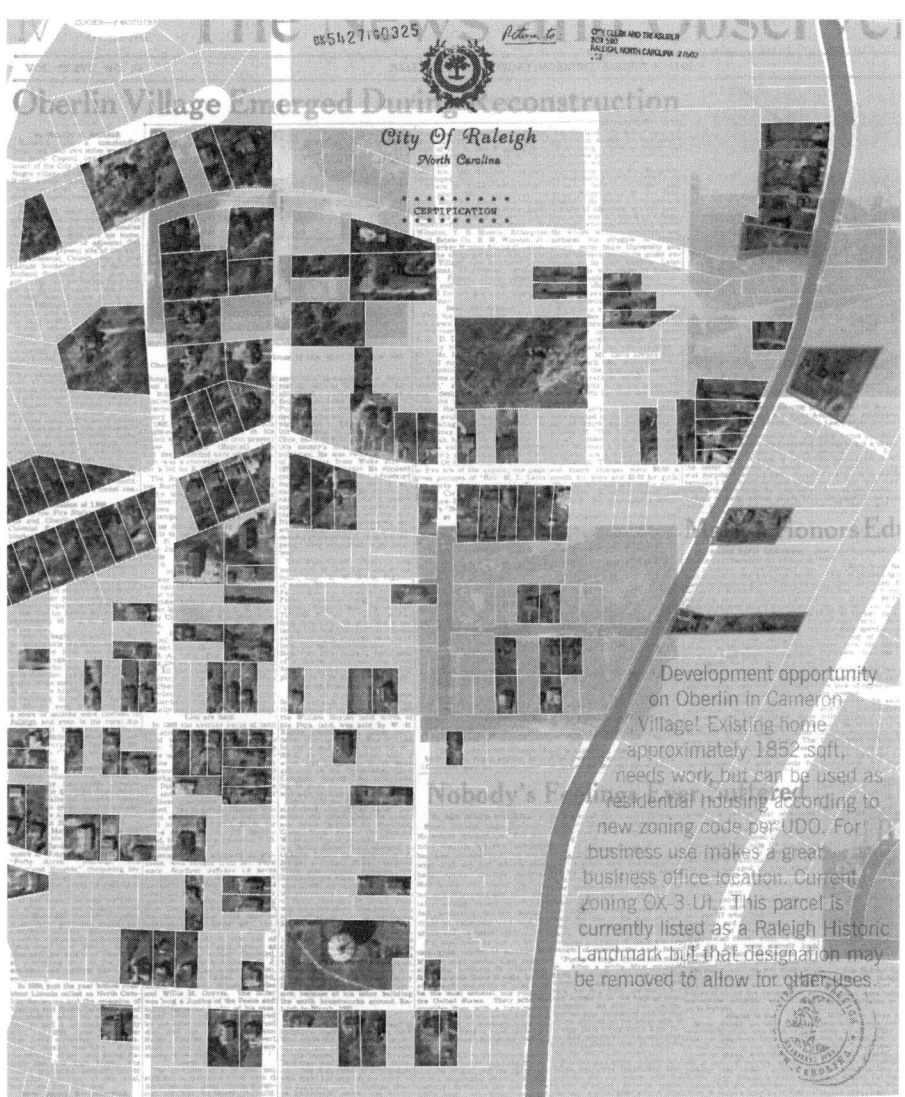

Figure 7.4

Experiencing
Oberlin Village,
the first Freed
Slave community
in Raleigh, NC.
Image courtesy of
Rebecca Ryan

The first map series focused on historical and contemporary GIS data along with historical maps and census information to start to frame an understanding of urban development over time. The second map moved out of the geospatial realm, focusing on networks and associations to deepen the reflection on how a specific topic—education, for instance—has been influenced by, as well as influenced, the ways in which the city expanded. Finally, to compare the research the students had done as a removed observer, students created their final maps as "thick descriptions" of a particular site related to their topic. These final maps required students to visit the site and spend time observing and investigating scenes based on location, adjacencies, and social territories. One student, a master's student in Architecture, began her research by looking specifically at the relationship between education, school locations, and education quality related to property value in downtown Raleigh, where NC State is located. This initial research revealed an inequality between where lower-income students were living, and how close or far they were to a quality school. Schools that they were natural assigned to often times were rated lower, and the only options for them were to attend a school that was much further away, and often involving long commutes. Through the research, the student also revealed a connection between the neighborhoods that the students were coming from and historic issues of segregation prevalent in the American South until the mid to late 1960s. Finally, the student went to one of the oldest African American neighborhoods—the first freed-slave community in Raleigh, and one where education was initially valued quite highly and where the first African American schools were built right after the US Civil War. In creating her final observational maps, she tracked where evidence of this rich history was evident based on what she knew had existed previously. The result of this student's research revealed a rich network of policies that tied education with property value and revealed how critical that relationship was when considering how urban development in a city like Raleigh should move forward.

> To see more information about this and other research projects that use mapping and visualization as a research tool, go to design.ncsu.edu/co-lab.

Arcades in Thessaloniki, Greece: networks of memory and emerging entrepreneurialism

The city of Thessaloniki on the northern coast of Greece has seen several old commercial arcades transform into cafes, bars, and restaurants. Increasingly attracting (usually young) locals' attention, online, and print press, blogs, and anecdotal evidence are referring to these arcades as the "new hotspots" representing a new creative entrepreneurialism, and promising a step forward for economic and cultural progress (Gerolympou-Karadimou, 2014, Koukoumakas, 2015). Sometimes these "new hotspots" coexist with old businesses, thus revealing the long-standing entrepreneurial and intergenerational character of arcades. Very often, however, passersby are confronted with a picture of abandonment and dilapidation, visible signs of the socio-economic decay that hit Thessaloniki among other urban centers in Greece particularly during the last decade during the economic crisis and a general transformation instigated by globalization and increased technological connectivity which has spawned many new forms of work and production (Patsarika, 2005).

    An international collaboration between a professor at Thessaloniki University in Greece, Maria Patsarika, and North Carolina State University, Scott Townsend, engaged students in a prolonged study of these spaces, focusing on how these new entrepreneurial ventures are being accepted and integrated with the more traditional shops that still occupy the markets. As Patsarika explained it, the project:

explored place identity and entrepreneurial practices, as perceived and experienced by entrepreneurs themselves, and in light of the social and economic changes Greece has experienced in recent years. These have been marked by debates over innovation and a new entrepreneurial culture as conditions for economic growth and revival of the Greek society (Bouikidis, 2014). The project also aimed to problematize such debates through the lens of memory and heritage, values which arguably have the potential to reinforce cultural continuity and intergenerational understanding, in tandem with societies' economic growth (Rosenberg, 2012, Seedat, 2014); and to explore ways to engage local communities in dialogue, community design and social innovation.

As a networked study, students used many different tools and platforms to record and make sense of the many dimensions of identity and histories evident in the space in and around the arcade. From interviews, video, and photographic collection to ambient noise, the student researchers created a rich and textured network of evidence regarding personal and historical identity. As part of the field diaries, one student wrote:

> What Malakopi arcade (stoa) means to [Mr. Voskidis] cannot be explained in few words. It is the place where his dreams are being gradually metamorphosed into tangible objects. The locus, itself, is not a stimulus of inspirations but a nest of memories—as he advocates. It is the reference point where remarkable achievements are accomplished and revitalise his duty to behave with integrity and discretion.

One of the main goals of the project was to display and present the research findings back to the arcade stakeholders, those business owners—old and new—who were occupying the space as a way to start conversations about how the market was changing, and the role that identity played in how both customers and shop owners viewed and related to the market. Back in the US a group of sophomore graphic design students led by Scott Townsend took the interviews, field diaries, photographs, and other kinds of documentation that Patsarika and the other students had done and designed knowledge maps to be used in further discussions with people in the community. As Townsend explained it:

> the students were also being introduced to "people, designed objects and contexts of use" through research, analysis, and interpretation, while learning about and refining formal ways of visualizing & communicating your research through graphic design artifacts. In other words, the students were engaging in research *through* design.

As a part of the process, students created a comprehensive in-progress overview of the space by printing out and assembling all the archived materials on the studio wall. Because many of the students in the class had never been to the site, and so were engaging in research "from afar," each student needed to locate where individual shops were as well as where the interviewees could be found in the space as a way to visualize the arcade and give them a deeper understanding of the physical and cultural space. Each team then took one

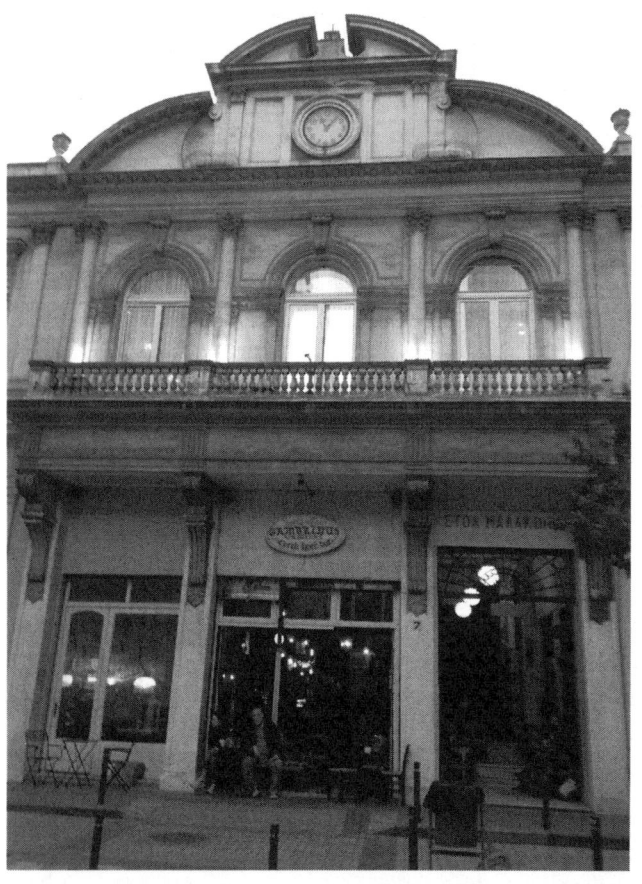

Figure 7.5

Malakopi Arcade today. Image courtesy of Maria Patsarika

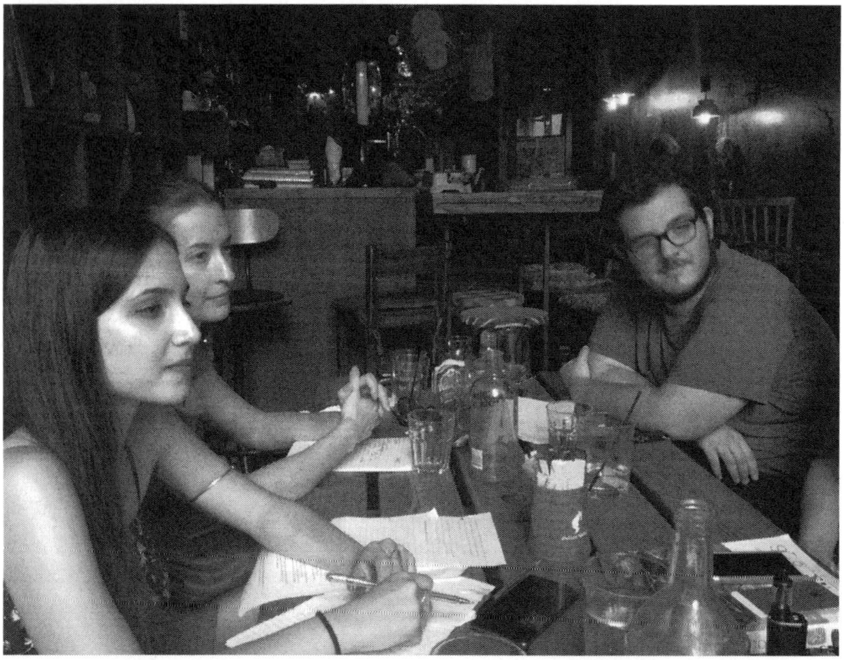

Figure 7.6

Students doing research. Image courtesy of Maria Patsarika

Visualizing the invisible

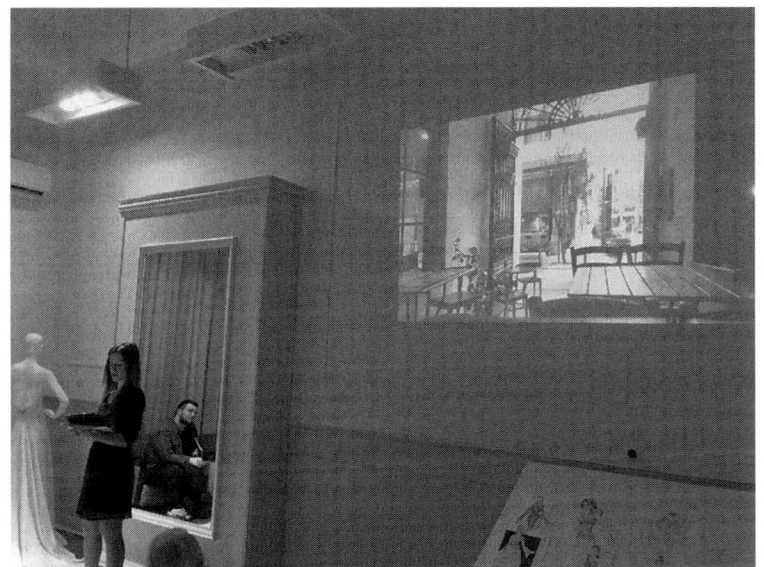

Figure 7.7
Student presenting research findings. Image courtesy of Maria Patsarika

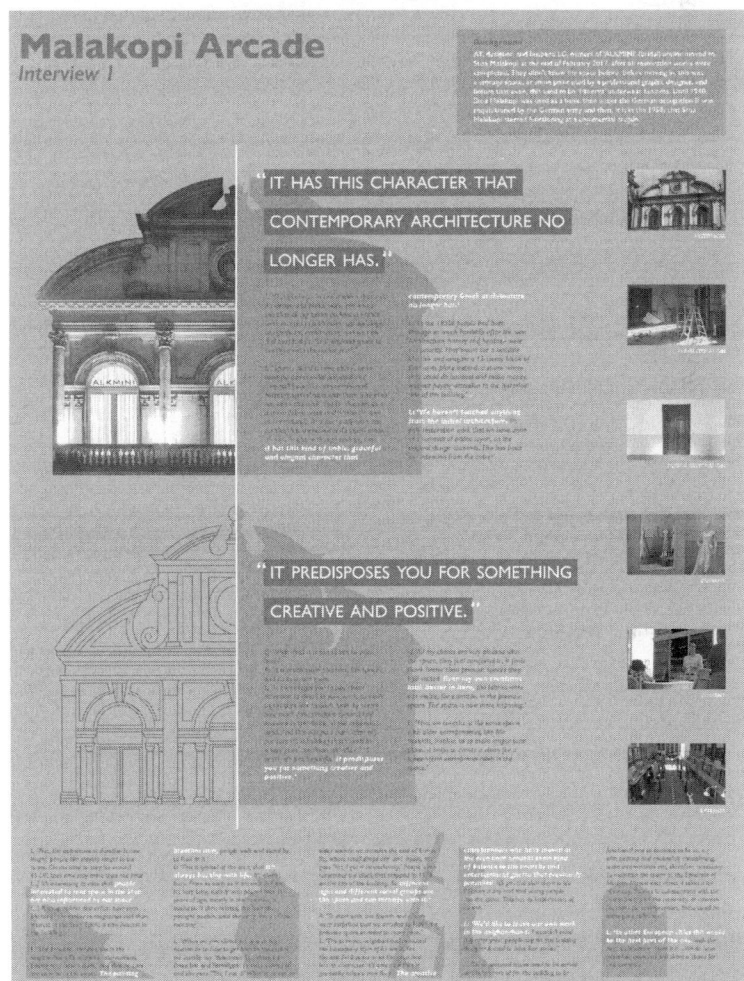

Figure 7.8
Interview 1 knowledge map. Image courtesy of Scott Townsend

Visualizing the invisible

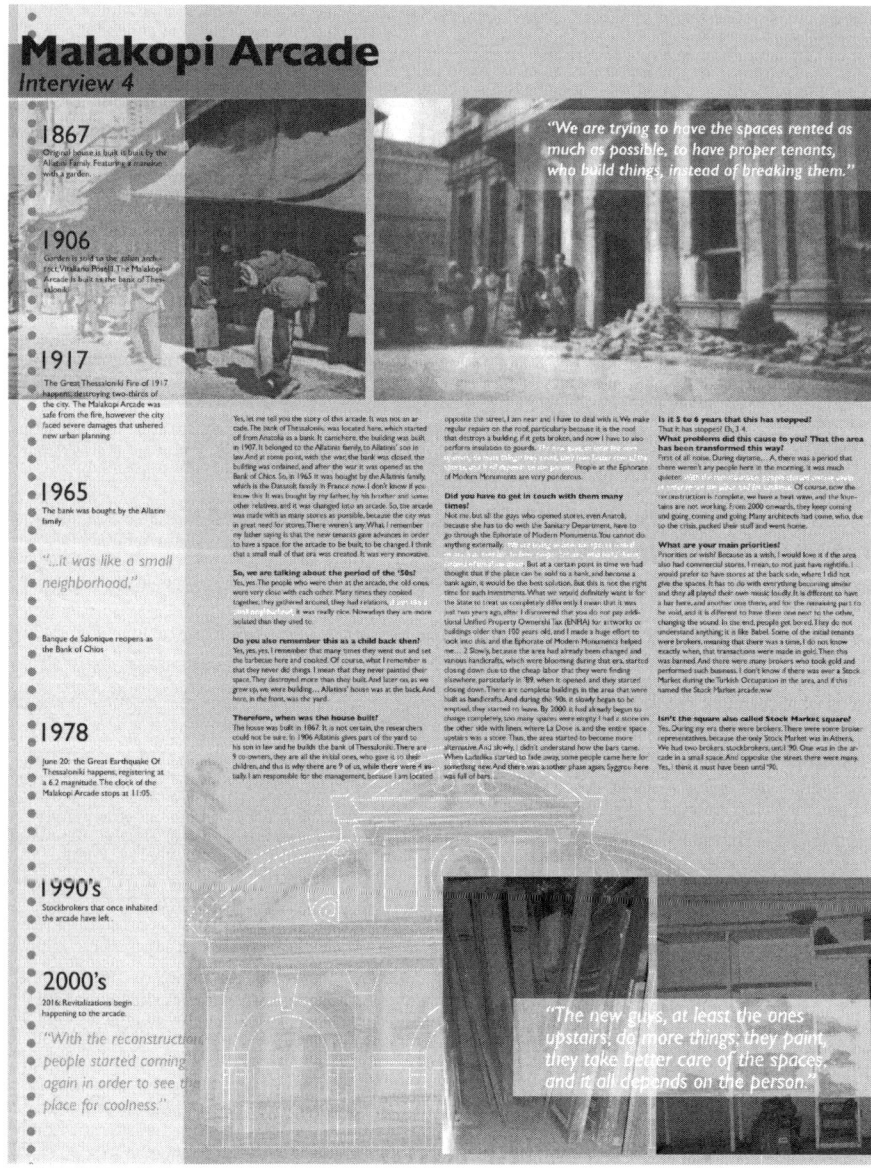

Figure 7.9
Interview 4 knowledge map.
Image courtesy of Scott Townsend

interview, and along with photos of the interviewee's space and the facade panorama, highlighted its location within the larger arcade context to create a specific documentation map. These maps then became important tools that Patsarika's students could use in their final community meetings, as visual evidence of the research, and also to start or continue conversations about the future of the arcade, and how the changing usage might accommodate the historical nature of the old arcade with the shifting landscape that was informing its current and future development. The ultimate goal of the work was to bring together business owners, urban planners, and citizens to find ways to work together to renovate the city space and the knowledge maps became key tools and artifacts through which to have those conversations.

Visualizing the invisible

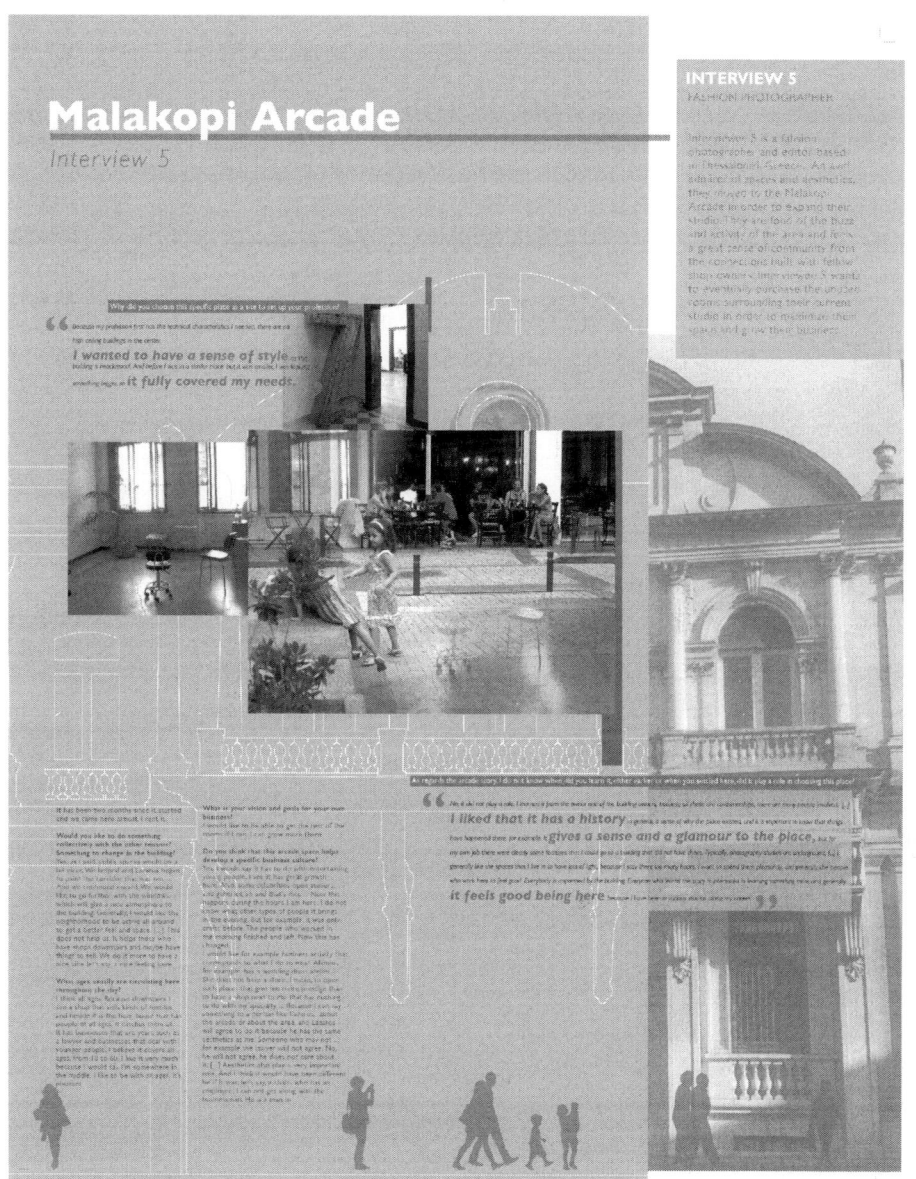

Figure 7.10

Interview 5 knowledge map. Image courtesy of Scott Townsend

Engineering serendipity: Terra Incognita and digital literacy

An extension of participatory design, relational or adaptive design sets up conditions for users to participate in the narrative or story that is being created through the design experience. Whereas participatory design and co-design use a collaborative process with users to define the terms of the design and in certain instances work in partnership with users to transform these ideas into a final design artifact or experience, Relational Design utilizes the experiences, situations of the environment and the user to reframe and reform the design itself. Relational Design privileges the individuality of the user who encounters the building, the museum exhibition, or the web environment to encourage the inclusion and utilization of it based on what is meaningful to that person, on within that particular context. This could be realized in the generation of content, as seen on Facebook, or in the work of Rafael Lozano-Hemmer who uses large scale multimedia installation to capture and re-present travelers through public space or the architect Teddy Cruz's project Manufactures Sites, which "offers a simple, prefabricated steel framework for use in the shantytowns on the outskirts of Tijuana—a structure that participates in the vernacular building practices that imports and recycles the detritus of Southern California's dismantled suburbia" (Blauvelt, 2008). Relational Design "relinquishes the crowd in favour of the assembly" (Druckery, 2003, 71). In other words, it is not about the masses that modernism attempted to appeal to, but in the collection of diversity of perspectives, uses, or enactments. In 2008, Andrew Blauvelt, of the Walker Art Center in Minneapolis, characterized Relational Design as:

> a multitude of contingent or conditional solutions: open-ended rather than closed systems; real world constraints and contexts over idealized utopias; relational connections instead of reflexive imbrication; in lieu of the forlorn designer, the possibility of many designers; the loss of designs that are highly controlled and prescribed and the ascendency of enabling or generative systems; the end of discrete objects, hermetic meanings, and the beginning of connected ecologies.
>
> (Blauvelt, 2008)

Relational Design can be used to challenge assumptions and to change mindsets of those who engage with it. It can be used to showcase the connected ecologies Blauvelt defines, and to help users see them in new and unexpected ways. This is the aim of Terra Incognita, a project by Catherine D'Ignazio, Ethan Zuckerman, and Matt Stempeck at the MIT Center for Civic Media. Explaining the project in a *Huffington Post* article, D'Ignazio (2014) wrote:

> We imagine ourselves to be citizens of the world but in fact we are drawn to people like us, to familiar experiences and to information that confirms our biases. This is the phenomenon Ethan Zuckerman calls "imaginary cosmopolitanism." We could potentially read the daily news from Lagos, Nigeria on our laptop while we're wearing pajamas. We could follow trending tweets from Turkey. But the imaginary part of the cosmopolitanism is that we don't.

As the name suggests Terra Incognita seeks to introduce users of it to new lands and new information and make visible what is ignored. Terra Incognita was a term used by early explorers to designate lands that were unworthy or devoid of inhabitants. Conceived as a global news recommendation system and game, Terra Incognita replaces the user's home page with a map and suggestion for worlds that remain unexplored.

Visualizing the invisible

To this end, we created a game called Terra Incognita: 1,000 Cities of the World after the "unknown lands" label that was inscribed on ancient maps. The program incorporates itself into the Google Chrome web browser when you download it. And each time you open a new tab, it creates a kind of "gateway" home page that gives you a map of and links about an international city Americans tend to ignore or where the mainstream news coverage is oriented to conflict and violence. Sumqayit (Azerbaijan), Ürümqi (China), Aguascalientes (Mexico) and Algiers (Algeria) are a few of the places you might end up exploring.

(D'Ignazio, 2014)

The momentum continues as the user explores new terrain, showcasing what others have explored and suggesting new, related lands and cultures. From a technological

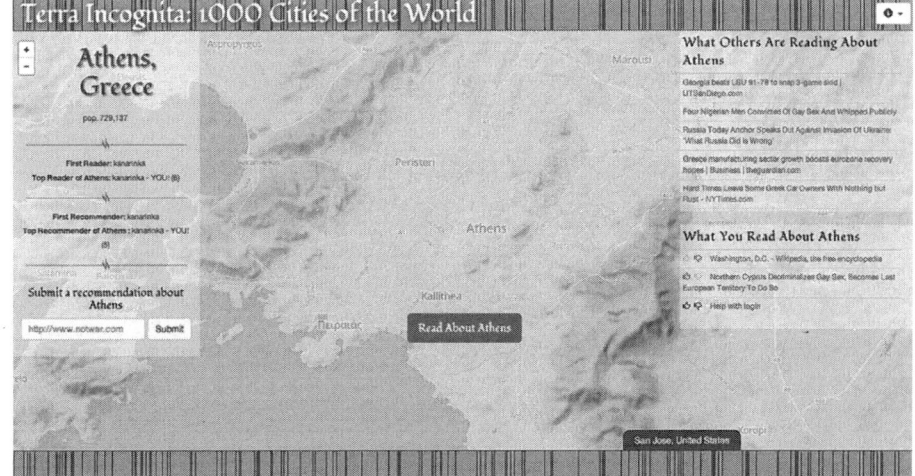

Figure 7.11

Screenshot of landing page from Terra Incognita. Images courtesy of Catherine D'Ignazio

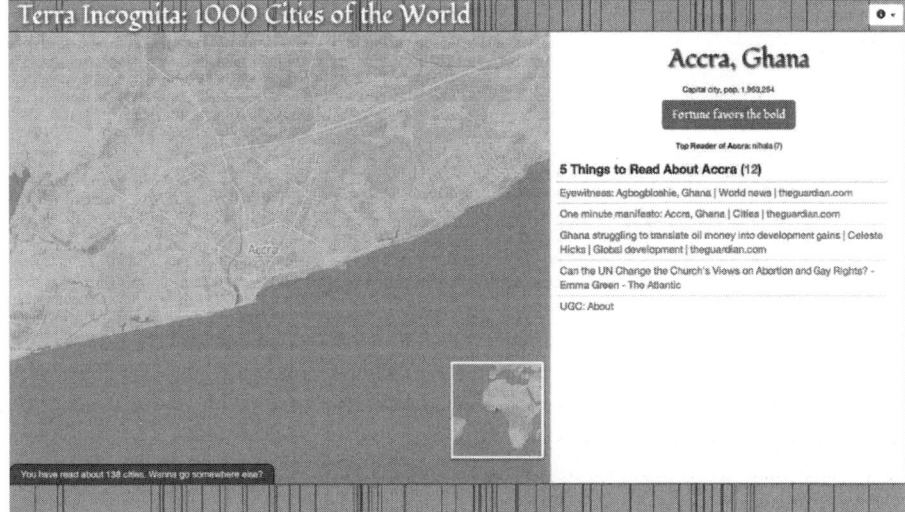

Figure 7.12

Screenshot of entry page into a new location, from Terra Incognita. Images courtesy of Catherine D'Ignazio

97

perspective, the project learns from each individual browser, making each exploration situation and user specific. As more lands are explored, the programs learns from these explorations and seeks out new lands, constantly fluctuating between individual and systematic scale. There is also an element of competition in the game, by showing users those people who have read the most about the gateway that they are currently exploring. For example, a user "visiting" the city of Tripoli might see at the bottom of their browser window another user who has read the most entries about that city, ideally inspiring you to explore more.

As with most projects (technology or otherwise), D'Ignazio and her team made some key discoveries about the project and how people interact with technology. One key discovery is the inherent difficulty of "engineering serendipity." As D'Ignazio outlined in an article for the *Huffington Post* (2014), some of these difficulties include the fact that there are still many "blank spots" on the internet, where information does not exist. From a technological perspective, D'Ignazio also acknowledges the difficulty of programming computers to detect the nuances of a story and what it's about—something that can be relatively easy for a human to do quickly. It is also inherently difficult to anticipate what people will actually want to know about—so when encouraging random connections that have some structural background to them, there is no way to fully anticipate an interest in that subject matter. And finally, the difficulty of incentivizing wandering over "what you want." As D'Ignazio herself stated, "Wandering on the Internet is a concept that sounds romantic until you are actually lost and become terrified, baffled or bored."

While Terra Incognita focused on news and media literacy, D'Ignazio and her collaborator Rahul Bhargava are also tackling the gaps in data literacy through another project, DataBasic.io, which is a suite of four tools and activities that help educators, journalists, policymakers, and citizens gain critical experience with data analysis without having to know the complex code or programming that often goes along with data analysis software. As D'Ignazio and Bhargava et al. (2016) explain it, the need and expectation for data driven research and for students, educators, and professionals to "speak data" has not been offset by the necessary tools and resources to help with the data literacy and competency needed to draw meaningful conclusions.

> Reading data involves understanding what data is, and what aspects of the world it represents. Working with data involves creating, acquiring, cleaning, and managing it. Analyzing data involves altering, sorting, aggregating, comparing, and performing other such analytic operations on it. Arguing with data involves using data to support a larger narrative intended to communicate some message to a particular audience.
>
> (Bhargava et al., 2016)

There are four tools that are a part of DataBasic.io. WTFcsv is a web application that takes a data table or file and returns a summary of the fields, their data type, range, and basic descriptions. WTFcsv is particularly focused on assisting with the beginning of the data summary. WordCounter is a basic word counting tool that takes unstructured text as input and returns word frequency, bigrams (two-word phrases) and trigrams (three-word phrases). SameDiff is a tool that gives users various ways to compare two text documents, to see how they are similar and/or different. For example, how the song lyrics of Beyoncé and Aretha Franklin share common or diverging words and ideas. Finally, Connect the Dots introduces the basics of network analysis for analyzing social media or any data that consists of discrete elements (or nodes) and relationships between those nodes (links).

The key principles guiding the design of all four of these tools, and what D'Ignazio and Bhargava argue are critical for reducing barriers to data literacy and analysis, include being focused, guided, inviting, and expandable. By being focused the tools are easily accessible to new users and require a minimal amount of guidance. To varying degrees, the tools offer guidance—especially at the beginning stages of interaction—to help new users grasp the fundamentals of the tool and of data literacy.

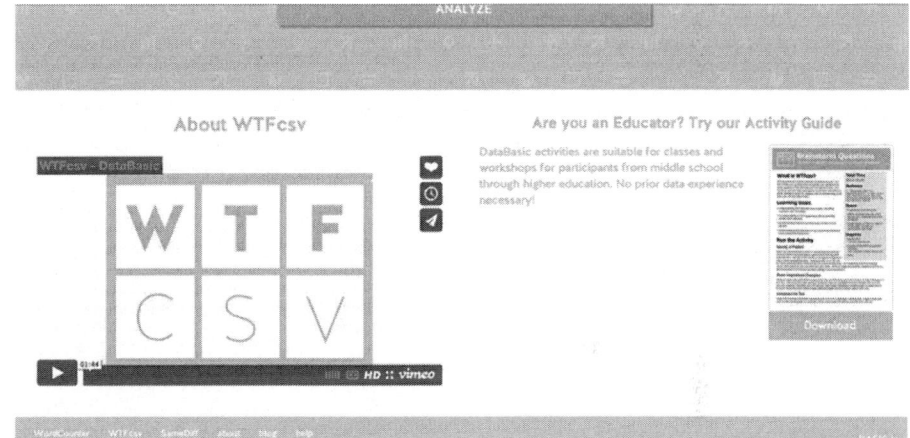

Figure 7.13

WTFcsv home screen. Screenshot courtesy of Catherine D'Ignazio and Rahul Bhargava

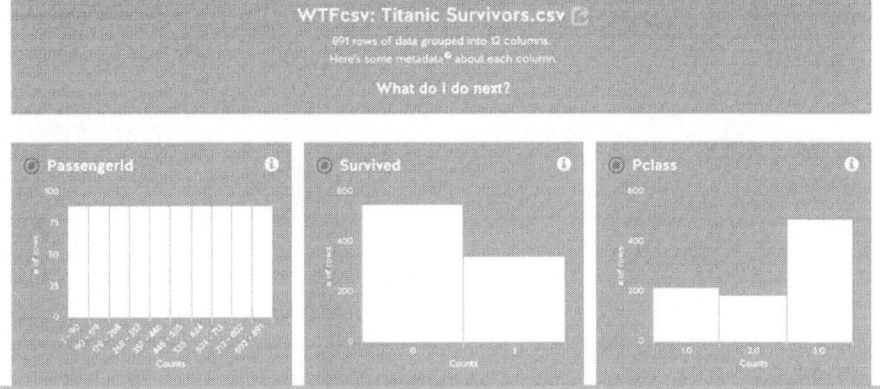

Figure 7.14

WTFcsv visualizations. Screenshot courtesy of Catherine D'Ignazio and Rahul Bhargava

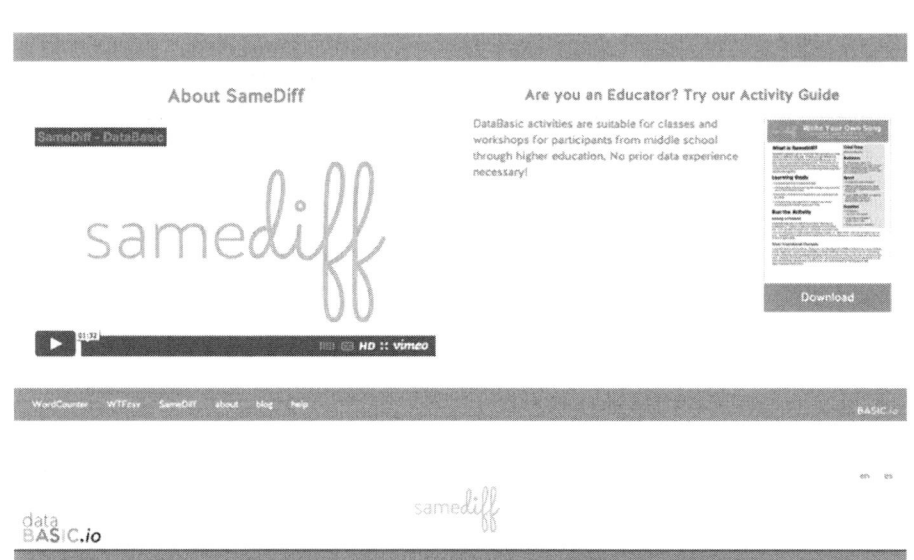

Figure 7.15

SameDiff home screen. Screenshot courtesy of Catherine D'Ignazio and Rahul Bhargava

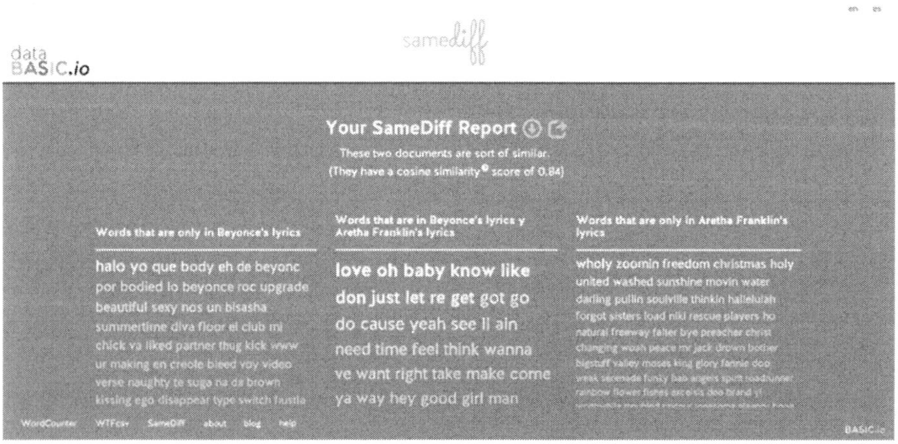

Figure 7.16

SameDiff data input. Screenshot courtesy of Catherine D'Ignazio and Rahul Bhargava

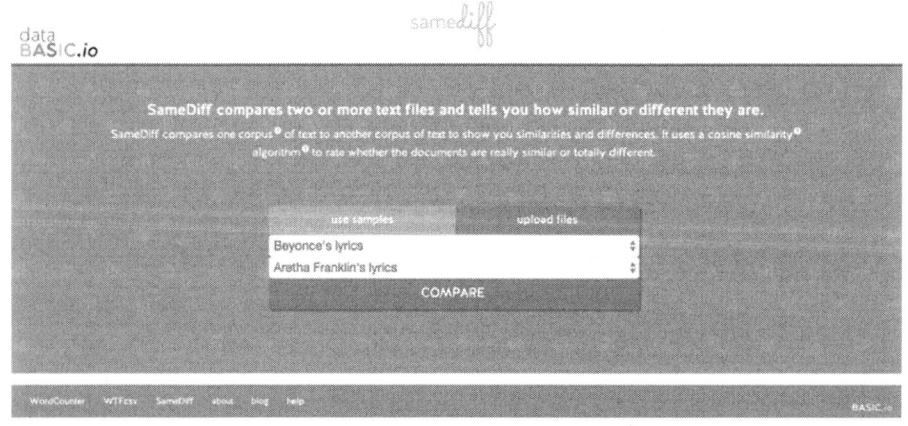

Figure 7.17

SameDiff report. Screenshot courtesy of Catherine D'Ignazio and Rahul Bhargava

The third principle of being inviting acclimatizes and even incentivizes learners and users by allowing them to use data and information that is meaningful to them. Finally, the principle of expandability means that the tools can grow in complexity and sophistication as the learner does. As more and more data visualization software and platforms are introduced, DataBasic.io offers a much-needed alternative to the landscape—one that is heavily weighted with platforms that make things look pretty or are incredibly powerful and require a steep learning curve. Through DataBasic.io, data literacy and criticality are given emphasis in a way that does not sacrifice the importance of visualization and visual thinking as a part of the analytical process.

Revealing our relationship with technology: Jonathan Harris

The technologist and artist Jonathan Harris has long been interested in how new technologies are shaping our experiences. The project We Feel Fine, which he created with Sep Kamvar in 2006, was an exploration of early social media in the form of blog posts. Scanning the internet, the program tags and include any and all blog posts with the word or words "I feel" in them and then creates an new constellation of these posts. Users of the site can then sort these messages according to location, gender, age, and even the weather in the original location of the post. As a new window into this writing, the site is both an exploration and an examination of how and what people share in these new online environments. Aggregating the data, the site also allows the user to explore metrics and make connections and meanings between the posts—such as comparing how many more times we feel is followed by "crazy" (3.8 times the average level) or "alive" (3.1 times the average level). Harris and Kamvar are not trying to create a scientific investigation but to help reveal patterns that exist in seemingly disconnected

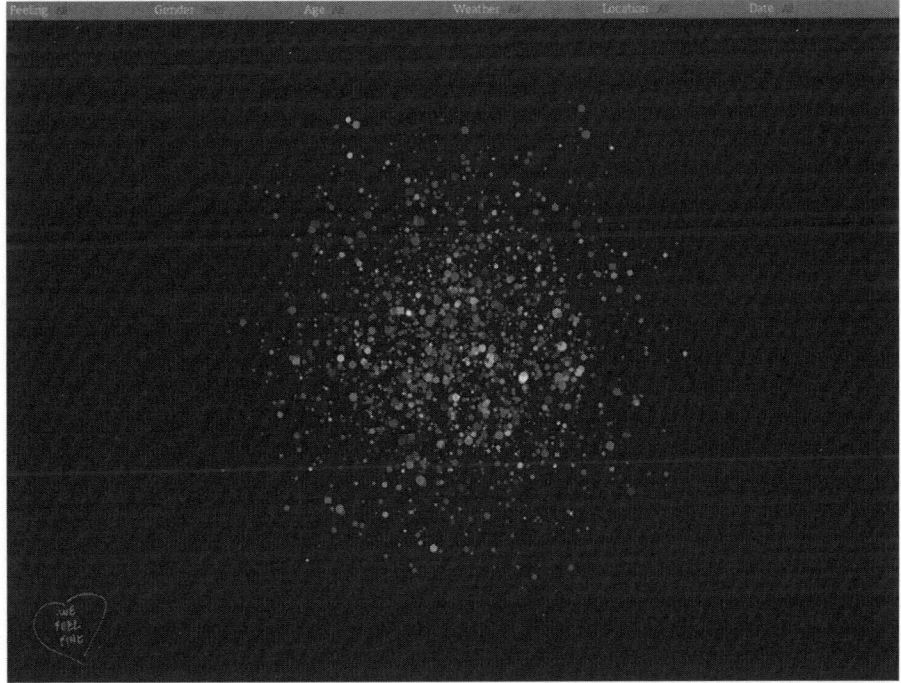

Figure 7.18

We Feel Fine landing page. Image Courtesy of Jonathan Harris

Visualizing the invisible

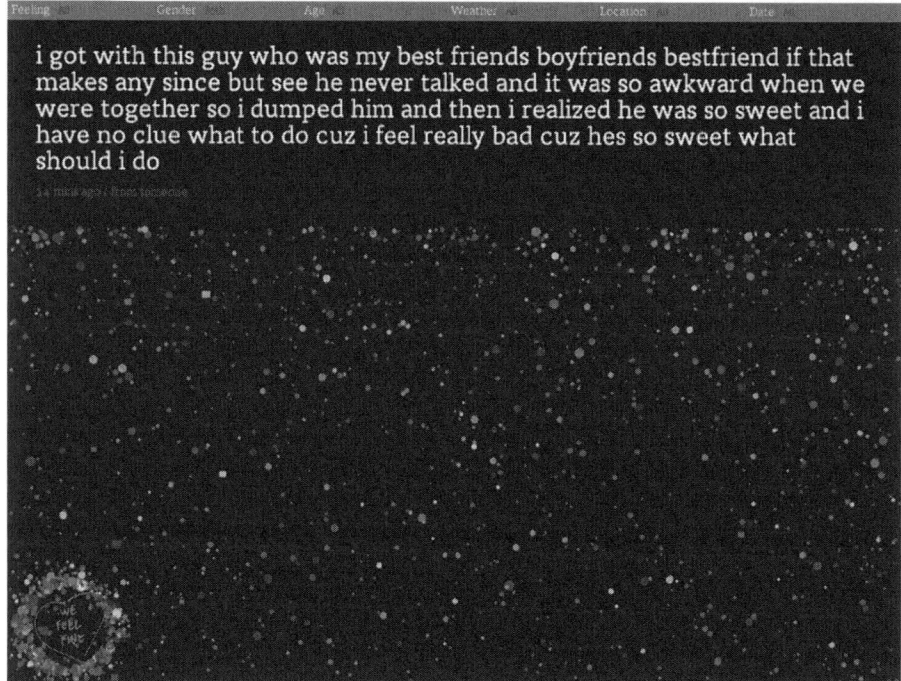

Figure 7.19
We Feel Fine. Rolling over a node in the galaxy reveals a "feeling." Image courtesy of Jonathan Harris

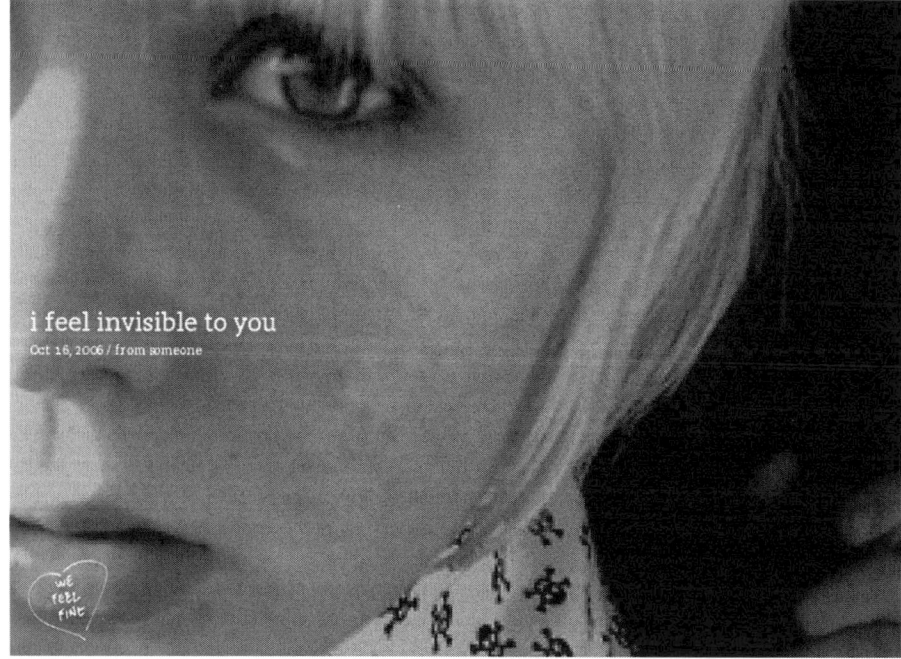

Figure 7.20
We Feel Fine montage of image and text. Image courtesy of Jonathan Harris

Visualizing the invisible

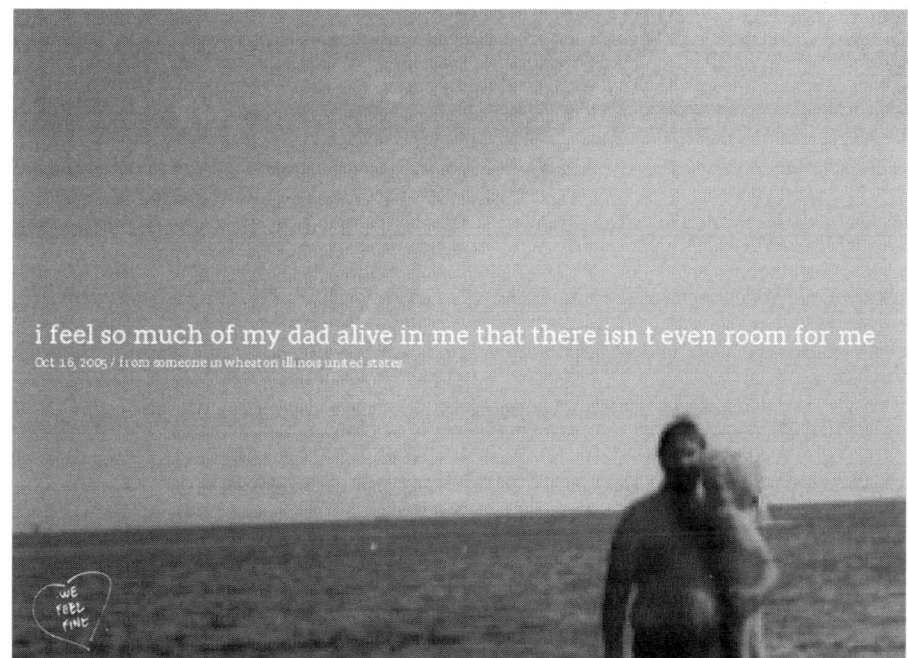

Figure 7.21

We Feel Fine montage of image and text. Image courtesy of Jonathan Harris

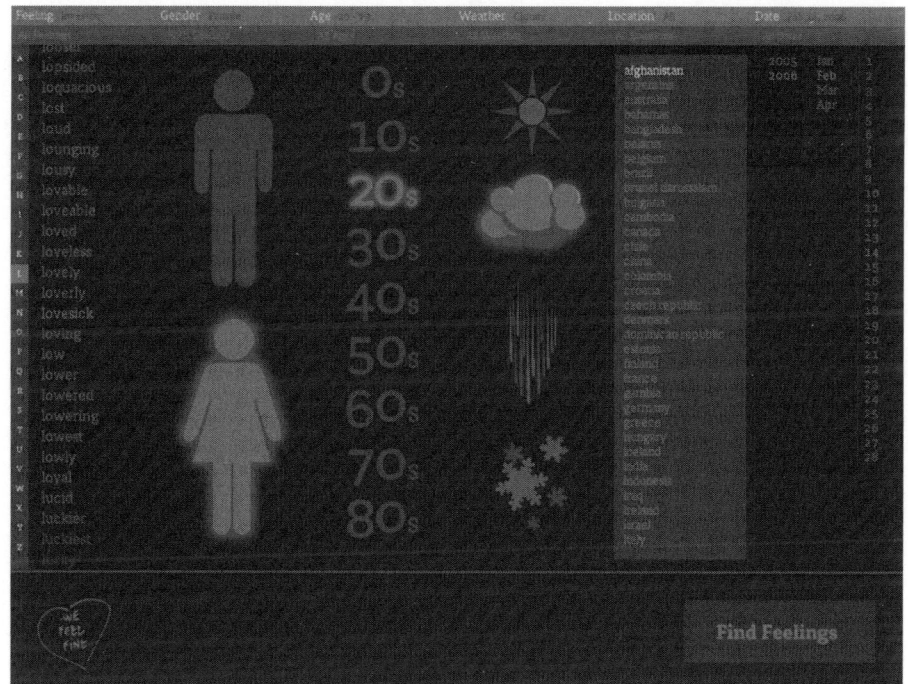

Figure 7.22

We Feel Fine sorting metrics. Image courtesy of Jonathan Harris pieces of information. We Feel Fine is as much a social exploration as a technological one—it highlights how our physical and virtual environments affect what we share and how we share it.

More recently, Harris has embarked on more critical projects like Network Effect:

> The Internet is a miraculous tool, but all too often, it affects us like a drug. Many of its popular apps, news websites, and social networks have been carefully designed to addict and distract, so they can harvest human attention like the natural resource it is.
>
> (Harris, n.d.)

Through this project, users are exposed to the intoxication of stimuli that the internet offers, but are given only seven minutes to explore it all. Through bigger themes such as dance, kiss, knit, shoot, the program curates videos, audio, and articles that you are "fed" through the interface. But the limited time is meant to remind you of the world that you are missing while being transfixed with this project. As Harris explains is, "We need time and space and silence to remember who we are, who we once were, and who we can become. There is a way, and every one of us contains the potential to find it." (Harris, n.d.). As with We Feel Fine, Network Effect encourages the user to explore the metrics that are defining the videos that Network Effect is displaying—how many people are "knitting" or the gender of those who are "knitting" all encourage them to think about the internet not as a singular experience, but as a common one. It also serves to emphasize the need for the user or surfer to actively stitch together meaning—about our experiences, our values, and our similarities. Pulling the user in and out of the immersion that is new media and the internet. In a 2015 *Washington Post* article, Harris explained the projects basis:

> I think one thing we have in common is a very deep need to express ourselves . . . I think this is a very old human desire . . . What's new is that in the last several years a lot of these very traditional physical human activities, these acts of self-expression, have been moving onto the Internet.
>
> (Dewey, 2015)

And on the Network Effect website, Harris explains the project further by saying, "We need time and space and silence to remember who we are, who we once were, and who we can become. There is a way, and every one of us contains the potential to find it."

So, what do these projects like these tell us about the ways that designers interact with and utilize technological systems? In many ways, they reinforce the basic premise of this chapter which is the dual, and sometimes conflicting, role of technological systems in design. As a tool for liberation, technology has the power to create entirely new experiences and connections for users as well as to help designers create new and open spaces for collaboration between users and designers. As a limitation,

Visualizing the invisible

the logic of technology can lure us into forgetting about the natural, organic, and often surprising needs and wants of people. It is up to the designer to recognize and balance these two forces and explore ways to capitalize on the assets inherent in each of them.

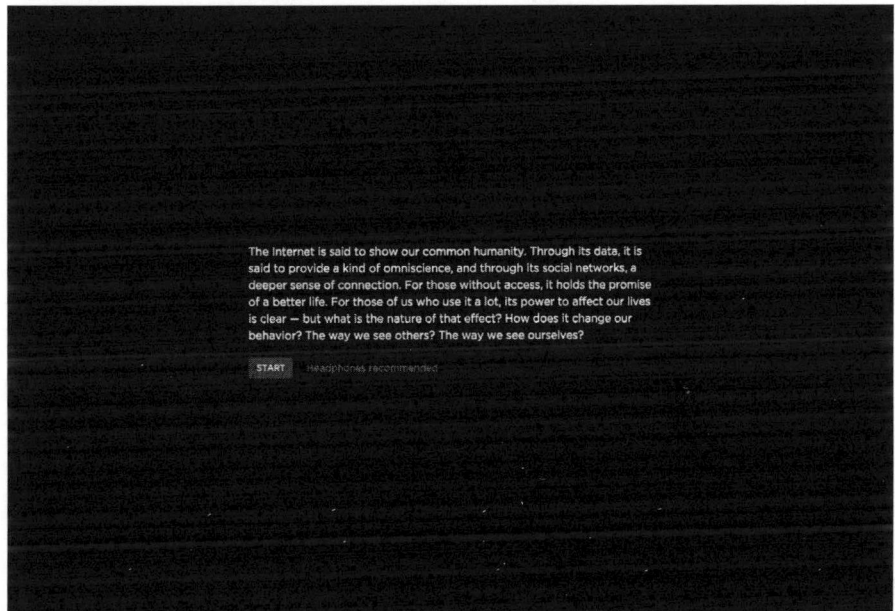

Figure 7.23

The Network Effect prologue. Image courtesy of Jonathan Harris

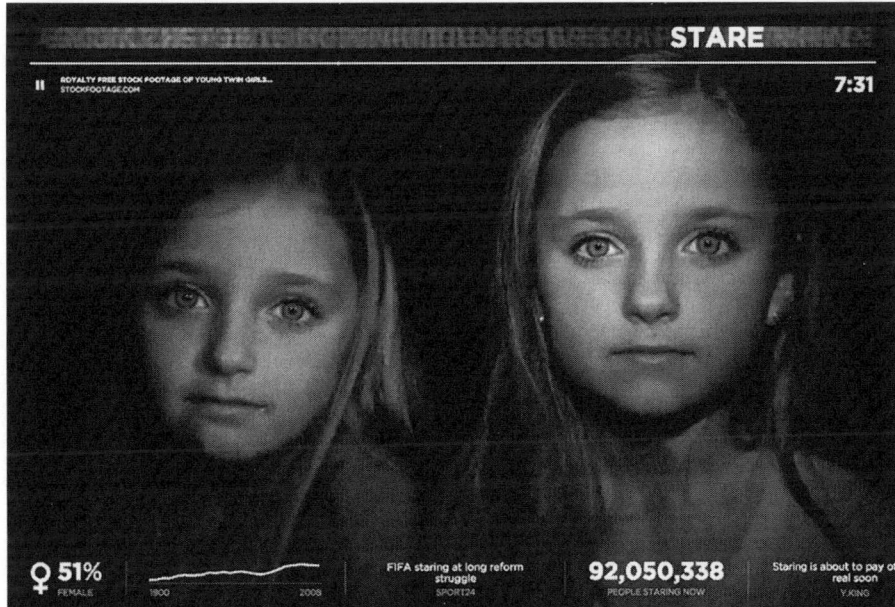

Figure 7.24

The Network Effect detail, "Stare". Image courtesy of Jonathan Harris

Visualizing the invisible

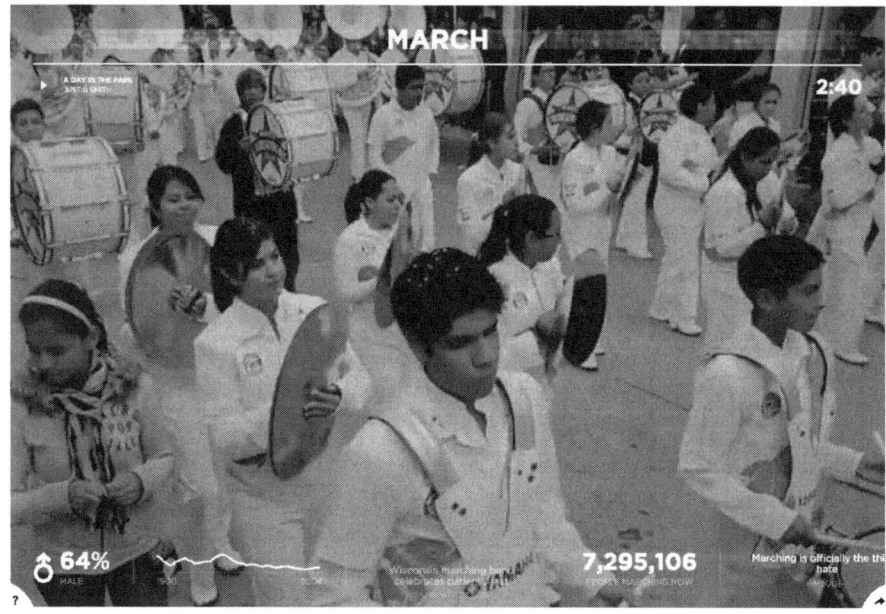

Figure 7.25

The Network Effect video, "March." Image courtesy of Jonathan Harris

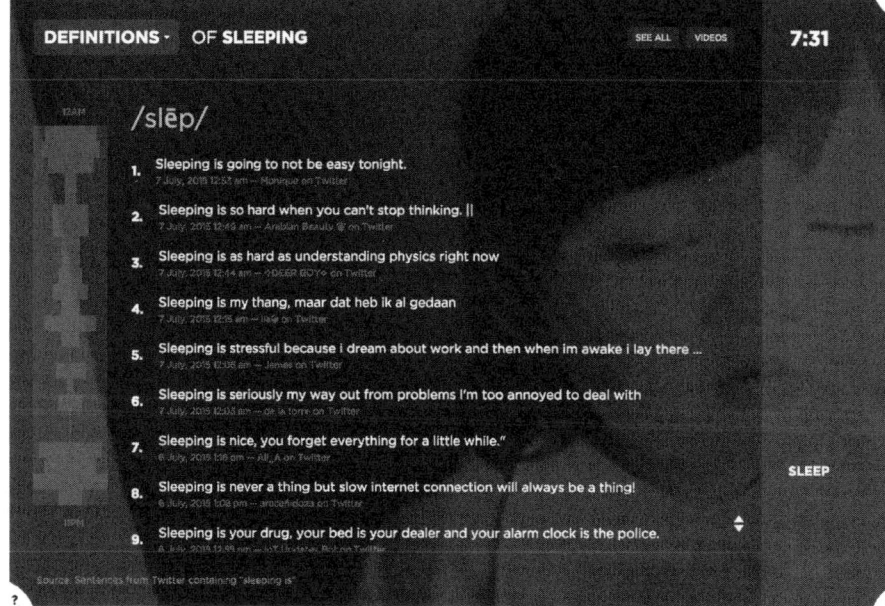

Figure 7.26

The Network Effect, definitions. Image courtesy of Jonathan Harris

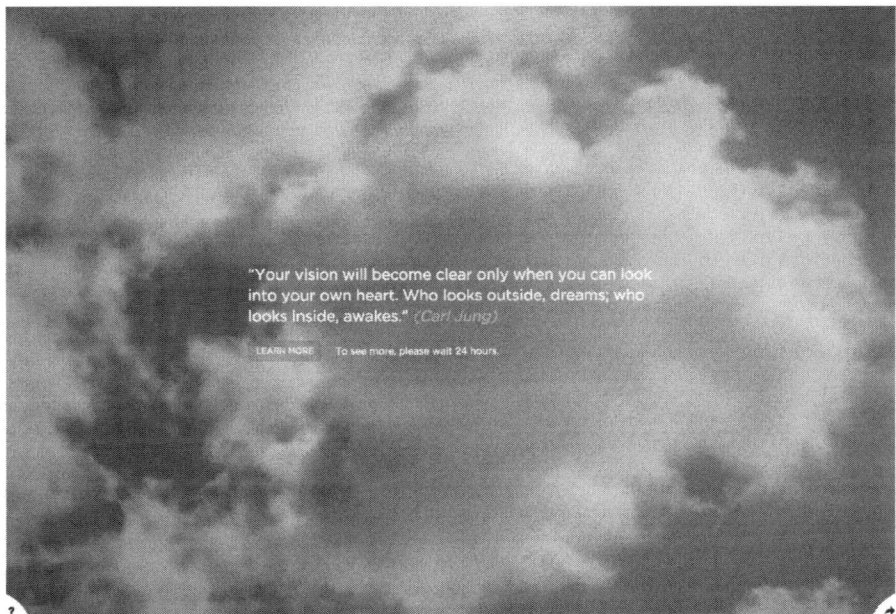

Figure 7.27

The Network Effect, epilogue. Image courtesy of Jonathan Harris

References

Bhargava, Rahul et al. "Data Murals: Using the Arts to Build Data Literacy." *The Journal of Community Informatics*. October 26, 2016.

Blauvelt, Andrew. "Towards Relational Design." *Design Observer*. November 3, 2008. Retrieved from https://designobserver.com/feature/towards-relational-design/7557. Accessed September 22, 2018.

Bouikidis, Aphrodite. "3 Ways Social Entrepreneurship Can Create a Resilient Ecosystem in Greece." *Forbes*, November 6, 2014. Retrieved from www.forbes.com/sites/ashoka/2014/11/06/3-ways-social-entrepreneurship-can-create-a-resilient-ecosystem-in-greece/. Accessed June 10, 2015.

Corner, James. "The Agency of Mapping: Speculation, Critique and Invention." In Denis Cosgrov, editor. *Mappings*. London: Reaktion Books, 1999, pp. 231–242.

Crouch, Christopher and Jane Pearce. *Doing Research in Design*. London: Bloomsbury, 2015.

Dewey, Caitlin. "How the Internet's Most Earnest Evangelist Became its Fiercest Critic." *The Washington Post*. October 25, 2015.

D'Ignazio, Catherine. "This Online Game Forces You Out of Your Bubble by Taking You to Places You've Never Heard Of." *Huffington Post*. October 4, 2014. Retrieved from www.huffingtonpost.com/catherine-daignazio/terra-incognita_b_5643012.html. Accessed September 22, 2018.

D'Ignazio, Catherine and Bhargava, Rahul. "DataBasic: Design Principles, Tools and Activities for Data Literacy Learners." *The Journal of Community Informatics*, 12(3), 2016, pp. 83–107.

Druckery, Timothy. "Relational Architecture: The Work of Rafael Lozano Hemmer." *Debates & Credits. Media / Art /Public Domain*. Amsterdam: De Batie Centre for Culture and Politics, 2003, pp. 69–72.

Gerolympou-Karadimou, Alexandra. "Στοές και περάσματα στην αγορά." ["Arcades and passages in the market."] *Parallaxi Magazine*, January 1, 2014. Accessed June 10, 2015. Retrieved from http://parallaximag.gr/thessaloniki/stoes-kai-perasmata-stin-agora. Accessed March 1, 2019.

Harris, Jonathan. "We Feel Fine" and "Network Effect." (n.d.). Retrieved from http://number27.org/networkeffect. Accessed March 1, 2019.

Koukoumakas, Kostas. "Στις στοές της Θεσσαλονίκης." ["In the arcades of Thessaloniki"] *Kathimerini*, February 2, 2015. Retrieved from www.kathimerini.gr/801932/article/ta3idia/sthn-ellada/stis-stoes-ths-8essalonikhs. Accessed June 10, 2015.

Patsarika, Maria. *Iconic or Ironic? Multiple Perceptions of the Baltic Centre for Contemporary Art, Newcastle upon Tyne*. International Centre for Cultural and Heritage Studies, the University of Newcastle. Unpublished MA dissertation, 2005.

Rosenberg, Elissa. "Walking in the City: Memory and Place." *Journal of Architecture*, 17(1), 2012, pp. 131–149.

Seedat, Mohamed. "Oral History as an Enactment of Critical Community Psychology." *Journal of Community Psychology*, 43(1), 2014, pp. 22–35.

Part 3
Design and sustainability
Killing messengers

8 Paradigm shifts
Designing resilient systems

Designing sustainable futures requires more than new ways to manage our waste, and also necessitates moving beyond the paradigm of finding alternative resources. It requires different attitudes about consumption in general; for us to be lighter, slower, smarter, and more convivial (Thackara, 2005). This will not be easy for designers to do because at the heart of design is still the connection to the product—whether it be a building, a website, or a campaign. Production of any kind requires resources. The key, in this chapter, is to rethink our assumptions about sustainability; and to move beyond what are ideas focused on management and finding alternative resources and towards ways that designers can actively participate in the reduction of consumption in the first place.

John Thackara, author of *In the Bubble* (2005), calls for a paradigm shift in "innovation driven by science fiction to innovation driven by social fiction" (4). What Thackara means by this—something that we have already explored a bit in this book—is that for design to truly address issues of sustainability necessitates a change in how we define innovation, and move beyond what we *can* do to what we *should* do. The earth, and our time on it, is not infinite. And no matter if one believes in climate change as a real, critical phenomenon or not, our impact on the earth is not disputable. If we take more trees than we plant, we are affecting the earth; if we put chemicals into the air or the sea or distribute it around the earth we are making an impact that the earth cannot recover from at the speed with which we continue to distribute those things. We don't need to be confronted with the huge landfills that pocket our earth, or pictures of the Great Pacific Garbage Patch (although it is shocking and profound) to understand that what we consume has to go somewhere. Thackara argues that in order for us to truly mitigate our impact on the earth, we need to change our attitudes about how fast and to what degree we consume by consuming less, and sharing more. These ideas are not entirely novel, but especially in the United States, where the "average American will drain as many resources as 35 natives of India and consume 53 times more goods and services than someone from China" (*Scientific American*, n.d.), and as more and more of these emerging markets start to emulate the US in terms of production and consumption, it's easy to understand how the earth will be unable to handle that type of growth. So, what is design's role in addressing these issues of sustainability? Specifically are there ways that designers can shape new attitudes and expectations when it comes to sustainability, in the field of design itself, and related to how and what we are designing?

But is it realistic to work towards this type of response to sustainability? After all, we live in a modern society that relies on advanced products. We can't go back to living in lean-tos made from sticks we found on the ground. So the idea of reduction has to also be counterbalanced with a responsible approach to manufacturing in the first place. In *Cradle to Cradle* (2002), authors Michael Braungart and William McDonough call for a "new industrial revolution" where the items that are manufactured go through as rigorous a sustainability evaluation as they do for cost efficiency.

The sustainability of living systems

Contextual systems

One of the most important aspects of current design theory and practice is the idea of context. Context can have many different interpretations and relevance for design. Obviously a design lives within a physical context—a carrot peeler might be used in a kitchen. But there are also economic, social, cultural, environmental, and even political contexts to consider within any design. How much will the peeler cost to make? How much can people afford to pay for it? How much of the carrot is wasted by using the peeler? Will people know how to use it? What sort of environmental impact will it have? This might not seem particularly revolutionary, but when looking at it within the legacy of western design, and specifically European design, championing context is in almost direct opposition to the roots of modern design, which specifically aimed to decontextualize and universalize it. Much of these attempts came from a place of elevating and standardizing design to give it deeper roots and credibility. Charles and Ray Eames, notably the most experimental and innovative designers of the modern era, wanted to provide access to good design—to standardize design and by extension the manufacturing process that good design could be produced within, less expensive and accessible by more people. Universal design solutions were championed for their efficiency and transferability. Why design a kitchen for a German family different than for a Japanese family? Ignoring for a moment the overarching colonialist mindset that was at the root of this perspective, modernism's focus on universal systems inherently ignored the context in which design existed. Rather than design responding to a context, it was meant to shape and form the experience people had with it.

In the United States, one of the most famous examples of design not responding to a context can be seen in Las Vegas. The palaces that line the Las Vegas strip, the lawns that residents want to keep green and lush, and the many golf courses that operate in and around Las Vegas all put an inordinate tax on an environment not designed for this type of usage. As a result, the city is constantly negotiating how and where to import water. Because water is such a commodity, this also leads to unfair "water grabs" with smaller businesses and individuals (like farmers and ranchers) at a severe disadvantage.

Paradigm shifts

But on a more fundamental, and even more basic level, when the design of a city such as Las Vegas which operates by creating a fantasy or "mirage" within a desert, we must question how the environment will support such a fantasy. Looking globally, we can see evidence of the same perspective in places such as the Palm Islands in Dubai which are the world's only entirely artificial man-made islands—there are three of them either finished or under construction. One of the goals of the project was simple—to increase the amount of waterfront property in Dubai to increase tourism and luxury real estate. One of the side effects of this project, however, has been to drastically alter the ecosystem within the water. "The massive dredging required to build the island has drastically changed the wave, temperature, and erosion patterns in the Persian Gulf, and a whole square mile of coral was killed" (Jennings, 2015) and even those attempts to recreate the reefs have proved slow to remediate the damage done.

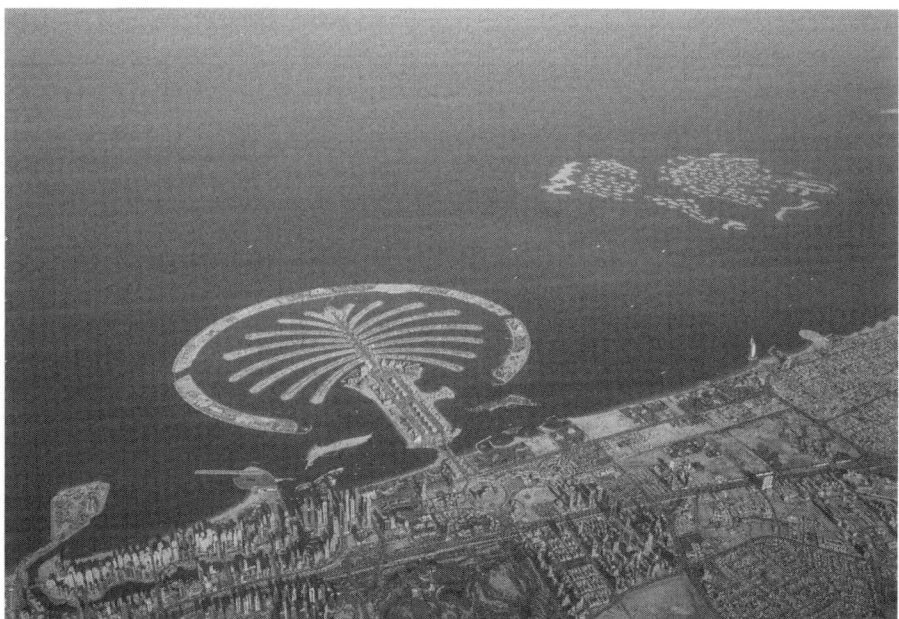

Figure 8.1

Palm Island aerial shot, Dubai, UAE

Nowhere is the relationship between design and context better examined than through the contemporary struggle to keep modern cities from flooding due to climate change, increased sea levels, and other factors making cities situated close to rivers, which were once used for transportation and shipping, vulnerable to increased damage from the rising waters. Anuradha Mathur and Dilip da Cunha astutely describe in *Mississippi Floods: Designing a Shifting Landscape* (2001), the Mississippi River as a "landscape of conflict, result of efforts to prevent flooding, while exploiting . . . [it's] navigational potential and . . . valuing it's ecological role . . . The sense of permanence, security, and prosperity and designed interventions have promised is being increasingly questioned" (2). As one of the main waterways in the United States, extending from northern Minnesota all the way to the Gulf of Mexico, the river has been instrumental to travel, shipping, and irrigation. As a result, much effort has been placed on controlling

Paradigm shifts

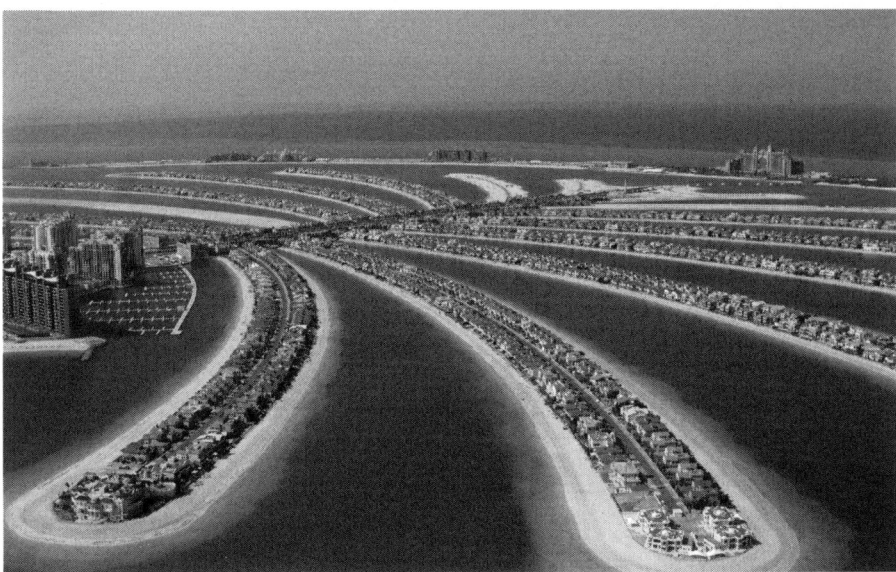

Figure 8.2
Palm Island close up, Dubai, UAE

its boundaries, attempting to keep the river from flooding and protecting the boundaries of the river itself. But this approach is being questioned more and more, and in the most extreme examples, recommendations to let the river run completely free. We can see similar results of Hurricane Katrina in New Orleans, Hurricane Matthew in North Carolina (among others) to better understand that a new, more resilient approach to flooding mitigation is needed. In some cases, this might mean moving out of the floodplain, or designing for the potential of flooding or considering how the environment might be used to help mitigate the potential of flooding in the first place. The challenge for designers in the constantly shifting landscape to which Mathur and da Cunha relate, is that this shifting landscape is not only physical and environmental, but it's also social, economic, political, and cultural. Designing for sustainability is really about responding to these shifts, and imagining design interventions in a variety of different states and contexts and to design products, services, and environments that are resilient, adaptable, and flexible.

Behavioral systems: from cradle to grave to cradle to cradle

The mindset that is driving the building of such structures in an environment that cannot sustain them naturally is the same basic premise that Braungart and McDonough (2002) argue drove the Industrial Revolution and encouraged fundamental misperceptions that (a) people could control nature, (b) that resources were unlimited, and (c) context was less important than people's activities within those environments. The authors argue that if we were to look back and design a system of production of the likes of the Industrial Revolution, we would say that should be a system that:

puts billions of pounds of toxic material into the air, water, and soil every year; produce some materials so dangerous they will require constant vigilance by future generations; results in gigantic amounts of waste; puts valuable materials in holes all over the planet, where they can never be retrieved; requires thousands of complex regulations . . .; measures productivity by how few people are working; creates prosperity by digging up or cutting down natural resources and then burying or burning them; erodes the diversity of species and cultural practices.

(18)

While this might seem a rather dystopian assessment, there is much truth to it. And what is particularly relevant is the impact that this perspective has had on many other features of human life than just the natural environment. It has changed our whole model of life and productivity, and begs some deeper questions about why we are doing it at all? It is time for design to lead the charge to change the face of consumerism, and to fundamentally rethink not just the products themselves, but also the systems of production that surround them. This applies to all forms of design—from the size, scale, and scope of our built environment, to the ways that we design our natural environment for people to enjoy and make use of, to the products and communication strategies driving the values that people place on the world around them.

While early industrialists might have literally believed this, modern industrialists believe we can find alternative resources to supplement the ones we are currently using. This is a dangerous position, for by relying on the artificial production of new resources, we are simply falling into the same mindset of the early industrialists. As Braungart and McDonough (2002) argue, the cradle to grave mentality is problematic on a number of levels. As consumers, we actually consume very little—and much of what we do consume is discarded. Much of what is discarded has the potential to contribute back into the environmental cycle, creating new fossil fuels but when it's discarded into landfill, that positive contribution is lost. This mentality is still in evidence when we are trying to package industrial waste so that is less harmful to the environment. We are relying on previous mental structures of that cradle to grave mentality rather than reframing and reinventing the very paradigm that is driving it. The desalination products discussed earlier in this book are typical examples of this type of alternative-resource thinking approach. But wherever there is consumption, there is by-product. As in the desalination process, the by-product is additional salt, which is either channeled back into the water or disposed of somewhere else. In either case, there is additional non-natural components put back into the environment and needing additional mitigation.

The future of design is in designing less, better. How can we design products that need little to no artificial packaging? How can we design packaging that is reusable, up-cyclable? These are the challenges that require new innovations. Some might see this as daunting, but there is also great opportunity for new and innovative ways of thinking about design.

Paradigm shifts

Human systems: design for the other 90%

Another important component of sustainability is to think for whom we are designing and where new innovations can be best applied. One of the key features in global agreements to limit greenhouse gases takes into account developing countries need for fossil fuels to help them compete with already established countries with established industries that are better prepared to implement newer technologies. Think, for instance, of the traditional car vs the electric or hybrid car. Manufacturing of those traditional cars is cheaper and easier to do . . . But it's interesting to use the cellular phone as a model to think of new ways to bridge the gap between countries at different levels of development. In many ways, developing countries were able to leapfrog over the hard wired telephone with the rapid advance of cellular technology that could reach and connect people without the necessary, bulky infrastructure (like phone lines) that those countries were lacking. In what other ways could the design of new components of a system help redesign the system itself? One of the first things that designers can do it to simply consider for whom we are designing and to what end. To this day, the majority of design attention is still placed on those high-end consumers in the world that can afford well-designed products. There have been inroads into design products for non-traditional consumers, and those who are not always at the top of the pay scale, but often they are seen as novelties, or pro-bono projects rather than the mainstay of an innovative design practice. In 2007, the Cooper Hewitt Design Museum in New York City created an exhibition of many of these products—from individual water filtration devices to water pumps and power tools. As the Cooper Hewitt explained it:

> Of the world's total population of 6.5 billion, 5.8 billion people, or 90%, have little or no access to most of the products and services many of us take for granted; in fact, nearly half do not have regular access to food, clean water, or shelter. *Design for the Other 90%* explores a growing movement among designers to design low-cost solutions for the other 90%.
>
> (Cooper Hewitt Archive, 2007)

What this showcased was the myriad ways that design creativity could be used to solve alternative problems in emerging markets. One of the projects included in the exhibition—the PlayPump, invented in 2005—promised to use the energy of children to pump water for an entire village. Conceived as a merry-go-round that was linked to underground well-water, the PlayPump would draw water into a reserve that the entire village would then have access to. But just five years after its invention, PBS's *Frontline* ran a piece that showed many of the pumps lying idle. The causes for this were varied, but Daniel Stellar of the Earth Institute at Columbia suggested that the PlayPump relied on a number of critical assumptions. First, that there was sufficient groundwater, and that the groundwater was clean and drinkable. If either of these two criteria were not in place, then the PlayPump doesn't work as planned.

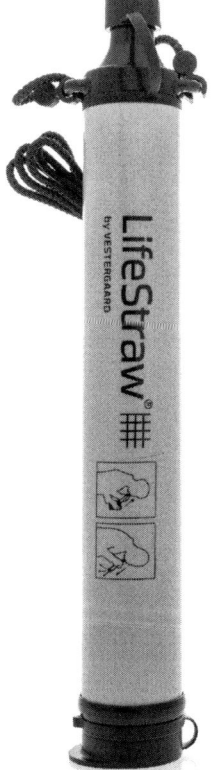

Figure 8.3
The LifeStraw

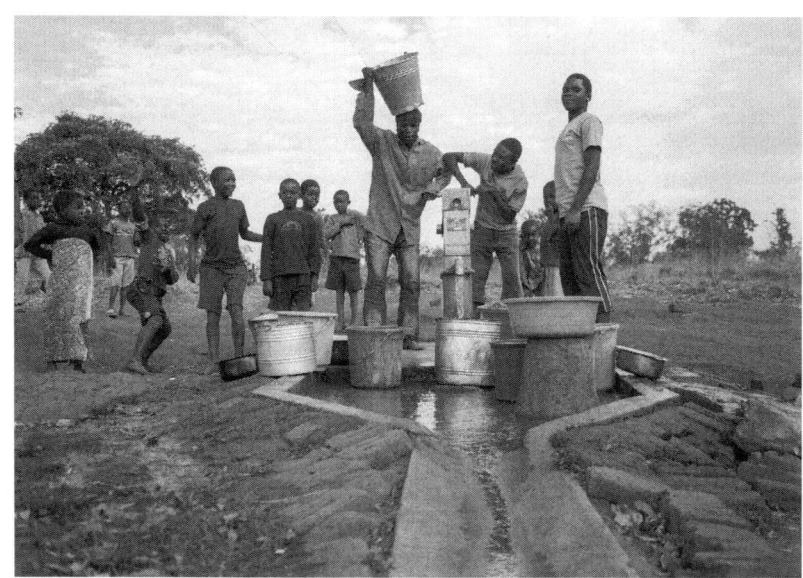

Figure 8.4

Traditional ways for collecting water

The failure of PlayPump points to a huge problem in meeting water challenges—simply put, there is no panacea. Water problems are very complex and come in a multitude of flavors. In some very specific situations, PlayPump may be the right type of solution. In most situations though, it is imperative to first really understand the problem and to then design appropriate, tailored solutions. It's also necessary to focus on the big picture, with an emphasis on water supply. If sufficient supply isn't available to start with, no amount of pumping, no matter how playful it may be, will help.

(Stellar, 2010)

Since 2010, PlayPumps have focused on bringing their innovations to schools that have historically relied on students bringing water from home. As an example of the innovation needing to be matched within the context of use, this small modification to the strategy illustrates the need to look holistically not just at the problem, but also at the solution.

Another well-known product from the Cooper Hewitt exhibit—the LifeStraw designed by the Swiss designer Torben Vestergaard Frandsen—was a straw with a filter built into it. The straw mitigated the need to carry and boil larger amounts of water from areas with less-safe drinking water. One of the critiques of the LifeStraw, and the concept of *Design for the Other 90%* in general, was the very nature of the problems it was addressing. Does using design to mitigate the outcomes of a more deep-seated problem—such as the fact that people in developing worlds don't have the basic necessity of access to clean drinking water—mask the root problems in favor of ingenious solutions? This is a fundamental question that any designer must ask, but especially when working in the realm of sustainability where solutions to existing problems have the real potential of avoiding the harder questions that are at the root of those problems. But both of these projects point to the importance of design contributing to the way that we address these large scale problems, and to give means and opportunities to experiment with solutions at many different scales.

Convivial systems

In the book, *Tools for Conviviality*, Ivan Illich argues for the decentralization of tools and technology in order to provide access and an antidote to industrialization and mass production. Using the field of medicine as an initial example, he laments the inverse relationship between the increased simplicity and accessibility of the tools of medicine and the decreased access to these tools by everyday people. The idea of conviviality, Illich argues, describes a "society in which modern technologies serve politically interrelated individuals, rather than managers" (1973, 12). Specifically, Illich considers the importance of conviviality in the nature of sharing. For instance, tools that people use infrequently—a snow plow, or even a leaf blower—don't need to be individually owned. But industrialization and mass production has conditioned consumers to not even question some of these fundamental assumptions of ownership. As designers, there are new opportunities to reconsider these basic assumptions. Sites like BookMooch (bookmooch.com) have spawned much conversation and speculation about the future of business and sharing. An online site that is free to join and use, BookMooch connects those who have books to "give" with those who have books they want. The cost is minimal (or free) mostly paying just for shipping. The system works on points, where users get points by sending and/or listing books to exchange through the site and system. In the book, *The Sharing Economy* (2017), author Arun Sundararajan catalogues the many ways that our society and economy are transitioning to an "asset-light" existence. When Sundararajan wrote the book in 2016, reminiscing back only to 2011, things like car-sharing were just emerging. Now, a few short years later they are in full swing with projections that they will dominate new car sales in the near future. The sharing economy has expanded beyond physical objects to services and even money lending and gifting—peer to peer loans and crowdsourcing are growing in more popularity. Imagine designing a car with the sole purpose of being shared among multiple drivers, or an apartment or house whose sole purpose was to be part of Airbnb? How might this capacity for sharing impact how and what we design? Are there opportunities for new environments (physical or digital) where this sharing might take place? While it might not be immediately visible, emphasizing the sharing economy as a driving force in design production has the capacity to dramatically diminish our consumption and waste. This system of decentralization also has another important component to it, where the assets are spread out over multiple users, the dependence on one central source, or as Illich would call it, a "manager," makes the entire network stronger. Because many users are supporting the maintenance of the car, for instance, no one person is responsible for that large repair when it happens. Similarly, when a person who has opted into the system has to opt out, the entire system doesn't crumble. The self-sustainability of the system is stronger and more resilient.

References

Braungart, Michael and William McDonough. *Cradle to Cradle*. New York: North Point Press, 2002.

Cooper Hewitt Archive. "Design for the Other 90%." Cooper Hewitt Design Museum. 2007. Retrieved from http://archive.cooperhewitt.org/other90/other90.cooperhewitt.org/about/index.html. Accessed December 15, 2018.

Illich, Ivan. *Tools for Conviviality*. New York: Perennial Library, 1973.

Jennings, Ken. "The Real Story Behind Dubai's Palm Islands." Condé Nast Traveller. November 23, 2015. Retrieved from www.cntraveler.com/stories/2015-11-23/the-real-story-behind-dubai-palm-islands. Accessed September 22, 2018.

Mathur, Anuradha and da Cunha, Dilip. *Mississippi Floods: Designing a Shifting Landscape*. New Haven, CT: Yale University Press, 2001.

Scientific American. "Use It and Lose It: The Outsize Effect of U.S. Consumption on the Environment." *Scientific American*. (n.d.). Retrieved from www.scientificamerican.com/article/american-consumption-habits/. Accessed September 22, 2018.

Smith, Cynthia, editor. *Design For The Other 90%*. New York: Editions Assouline; ND Marginalized ed. edition, 2007.

Stellar, Daniel. *The PlayPump: What Went Wrong? State of the Planet*. Columbia: Earth Institute, Columbia University. July 1, 2010.

Sundararajan, Arun. *The Sharing Economy: The End of Employment and the Rise of Crowd-Based Capitalism*. Cambridge, MA: The MIT Press, 2017.

Thackara, Jonathan. *In the Bubble: Designing in a Complex World*. Cambridge, MA: MIT Press, 2005.

Troubled Water. Frontline. WGBH Educational Foundation, 2010.

9 Ecological design thinking

Thinking of a design problem as ecological naturally conjures up images of something that is ever-changing, in motion, and not static. This can be particularly helpful to consider the many contexts, environments, and situations that a design can exist within and encourages more possibilities for design to be dynamic and flexible. It also helps us better understand a specific design as part of a larger system that is also changing. In thinking about sustainability, we can envision our designs beyond the immediate context to consider a future or alternate state.

In his book, *Design for the Real World: Human Ecology and Social Change* (2005), Victor Papanek argued:

> To meet problems in a new and creative way has been part of the biological and cultural endowment of our species for millions of years. But, as we live in a society that places a high value on conformity, our creative processes have been blunted or stifled.
>
> (154)

As a result, design research methods need to focus not only on confirming the assumptions and ideas that are already a part of human culture, but also in revealing new and unforeseen alternatives to the complex issues that are embedded in sustainable design, and to help uncover and reframe some of the foundational paradigms, specifically those of the industrial age that are still very much embedded in western world perspective, especially related to the natural environment. Engaging in ecological design thinking—whether in the research or ideation phase, means embracing a perspective of openness and adaptability, and paying especially close attention to surprising discoveries that are revealed through the process.

Design research methods: using systems thinking to examine the broader context of design action

Phenomenological research

Human behavior and understanding is heavily reliant on phenomenological understanding of the world. We seek out patterns of behavior which help us understand why things are the way that they are. When looking at a system, with its myriad drivers and components, it is difficult to make meaning of anything within it without first searching for patterns of commonalities or differences. Phenomenological research is a qualitative research method that is primarily interested with how people understand the world and the objects that exist within it. As a designer engaged in phenomenological research, his or her goal is to try to better understand the patterns of behavior that people exhibit when coping with a specific situation. The goal of the researcher engaging in phenomenological research is to try to push aside his or her own biases in the activity of research itself. For example, if given a problem such as, "College students are spending more time on social media than on studying," a phenomenological study would seek to describe in detail the habits of the students in both social media and studying behavior, with the primary aim of illuminating patterns of behavior related to social media and studying. The researcher would attempt to ascribe no judgment to either of the activities, but seek to record, describe, and evaluate commonalities between social media behavior and studying behavior. As a designer, these types of studies can be incredibly valuable in that our preconceived notions about what is good or bad are intentionally put to the side to make room for potential solutions that we might ignore due to the biases or assumptions that we initially bring. For instance, when given that first problem, you likely thought that social media was bad and studying was good, and that social media was a distraction from studying and was the immediate "problem" that needed to be solved. This might indeed be the case, but by trying to stand back from the assumptions inherent in the way the problem is framed, we might begin to see some of the advantages and attractions of social media, and how those might be used to encourage other types of learning (for in reality, we are learning from social media, it just might to be the lesson our teacher wants us to learn!). Phenomenological research is also heavily tied to cognition, so the study above would also seek to better describe and illuminate why students spend more time on social media—what is satisfying about it?

Case study research

Case study research describes a type of research whereby new meaning and ideas are extracted from, and connected to real-world examples. Robert K. Yin, author of *Case Study Research* (2008) describes case study research as "used in many situations, to contribute to our knowledge of individual, groups, organizational, social political and related phenomena" (4). Case study research is bound by a specific context, yet the goal is to extract meaning that is applicable or transferrable to many different contexts. Why this type of research is valuable for design—and particularly valuable for thinking about issues of sustainability within design—is

Ecological design thinking

that the outcomes of design action never exist outside of a real-world context. Even when considering fictional futures, the real world is still the context through which to examine—with the aim of addressing or solving—the problem. When you are doing case study research, you can choose to look at one specific case study example to explore a number of different phenomena that might exist or you can compare multiple cases to find commonalities and differences. An example of a single case study examination was done by Phillip Lopate in *Places Journal* (2011) of the High Line in New York City. The project, which was initiated by the Friends of the High Line and designed through a collaboration between the landscape architect James Corner's Field Operations and the architecture firm Diller Scofidio + Renfro is a powerful example of how existing infrastructure can be rethought and recontextualized within

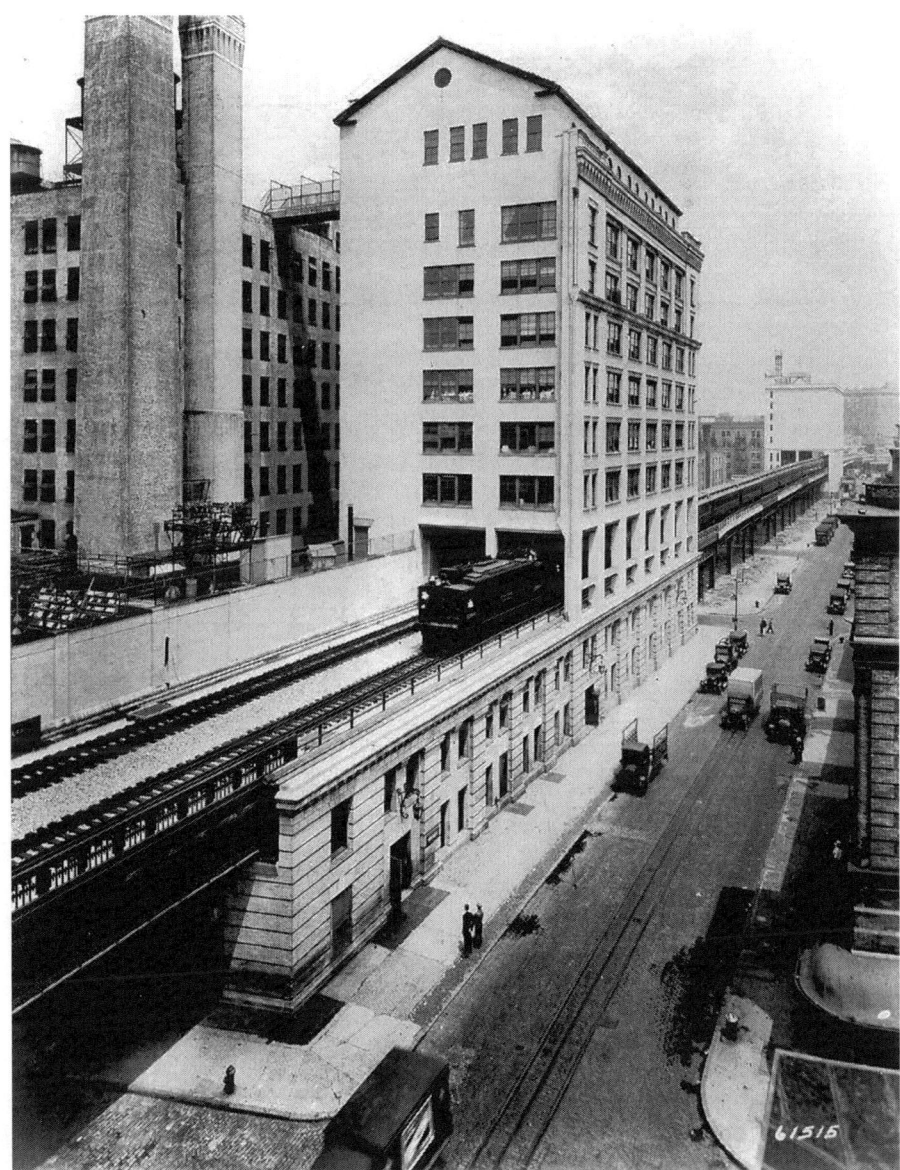

Figure 9.1

The High Line, circa 1930 (historical photo)

123

a contemporary context of need. Designed and built on abandoned elevated rail lines, Corner and DS + F created a much needed public space in the middle of Manhattan and New York City. Rather than demolishing and rebuilding, using the existing infrastructure foregrounded sustainability and reuse as a core component of the project. As a case study, the High Line can show other cities and designers how they might reclaim and reimagine the opportunities that exist in the reuse of buildings that on the surface might appear to be only limitations. Case study research can take the form of first-person examinations of a design. In Lopate's case study, he examines the High Line from a number of different angles including its history, the experience, and the potential future impact. In discussing the experience, Lopate wrote that:

> that modest extra altitude (18–30 feet high) made for a profoundly different peripatetic perspective: as in a dream where suddenly you can walk through walls, I was passing in and out of manufacturing buildings, staring into the backyards of private residences, saluting the Gothic Revival red brick fortress of the General Theological Seminary, and hovering within sight of the waterfront like a seagull.

Lopate's case study is particularly provocative and insightful because it involves his experience both before and after the High Line was rebuilt. From a first person perspective, his experience reads as a provocative narrative. From an historical perspective, Lopate traces the history of the High Line's original construction and vision and how that vision was resonant in the Friends of the High Line group that engineered the initial vision for an elevated promenade to make use of the abandoned structure. Lopate considers the inclusion of the High Line not in isolation to its environment but as a connective layer within it. The behaviors of users on the High Line—the constant movement and motion—is not unlike the movement happening on the streets below.

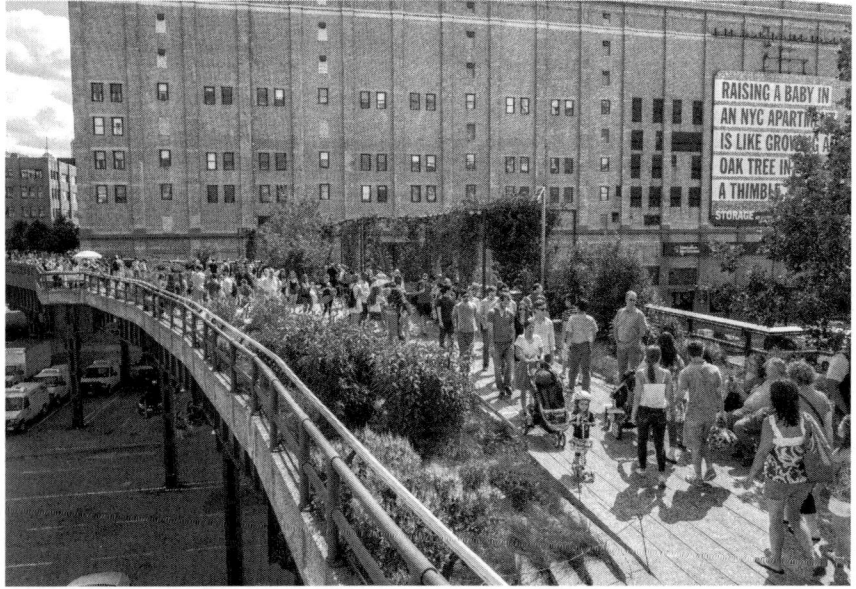

Figure 9.2

The High Line as an elevated park, 2010. Wikimedia Commons, photographed by La Cita Vita

Creating a case study

Creating a case study at the beginning of a project can be an excellent way to explore and examine phenomena that might be relevant to you. But how do you find the right case? What are the right questions to ask and how do you structure it? There are many ways to approach case study research, and the following can help provoke some answers to those questions.

Finding the right case

First, think about what you want to learn about the most, or challenge yourself to think about differently. Do you want to explore new materials and structures within the project? Are you interested in how a project might reuse existing materials in different ways? Do you want to see how technology might alleviate some of the burdens of production? Are you interested in how users themselves might participate in a co-creative process that reduces consumption or changes user perspective about some issue of production or consumption? Taking some time to articulate how your approach to the project itself will be different will help frame how you go about finding the case study in the first place.

Evaluating the case

Based on the questions that you asked yourself in order to select the right case study, you should create a structure through which you will evaluate your case. It's also important to understand some of the historical context of the project so doing some background research on its history, the history of the designer, even the political, social, and economic context in which it was created will help you better understand the need for the design in the first place. Write a list of what works well in the project and what is not working well. How did the designer (in your opinion) fulfill the goals of the project? What was your experience engaging with it? What is the significance of the project? Has that significance changed over time?

Structure

Depending on the ultimate goals of the case study, you can write it as a detailed outline, organized notes, or a more formal report. A common structure is to start with the history of the project, state (to the extent possible) the goals of the project and/or the vision of the designer, and then your assessment of what is or is not working within the project. Adding annotations and notes for yourself about what you might want to build off of in your own project is critical at this stage.

(continued)

> (continued)
>
> **Additional tips**
>
> - Look outside of your discipline. If you're an architect, look and see what graphic or industrial design projects might offer you for insight.
> - Your case study doesn't have to be a famous project. Your neighborhood park might offer you an opportunity to engage and examine it from a new perspective, and give you as much insight as visiting Central Park in New York City.
> - At the same time, look outside of your city, region, and country. Oftentimes, different cultures and cultural attitudes can be incredibly insightful in rethinking old ways of doing things.

Behavior mapping

In addition to the mapping strategies outlined in Chapter 6, behavior mapping is a useful strategy when trying to understand how people move through a physical, virtual, or natural system. The power of the map to act both as a catalyst for research but also as a tool for better understanding the data being collected is especially powerful when trying to understand the ecological systems that are underlying sustainable issues in design. Through the process of isolation, designers can look at one specific element that exists in one space of place. Through methods of overlay, it is easy to compare two isolated elements to see where there might be overlap, correlation, or causation. Using the map as a tool to visualize how people move through a space, where they rest, what they look at, and how they react can be particularly powerful visualizations to help us see patterns that we would not normally see. Behavior mapping uses the power of observation to look deeply into the phenomena driving human behavior and to help designers not only see how people act within an existing environment but also to potentially see how they might act in a future one. Described by Robin Moore, Nilda Cosco, and Mohammad Zahirul Islam behavior mapping is "an unobtrusive, objective, observational method for measuring actual use of space" that:

> can yield information about relationships between environment and behaviour and can answer questions such as, "Which settings or components are most heavily used?" or "Which physical components support significant amounts of physical activity, or social interaction, or interaction between children of different ethnic backgrounds?"
>
> (34)

Those who use behavior mapping regularly agree that there are two main types: place-centered and person-centered. In the most comprehensive uses of behavior mapping, both of these types are used as a way to cross-examine behavioral phenomena more closely.

Sampling

Before engaging in behavior mapping, you need to understand what, exactly, you are looking to map, or what sort of sample you are taking. Taken from observational research in psychology, sampling is a means by which to organize and structure observational research. Since observation is the first stage in behavior mapping, sampling provides a framework by which to decide what and how you are observing and recording behaviors. Are you sampling the number of people who are going in and out of a park during a specific period of time? Or the different types of activities people are doing in a particular area, or at different times of the day? There are a number of different types of sampling that you can use to provide structure around what you are mapping and also to explore and experiment with mapping different content and behaviors.

Time sampling: Time sampling uses specific intervals of time to record behaviors. there are two ways to think about time-sampling for behavior mapping. One ways is to look at all of the behaviors that are going on in a given interval of time and within a certain physical space or environment. For example, sampling how children behave on a playground, you might record all of the activities that are happening between 12–1pm on a given day (or series of days). The second way to engage in time sampling is to see how long it takes for a person, or people, to go through a certain set of events and record the time that they spend on each stage of the process. For example, by following a few children or families visually through the playground to see where they play and for how long.

Event or situation-sampling: Event sampling uses a particular event or situation to map as much about that situation as possible. Event sampling tries to record all of the behaviors and interactions that happen within a particular event. Time can be associated with the event, but the activities are the primary goal for content collection and mapping.

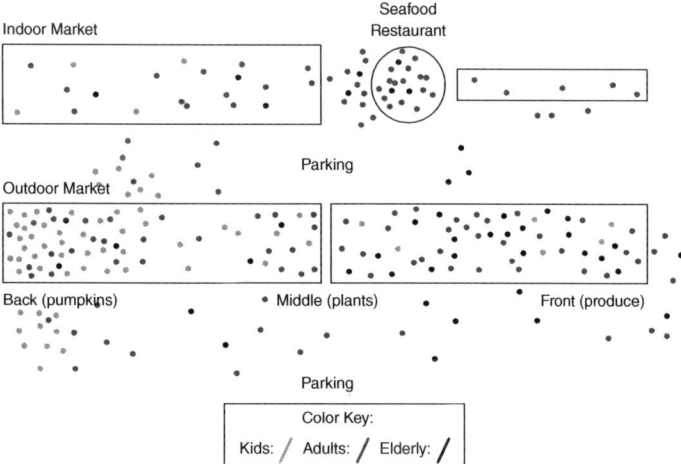

Figure 9.3

Sampling behavior at a flea market in Raleigh, North Carolina

Behavior mapping can use the element of time to observe and record how many "subjects" exhibit a certain behavior within that time frame. Conversely, they can follow a singular subject throughout a certain series of events to observe and record such things as the order in which they accomplished tasks, the pace with which they accomplished these tasks or any number of other observable phenomena.

Ecological design methods and processes: focusing on change as the only constant

Systems thinking

Since discussing the idea of systems so heavily in the introduction to this chapter, it seems particularly relevant to discuss the ways that we might think in systems as a part of the design process. In her book, *Thinking in Systems* (2008), Donella Meadows describes a system as:

> an interconnected set of elements that is coherently organized in a way that achieves something. If you look at that definition closely for a minute, you can see that a system must consist of three kinds of things: elements, interconnections, and a function or purpose.
>
> (11)

The basic interaction of a system, as Meadows explains, also consist of stocks and flows. Stocks are those elements that you can "see, feel, count, or measure at any given time" (17). Flows are those elements or triggers that might change what is in the system or what is going on in it. They can be inflows in the sense of adding to the stock or outflows which is taking away from it. Stocks can be tangible (like the water in a reservoir) or they can be intangible (like consumer confidence in the stock market). The inflows to a reservoir might be rainfall and the outflows might be consumer usage. Often in design, we focus on the stock (i.e. how can we get more water into the reservoir or how can we keep the river in place) rather than the flows. But by looking at the flows in addition to the stock, we open up a much broader range of intervention points, and we start to see how intervening in one area affects and contributes to the larger system. The story of Las Vegas mentioned in Chapter 8 is an excellent case study for how stocks and flows operate. As a city situated within a desert, where the natural water sources are far surpassed by the water need, the balance between stocks and flows is uneven. The stock of water—in the aquifer(s) on which the city draw—is inadequate for the use that has been built into the city. The casinos, hotels, golf courses, pools, and other amenities are huge water draws. In thinking about this problem from a systems perspective, the traditional solution has been focused on increasing the stock of water—importing it from nearby areas rather than thinking about reducing the inflows, which might range from looking at different materials for the greens, limiting the number of golf courses that can be within a certain area, or even instituting new recreational forms that are more aligned with what the environment can support. Systems mapping can help us see the relationships and impacts between the inflows, stocks, and outflows and encourage designers to challenge the premise of how they might be addressing the design problem in the first place. They can also help us see what is contributing to a problem and what the impact of that problem is—not just in the immediate sense but also one or two steps removed.

Systems mapping and wicked problems

Systems mapping can be a great way to better understand the components of wicked problems, and to outline not just the outcomes of those problems, but also what is potentially contributing to them in the first place. Systems mapping can be used for very specific problems or broader more universal ones. Systems mapping isn't easy and sometimes it can force your brain to stretch in uncomfortable ways, but by putting the time into it, novel and insightful answers to design problems can be revealed. The steps to creating a systems map are fairly straightforward, but how deep and broad you take the map is what is particularly important.

To create a systems map, take a blank piece of paper and divide it into three main sections. In the center, write down the main problem that you are addressing or has been given to you—this is the "stock." On the left, create a section for the issues that are contributing to that problem. Include issues that are more directly related to the problem closer to where you have written the main problem (or stock) and then work your way out to more tangential or indirectly contributing issues. On the right, write the issues are that an outcome of that problem, following the same strategy as with the inflows, with more directly related outcomes closer to the center of the page and more indirectly related issues as you move further away. This strategy can be used both as a brainstorming tool and to organize research around a topic. See the simplified example below.

Example problem: How can we get more people recycling on college campuses?

Backward systems: anti-solutions and worst-case scenarios

A pivotal part of thinking about systems—and in particular thinking about design as ever-changing and growing—is the evaluation and consideration of impact. While on first pass it might sound antithetical to design, which is often defined as taking existing conditions and transforming them into preferred ones (Papanek, 2005), but thinking about the impact of a system needs focus on the outcome first and foremost.

One technique for helping break down and examine problems in more detail is called anti-solution, or anti-solution brainstorming. For example, rather than asking the question, "How do we encourage people to recycle more?", we can reverse that question to ask "How can we discourage people from recycling?". The answers to that might be, "remove recycling containers, make it unclear what container to use, create openings that are too small for their containers to fit in, etc." In doing so, we can reveal the actual solution to the core problem. We can take this further, and rather than designing a system that encouraged people to recycle, what if we designed something that encouraged them to litter? Or to throw everything away? What would the impact be? And, if that were the system that we were designing, how might we actually use those behaviors (no matter how horrible) to achieve our recycling goal?

Similarly, thinking about the worst case scenario aligned with recycling can help identify different intervention points along a longer cycle of disposal. Asking ourselves "What would happen if we didn't intervene in this problem and let it continue on its current course?" can force us to think outside of the immediacy of the problem (or maybe enhance the immediacy of the problem!) by focusing on the larger picture. How will the problem become exacerbated, or compounded by doing nothing about it? If the landfills accrue more and more plastics, what are the outcomes? It might look a little like the Wes Anderson movie, *Isle of Dogs* (2018), where all the dogs in Tokyo are shipped to an island of trash in the middle of the ocean. Including a creative narrative around it can expand our minds about potential impacts and generally reveal creative intervention points that simple brainstorming might not get at.

Natural systems: using biomimicry to inspire new ideas

In her book, *Biomimicry: Innovation Inspired by Nature* (2002), Janine Benyus introduced the term biomimicry as "the conscious emulation of life's genius" (2). The biomimicry revolution, Benyus further argues, is a paradigm shift, "introducing an era focused not on what we can *extract* from nature, and towards what we can learn from her" (3). In many ways, it seems common sense that we should copy what has worked on the earth for billions of years, and long before humans appeared and began the rapid decline into depleting the natural resources. Nature has many insights to show us, about co-dependence, change and adaptation, and co-evolution. Nature shows us first-hand that we are all interdependent and reliant on one another, and that one action has an equal reaction to it. In their book, *Hypernatural* (2005), authors Blaine Brownell and Marc Swackhamer suggest that there are specific ways that we can use biomimicry to open up the potential for rethinking design problems. As they argue, *behavioral* projects use the biology inherent in the natural environment to expand material and fabrication possibilities before moving into the construction phase, and as a way to better consider how construction might take place. To explain this type of biomimicry, Brownell and Swackhamer point to the Silk Pavilion by The Mediated Matter Group at MIT's Media Lab because the project focuses on computationally derived designs matched with naturally inspired production. The Silk Pavilion used robots that spun silk in the same manner that natural silkworms do. By studying the silkworm habits, the group designed touchpoints similar to the "nodes" that silkworms would use in the construction of their cocoons matched with what was necessary to make the pavilion structurally sound. These nodes were then the structural cornerstones of the pavilion itself. The result was an organic structure that could be constructed on site and temporarily provide shelter using natural materials.

Genetic projects use biology to directly inform the construction of a project. When George de Mestral was walking in the woods of Switzerland with his dog in the 1940s, he noticed the burrs that were attaching themselves to both his pant legs and his dog's fur. He wondered how the construction of those burrs encouraged this attachment. By directly copying this construction with synthetic materials, he formed the basis of hook and loop fastening systems, otherwise known as Velcro.

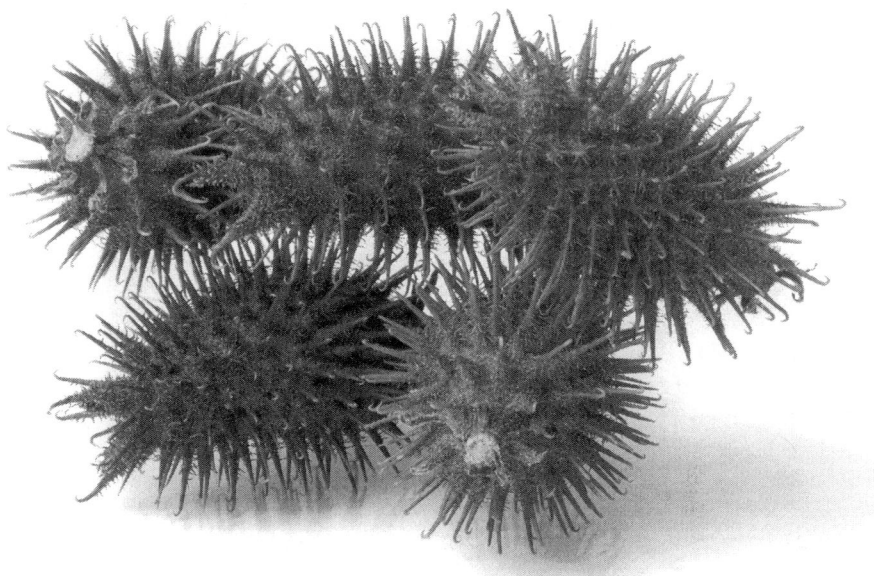

Figure 9.4

Hook feature of natural burr

Finally, *epigenetic* projects use biology, or principles of biology, to change the nature of the project after its construction. Designs that change with the environment are examples of these types of projects. One particularly compelling example of this type of biomimicry is from a group of textile designers in the Netherlands. The project, entitled Textile Reflexes, is a collaboration between Hellen van Rees, a textile and fashion designer, Angelika Mader, a creative technologies professional, and Geke Ludden, an interaction designer. Using robotic textiles to coach users to improve their posture, Textile Reflexes uses shape-changing sustainable textiles to give feedback to users as a sort of "coach." The first working prototype of this project is a posture correction coach. Designed as a vest that can be worn over regular garments, it measures when the user has an incorrect posture. It then pulls the flexible panel of squares at the back to subtly remind the user to sit back upright.

Ecological design thinking

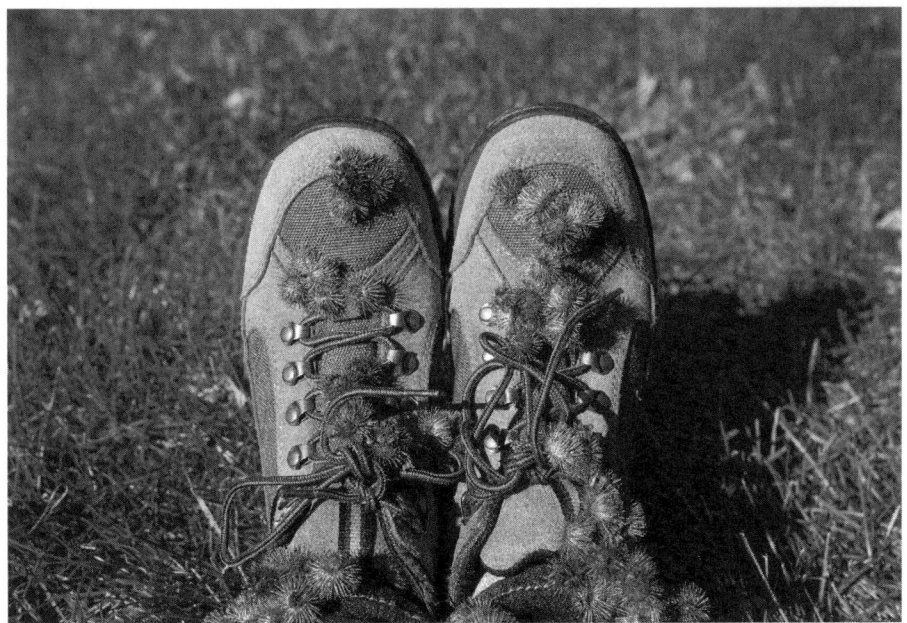

Figure 9.5

Natural burrs and synthetic fabric

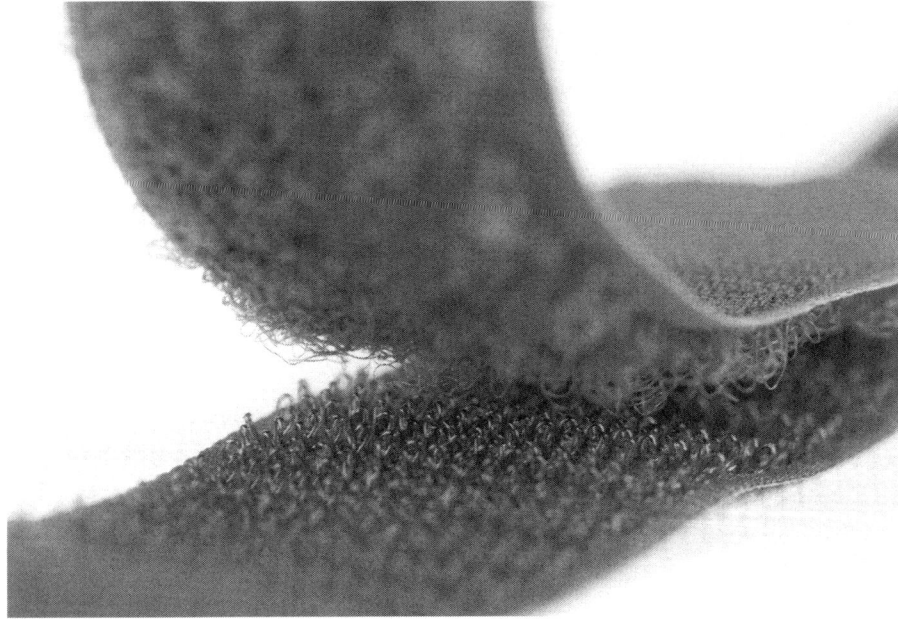

Figure 9.6

Closeup of Velcro, which uses the same technology

    The flexible textile is made of squares of post-consumer textile waste. Through a unique approach designed by Van Rees (2018), the different squares can move and respond to each other, creating a flexible, expanding and contracting surface. Through this effect a dynamic and playful texture emerges that easily adapts, leaving continuously changing open gaps between the squares. Van Rees was looking for a use for recycled textiles that she had begun turning into felt. Because the felt itself was thick and sturdy, there were some limitations to its usage. So Van Rees started to play around with modularly moving textile patterns that could be stitched together in such a way that they rotated, moved, expanded, or contracted. The basic shapes for the textiles were inspired by simple moving patterns found in nature. But as an example of an epigenetic biomimicry project, it is the response to posture that makes the project particularly compelling. The textiles are not a brace and they simply coach the wearer (as a reminder) through gentle compression, to sit up straighter.

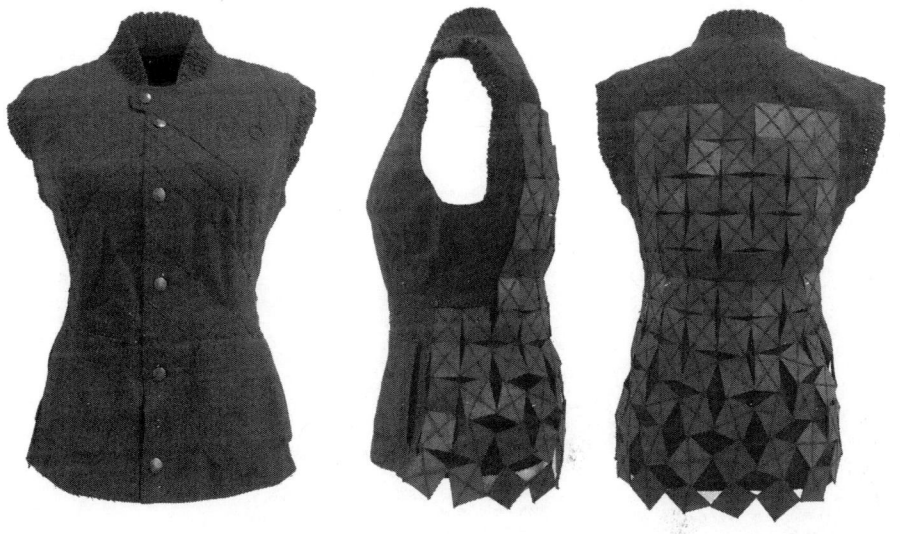

Figure 9.7

Textile Reflexes project. Image courtesy of Hellen van Rees

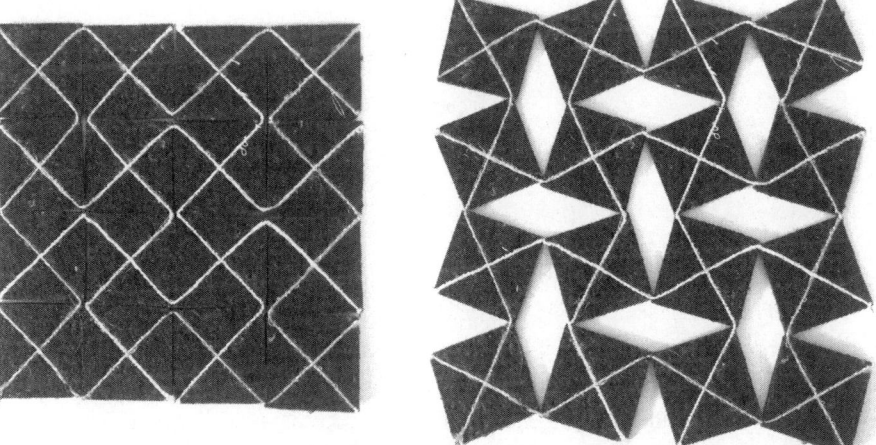

Figure 9.8

Textile Reflexes project. Image courtesy of Hellen van Rees

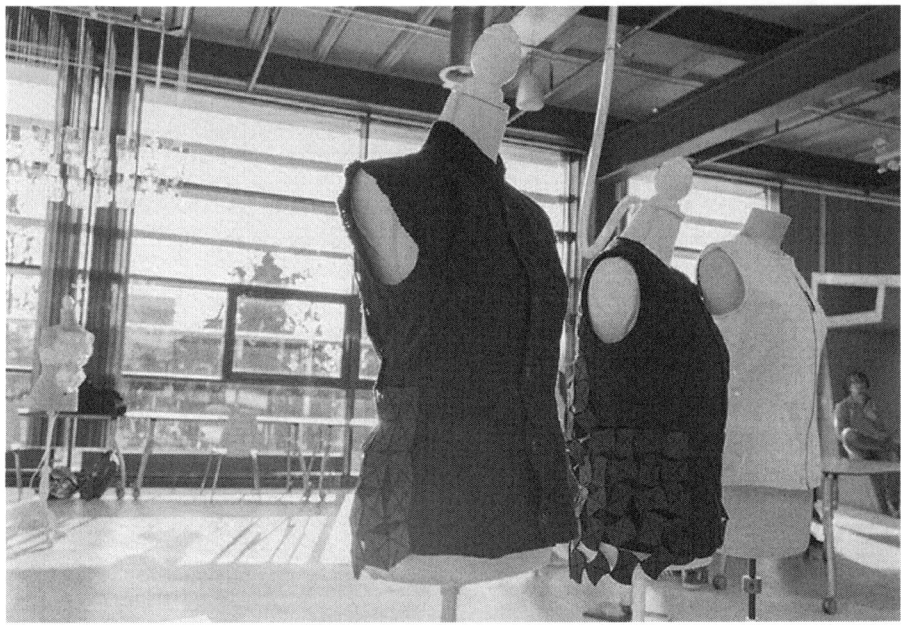

Figure 9.9

Textile Reflexes, detail. Image courtesy of Hellen van Rees

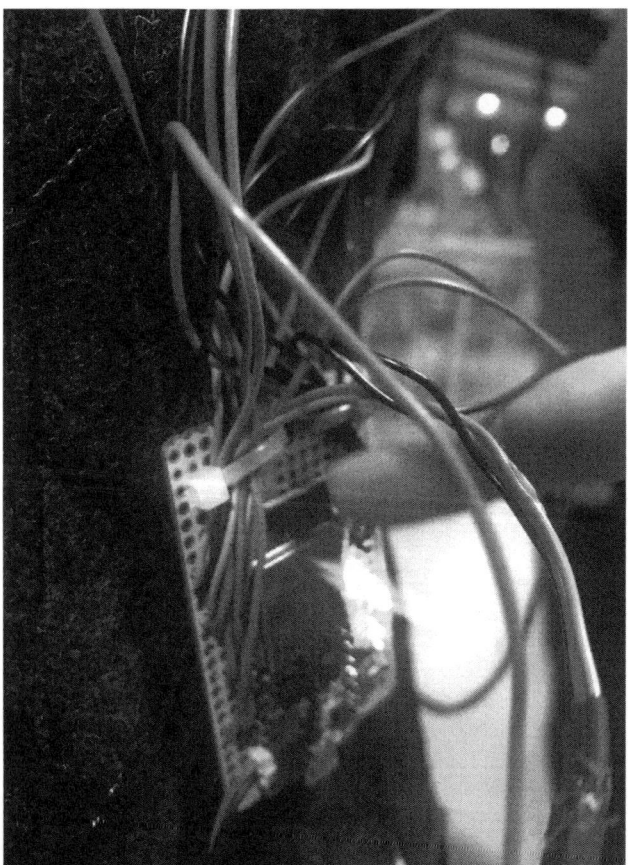

Figure 9.10

Wiring for robotic feature. Image courtesy of Hellen van Rees

What holds all of these methods together is an underlying perspective on the changing nature of design context—from the materials used to the principles of change and evolution that ideas are based on. Rather than avoiding the idea that a design might grow and change, building upon that constant—that change is constant—opens up entirely new ways of thinking about how and what is designed.

References

Benyus, Janine M. *Biomimicry: Innovation Inspired by Nature*. New York: Harper Perennial, 2002.

Brownell, Blane and Swackhamer, Marc. *Hypernatural: Architecture's New Relationship with Nature*. New York: Princeton Architectural Press, 2015.

Cosco, Nilda, Moore, Robin, and Islam, Mohammad Zahirul. "Behavior Mapping: A Method for Linking Preschool Physical Activity and Outdoor Design." *Official Journal of the American College of Sports Medicine*, 2010, pp. 513–519.

Lopate, Phillip. "Above Grade: On the High Line." *Places Journal*. November 2011. Retrieved from https://placesjournal.org/article/above-grade-on-the-high-line/. Accessed September 22, 2018.

Meadows, Donella. *Thinking in Systems: A Primer*. White River Junction, VT: Chelsea Green Publishing, 2008.

Papanek, Victor. *Design for the Real World: Human Ecology and Social Change*. Chicago, IL: Chicago Review Press, 2nd Edition, 2005.

Turner, J. Scott and Soar, Rupert C. "Beyond Biomimicry: What Termites Can Tell Us About Realizing the Living Building." First International Conference on Industrialized, Intelligent Construction (I3CON). Loughborough University, May 14–16, 2008.

Van Rees, Hellen, et al. "Textile Waste and Haptic Feedback for Wearable Robotics." *Design Research Society Catalyst*. University of Limerick, June 25–28, 2018.

Yin, Robert K. *Case Study Research: Design and Methods*. Thousand Oaks, CA: Sage Publications, 4th Edition, 2008.

10 Creating resilient futures
Case studies of ecological design thinking

Issues of sustainability are more and more common in the design studio. Paying closer attention to the full cycle of design, including production, construction, maintenance, and resiliency are common focus points for designers. And while systems thinking can be applied to the life cycle of a designed product or building, if we are to encourage the types of paradigm shifts that are advocated by John Thackara (2005), we need to also think about systems beyond the confines of the specific design object or experience being created. Part of that system is living, in the sense that people have the ability to interact, change and even carry forth the type of behavior and sustainable perspectives that are the only way real change will take root. Once we start thinking about the ecology of design, we realize that, much like the way that a plant or flower germinates, what we design is really just planting a seed—or possibly more so releasing a seed into the wind.

Designing sustainable futures in Qatar

While Qatar's environmental impact is small in comparison to world superpowers such as the Unites States and China, its per capita footprint is greater in many ways, particularly because of its oil-based economy and desert environment. As the 2012 UN Climate talks got underway in Doha, Qatar, the *Huffington Post* ran an article that outlined some of the more prevalent impacts that Qatar has on the world environment, the fact that the average citizen of Qatar use almost 2.5 times the amount of energy that American citizens do, reliance on energy intensive desalination plants to create drinking water, and the fact that its high temperatures require intensive energy resources to air condition its high rise hotels and office buildings. In Doha alone there are over 35 buildings over 150 meters high. For a city in the desert, that requires a remarkable amount of energy (McLendon, 2012). Additionally, because the government supplies free water and electricity, there is little incentive for citizens to engage in more sustainable practices. And because Qatar is still considered a "developing" country it does not have the same requirements as other large countries do, to curb emissions and be more sustainable.

At Virginia Commonwealth University's Doha, Qatar campus Denielle Emans is leading young graphic design students through a sustainability project where communication and behavior change is a core focus. Because of its desert location, solar energy is abundant, yet most of the urban development of the city has used traditional fossil-fuel energy. As solar energy technologies become more sophisticated and more accessible, focusing on that as a foundation for energy consumption makes logical sense. But this transition can still be challenging, as many urban developers are used to the traditional energy sources and technology. Starting from the ground up, and encouraging young designers to question the traditional means as a given, and to explore how alternative energies might be made more familiar and accessible can be a powerful first step in larger-scale paradigmatic change.

For this particular project, Emans encouraged students to explore the complexities of sustainability and the role of design in advancing systems of value in social, cultural, economic, and environmental terms. Following in-class discussions about design-led culture change, students honed in on a specific sustainability topic based on a combination of factors including, personal interest, partnerships with students in the United States, and data they gathered from primary and secondary sources in Qatar. Class discussions revolved around the idea that there is no "single" solution that can necessarily solve the complexities embedded within sustainability challenges. Why then, should designers think of their work in the same way, i.e. as one-off solutions, limited to a single outcome or format? Moving beyond the "single problem/solution" model and mentality prompted students to embrace multiple mediums and formats in order to communicate their message to a wider audience. The beauty of this approach is the freedom it inspires in the design process, to press beyond preconceived notions about a perfect "thing" that needs to be made. Instead, a systems thinking approach opens students up to the idea that designers can offer multiple channels for audiences to access information and make meaning for themselves. And as part of a cohesive system, each channel provides a new opportunity to help people rethink their behaviors or make more desirable decisions.

A critical part of the project was a prolonged initial research phase. Emans broke down the research into a series of primary and secondary research opportunities. Students read background literature as a first phase, and conducted small interviews with friends and family as they began to create a position on sustainability that would inform the larger project. By asking the students to engage in research, and by having them write an opinion paper, the students became engaged and took ownership of their own position and developed an engaged passion for the work they were doing. In a way, they became ambassadors for sustainability—however they defined it. Students were also asked to create surveys to conduct larger-scale interviews. Through a final opinion paper and presentation, students took an informed position on sustainability that would then inform their final project.

Outline of research and writing phase from Eman's sustainability project:

RESEARCH AND WRITING PROCESS

1.1 – SUSTAINABILITY: Dive into the assigned reading materials and research the idea of sustainability in Qatar, the MENA region, and in global terms. Examine your own habits and interview friends/family to understand what it means to be "sustainable." What does sustainability as a responsibility mean to you?

1.2 – INTERVIEW: Conduct three interviews to begin to understand the opinions surrounding sustainability from friends, family, community members, and external sources. Begin to outline a particular topic that interests you within the overall issue for further research.

1.3 – IDENTIFY: As an individual, identify a specific aspect of the sustainability issue in which to focus for the semester.

2.1 – SECONDARY RESEARCH: Use the VCUQatar library and academic databases to gather relevant journals/articles/books and synthesize information for your paper. Consider the interconnected issues embedded within the topic, making sure to note the relationship between people (social), planet (environment), and profit (economy).

2.2 – PRIMARY RESEARCH: Develop a questionnaire and/or survey to understand ideas/opinions towards your topic. Record and analyze findings. Choose interesting findings/narratives that support or refute your argument and integrate into your final paper.

2.3 – OUTLINE: Use the writing worksheet to outline your paper and help formulate your argument(s) based on primary and secondary findings.

2.4 – ABSTRACT: Write an abstract that serves as a brief summary of your research and your opinion for the paper. Consider including your motivation, problem statement, approach, results, and conclusion.

3.1 – OPINION PAPER: Write a two-page (double-spaced, 12 point) opinion paper on a sustainability topic supported by primary and secondary research. Make sure to include proper citations to a professional standard (MLA or APA style). Check grammar, use spell check, and employ the writing lab to ensure the highest quality of writing.

3.2 – ROUGH DRAFT: Turn in a rough draft for review. Please also hand in "Design Thinking Workbook" Intro and Section 1.

4.1 – PRESENTATION: Create a professional five-minute presentation (supported with visuals) demonstrating your research, findings, and resulting opinion.

Creating resilient futures

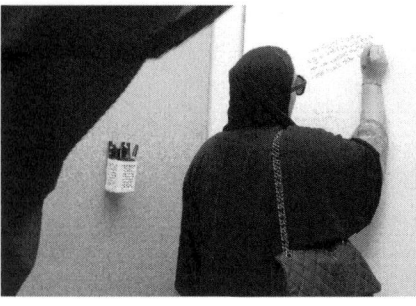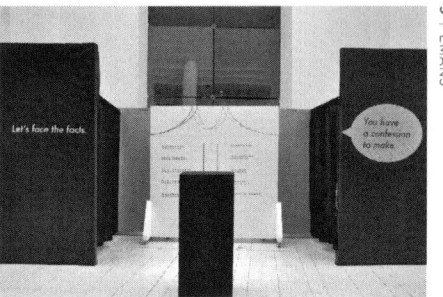

Mariam Al-Jufairi: A confessional style booth for children and adults to explore cultural sustainability issues in Qatar

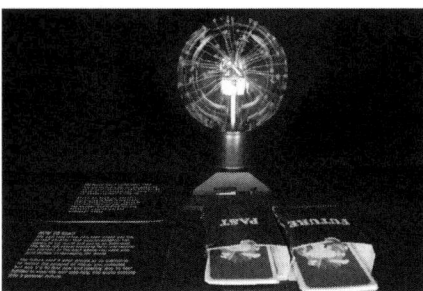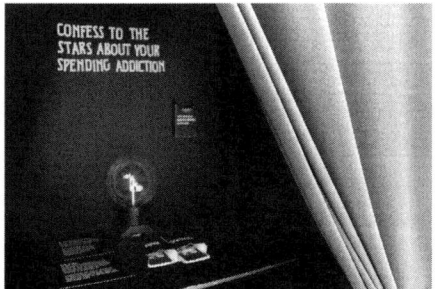

Nabilla Lubay: A tarot card booth that asks visitors to explore their personal spending habits

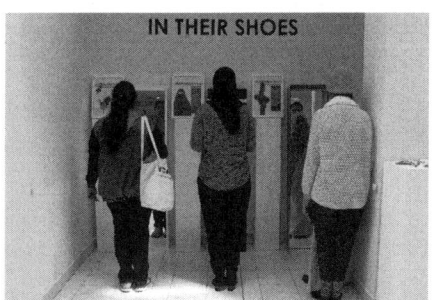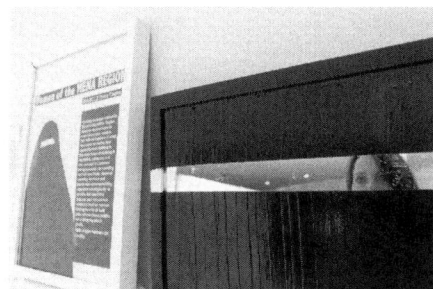

Aisha H Rasheed: An exhibition exploring the oppression of some women in the Arab world

PROJECT OUTCOMES
EXPERIENTIAL DESIGN

Each installation aims to raise awareness about a chosen sustainability topic that considers the Qatar 2030 national vision for development. The goal of this culminating exhibition was to introduce the audience to the collective findings of the course using multiple formats, mixed media and the elements of both 2-D and 3-D space.

Figure 10.1

Student work examples. Image courtesy of Denielle Emans

With this in mind, one student created a dynamic, interactive exhibition using multiple mediums and formats to help the audience consider how a city might switch to solar energy. This project engaged users in a game about fundamental ideas and information about solar energy and then asked them to decide how and where solar buildings might be best utilized within the urban planning process. In doing so, users were exposed to systems thinking on a number of different levels: as an environmental system users had to make decisions about how the solar panels would collect energy at different times of the day, or different seasons of the year. And as an urban system, users has to consider how various buildings and structures would collect, harness (and possibly even share) solar resources in an urban setting where other buildings may or may not have solar energy to draw upon. The project involves the design of an ebook, a newspaper expert, and a three-dimensional game to help players engage with solar energy and urban planning. Players explore how to implement solar energy in the city and take advantage of the sun by considering the relationship between the sun, panel location, building height, and location. The steps for the game are to 1) read the ebook 2) pick a building 3) attach a solar panel 4) pick a location 5) finish the urban planning. Players are also engaged in the game through multiple channels—through research and exposure to some of the underlying issues associated with solar energy and urban planning, and as a designer who must take what they have learned to make decisions that utilizes that knowledge to make the best decisions possible. As Emans conceived of the project, one of the primary goals was to engage and educate people through multiple sensory channels.

Naturally inspired design

At the core of the student project mentioned above is the rethinking of design projects to embrace and capitalize on what is natural to the environment in which we are designing. Since its construction in 1996, the Eastgate Centre in Zimbabwe is one of the most cited examples of biomimicry in architecture. Designed by Mick Pearce and Arup Engineers the project uses indigenous architectural principles and termite mounds to rethink temperature regulation in one of the largest office parks and shopping centers in Zimbabwe. Pearce, a South African architect, in particular was sensitive to the fact that most of the engineering principles driving African building construction was based on environments that were more temperate, and much cooler than those in Africa. As a result, he wanted to rethink some of the basic principles of heating and cooling that could take advantage of the African environment. The Eastgate building uses technology inspired from the termite mounds that are a part of much of the landscape in and around Africa. The termites,

> are themselves architects of sorts, building massive mounds that in some instances tower several meters high. The mound serves as climate-control infrastructure for the termite colony's subterranean nest. Pearce reasoned that the architectural principles of the termite mound, honed to sleek efficiency by the relentless refining of natural selection, could inspire buildings that perform equally well. By all measures, his vision succeeded brilliantly.
>
> (Turner and Soar, 2008, 1)

When they were first being studied, scientists believe that the termites constructed the mounds for a very practical reason—to keep the fungus that is their food source at a consistent temperature, even as the temperature outside fluctuated 50 or even 60 degrees between day and night hours. An article in *Inhabitant* explained that:

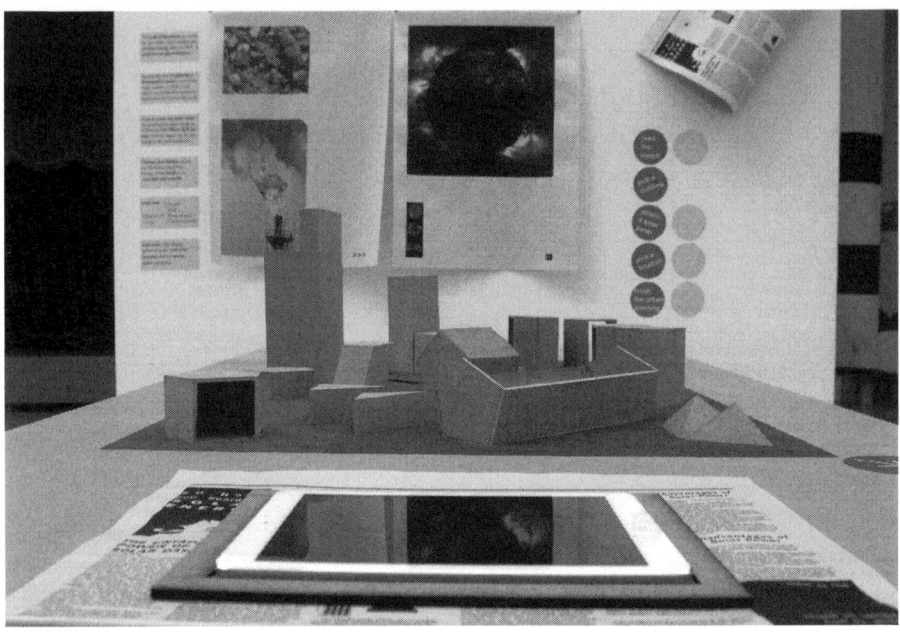

Figure 10.2

Bo Peng, Solar City game. Image courtesy of Denielle Emans

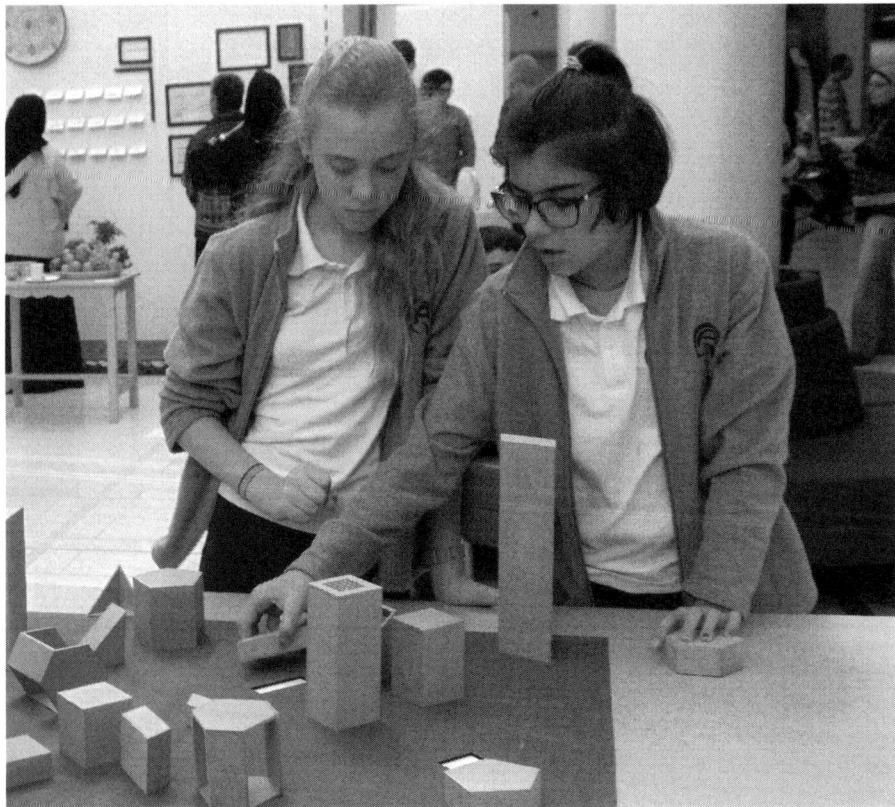

Figure 10.3

Children building a Solar City. Image courtesy of Denielle Emans

Creating resilient futures

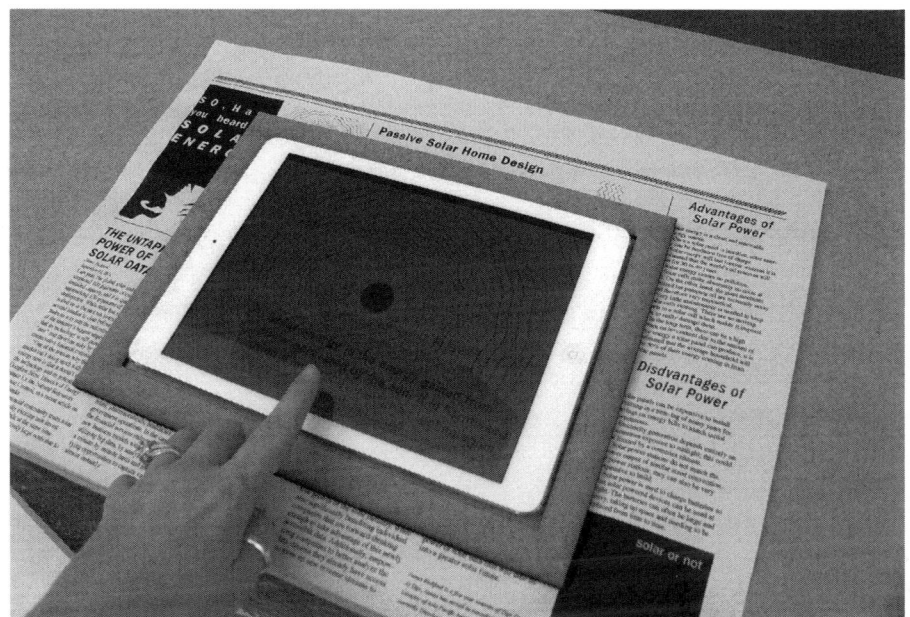

Figure 10.4

An interactive app gives users more information on the impacts. Image courtesy of Denielle Emans

The termites achieve this remarkable feat by constantly opening and closing a series of heating and cooling vents throughout the mound over the course of the day. With a system of carefully adjusted convection currents, air is sucked in at the lower part of the mound, down into enclosures with muddy walls, and up through a channel to the peak of the termite mound. The industrious termites constantly dig new vents and plug up old ones in order to regulate the temperature.

(Doan, 2012)

The Eastgate building is designed as two adjacent buildings separated by a large channel that draws in breezes from the surrounding area. The outer layer of the building is also porous in much the same way as the termite mounds are. As air is brought in, the large concrete mass that makes up the central corridor of the building either warms or cools the air, depending on whether the air is warmer or cooler than the concrete. The air is then moved back through the building to provide cooler or warmer air to the people inside. Air is then moved up through the building through a central chimney to avoid air from stagnating or becoming stale. This system has been incredibly economical as well as environmentally sustainable. The costs for heating and cooling to the building are almost 10% what it costs to operate a building of a similar size. One of the biggest challenges to this type of design is in the construction. Because of the modular nature of the building, many smaller parts are aggregated into a larger structure. Technologies like 3D printing can greatly offset the cost of creating so many independent pieces and greatly reduce construction materials and costs.

Since the building's design and construction, additional research into the way that termite mounds are constructed has revealed that the technology that some of the basic biomimetic principles that Pearce and Arup Engineers based their design upon was inaccurate. Namely, termites do not regulate the interior temperature in the ways that scientists previous thought and temperature within the mound could fluctuate 20–30 degrees Celsius. Additionally, while there was evidence of mound ventilation, there was actually no evidence of nest ventilation. Additional discoveries relating to the damping of air and regulation of wind flows around the mounds have also given way to new understandings of the complexities of these mound constructions. But, rather than diminishing the feat of Eastgate Centre, almost all who have surveyed it have agreed is an architectural and engineering success. This becomes a fundamental issue for biologically inspired design, where research will continue to uncover new and more sophisticated understandings of the natural world. And rather than discounting or disproving the work of Pearce and the Eastgate building, what this additional research points to is even more sophisticated engineering principles for architecture in the future.

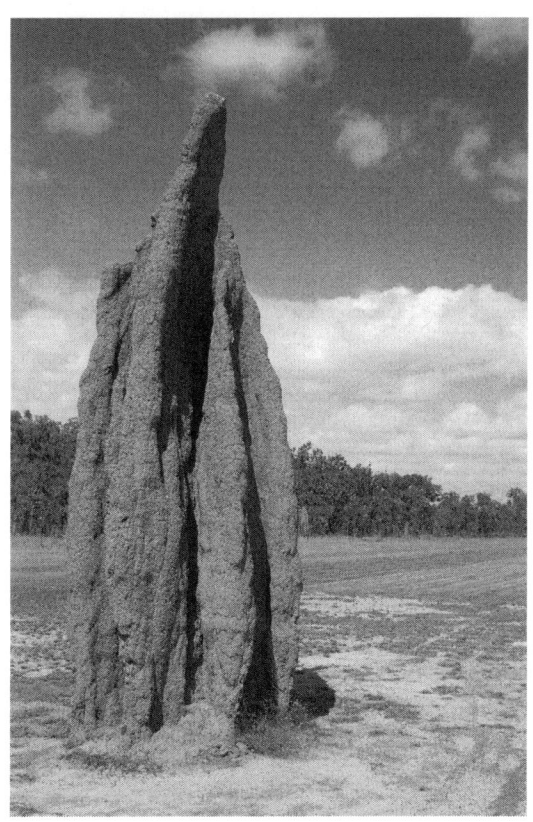

Figure 10.5
Cathedral termite mounds

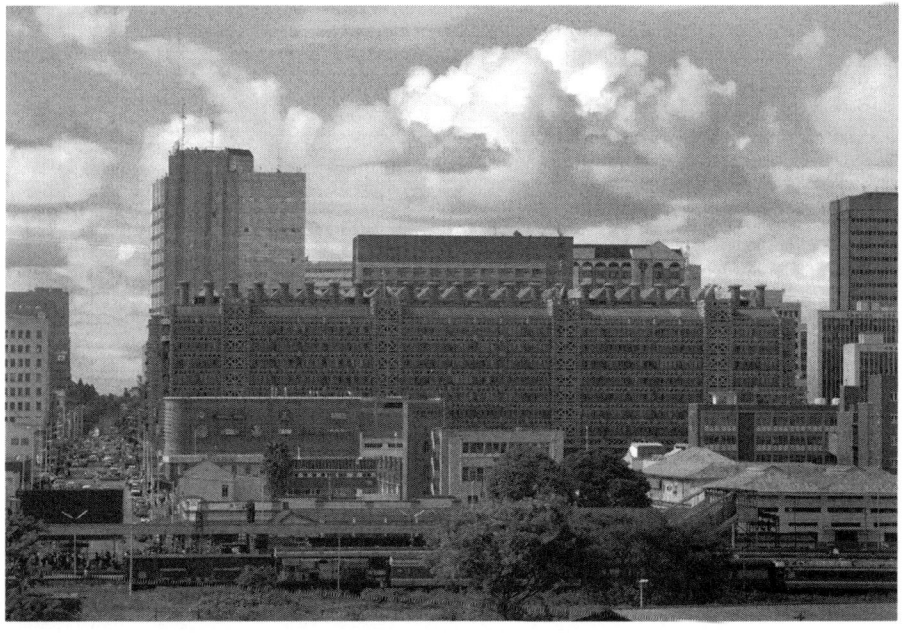

Figure 10.6
Eastgate building exterior, Wikimedia Commons. Image courtesy of David Brazier

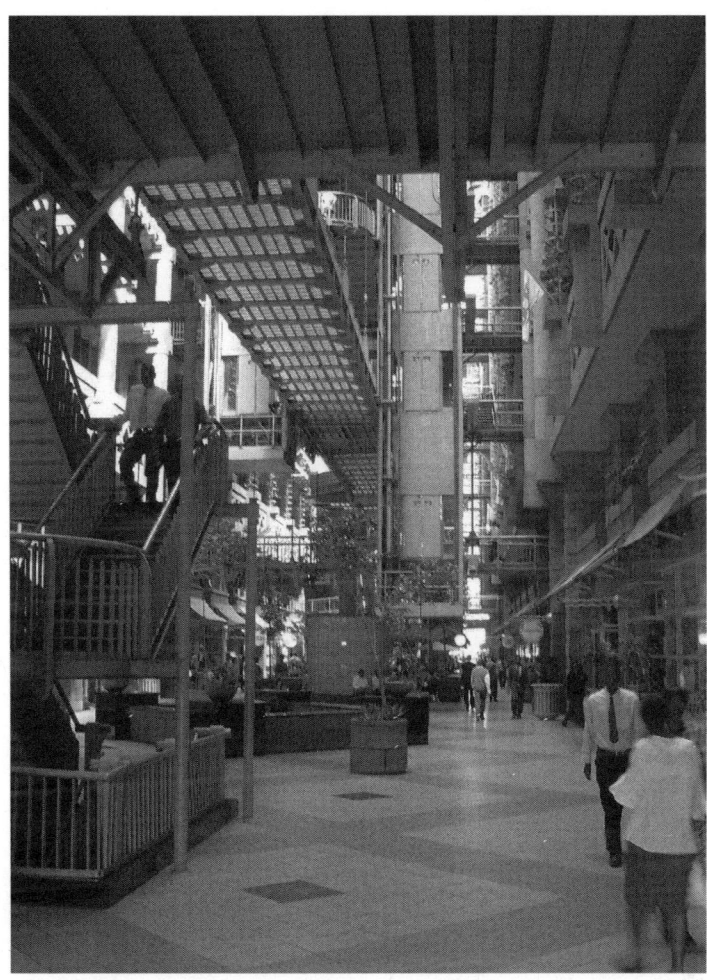

Figure 10.7
Eastgate building interior, Wikimedia Commons, photo by Gary Bembridge

Considering resiliency post-disaster: HomePlace and FloodPrint

Earlier in this chapter, John Thackara (2005) argued that true sustainability necessitates a paradigm shift in terms of productions, consumption, speed, and learning. While true, there are also real problems that we are facing globally as a result of the traditional thinking revolving around the exploitation and fallacy of never-ending resources. More and more, designers understand the larger system that design is operating within, and recognize the need for design to undergo a change in the fundamental approach to problem-solving. The paradigm shift driving the Coastal Dynamics Design Lab (CDDL) relates to fundamental decisions about how we respond to natural disasters—and specifically flooding. Led by Andrew Fox, a Landscape Architect and David Hill, an architect, the CDDL partnered with the Coastal Resilience Center at nearby University of North Carolina and the North Carolina Policy Collaboratory to engage North Carolina communities in rural areas hit hard by Hurricane

Matthew in 2016. The result of this engagement was *HomePlace,* a conversation guide aimed to support community decision-making on the allocation of federal funding for the rebuilding effort in six rural towns. *HomePlace* served not only to show how design could be used to think differently about resiliency at the individual, neighborhood, and community level, but also to explain the fundamental reasons why the flooding occurred in the first place so that community members could make more informed decisions about how and where to rebuild, or whether to rebuild at all. In most post-disaster rebuilding efforts, decision-making can be heavily driven by emotions, and the desire to get back to normal. According to the former head of the Red Cross in California:

> Losing a home can be like losing a limb . . . You may have worked on that house for 20 years, you may still be paying off the mortgage, you may never have the opportunity to own another home, especially if you're older. And later on, moving into a new home, it's not the same as an old home.
>
> (Brozan, 1983)

The approach to *HomePlace* was sensitive to these emotional realities and meant looking at a wide variety of factors in the design recommendations, and including sensitivity to the history and culture of the town—including the specific factors contributing to each town's flooding—while also looking at more pragmatic realities like affordability and sustainability for any refurbished or new structures that might be built in the future. As a result, *HomePlace* focused on locally distinct options for the redesign or rebuilding of individual houses, along with design strategies for yards, streets, and community greenspaces. All of the designs worked together toward the creation of responsive and resilient spaces that reflected local history and character. The guide also explained and illustrated key factors that community members might consider when making decisions about how and where

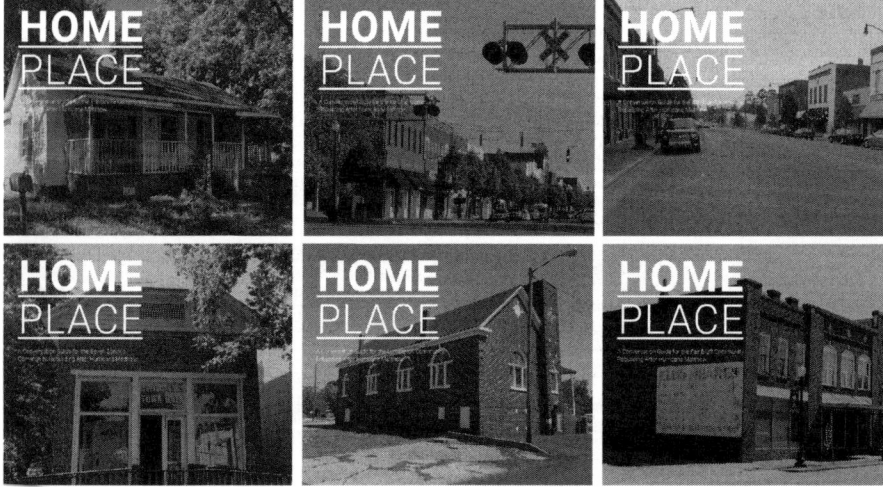

Figure 10.8

HomePlace covers of six communities. Image courtesy of the Coastal Dynamics Design Lab

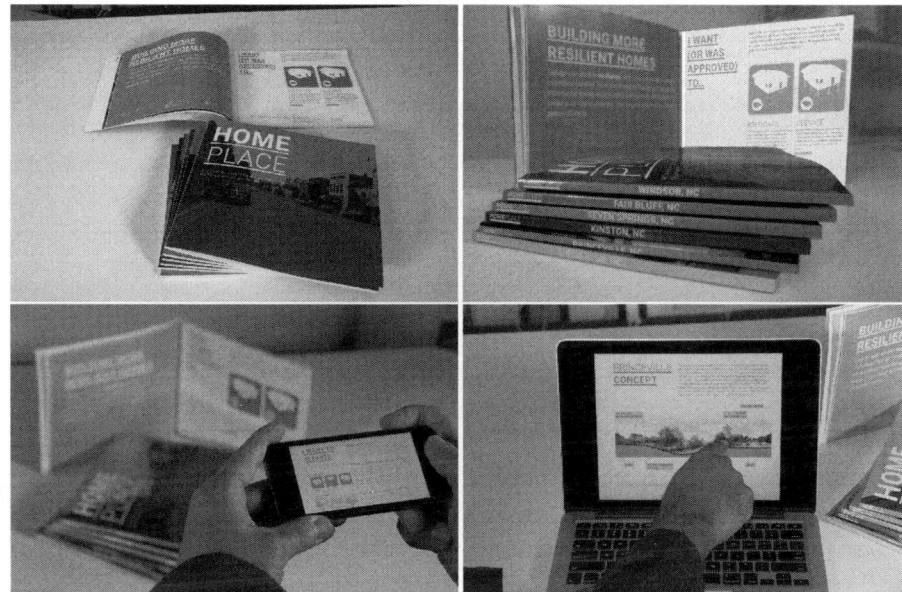

Figure 10.9

Accessing HomePlace in print and digitally. Image courtesy of the Coastal Dynamics Design Lab

to rebuild—including accessibility, curb appeal, affordability, comfort, efficiency, and flexibility (Boone et al., 2018, 5). The proposals included in *HomePlace* reflected the complex relationship every town had with the body of water that was ultimately responsible for the flooding that destroyed parts of them. On the one hand, the water provides sustenance—from trading and travel to recreation and tourism. On the other hand, the inability to control the changing climate and its impact on weather and rising sea levels increases the vulnerability of the town, making old ways of living and working at the constant mercy of the waterways themselves.

As a result of *HomePlace*—and specifically tackling the larger issues of vulnerability and vacancy caused in part by the impact of Hurricane Matthew, Florence, and other large storms that are increasingly impacting coastal areas around the world—the CDDL took on a more strategic project which looked at a single rural town that developed a framework for resiliency that could be applied to other areas around the world. The result, *FloodPrint*, aimed to reframe the notion of vacancy as necessarily negative, and to capitalize on vacant areas to identify and create resilient buffers that could be utilized by the community while also protecting it. Looking at these spaces as a network that could both move citizens around the town, provide resources that could be accessible by all, and elevate the heritage and culture of the town, *FloodPrint* designed a larger strategy for resiliency that focused on looking at flooding as part of a larger system that included learning from the past, responding to the present, and preparing for the future. As the *FloodPrint* document explained it, "Current research has shown that if managed properly, vacant land can act as a catalyst for reconnecting natural systems, creating connective social tissue, and providing ecosystems services to

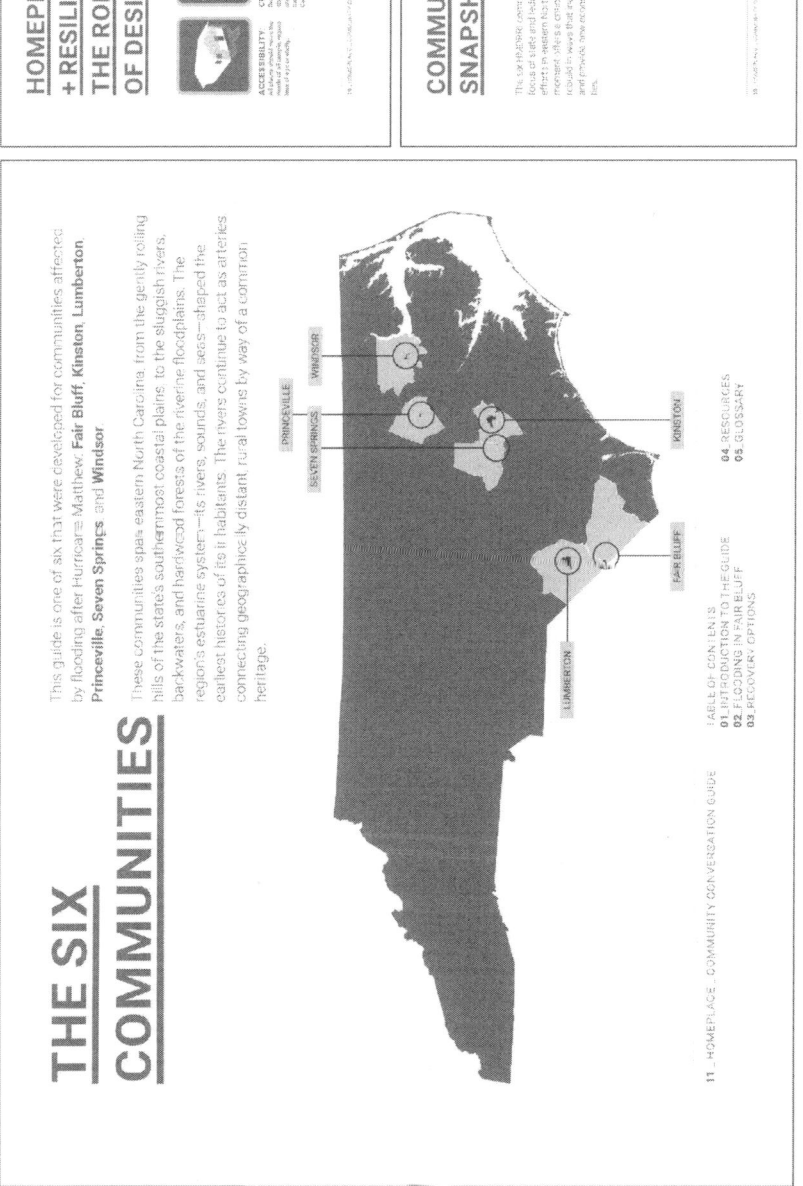

Figure 10.10

The six communities of HomePlace. Image courtesy of the Coastal Dynamics Design Lab

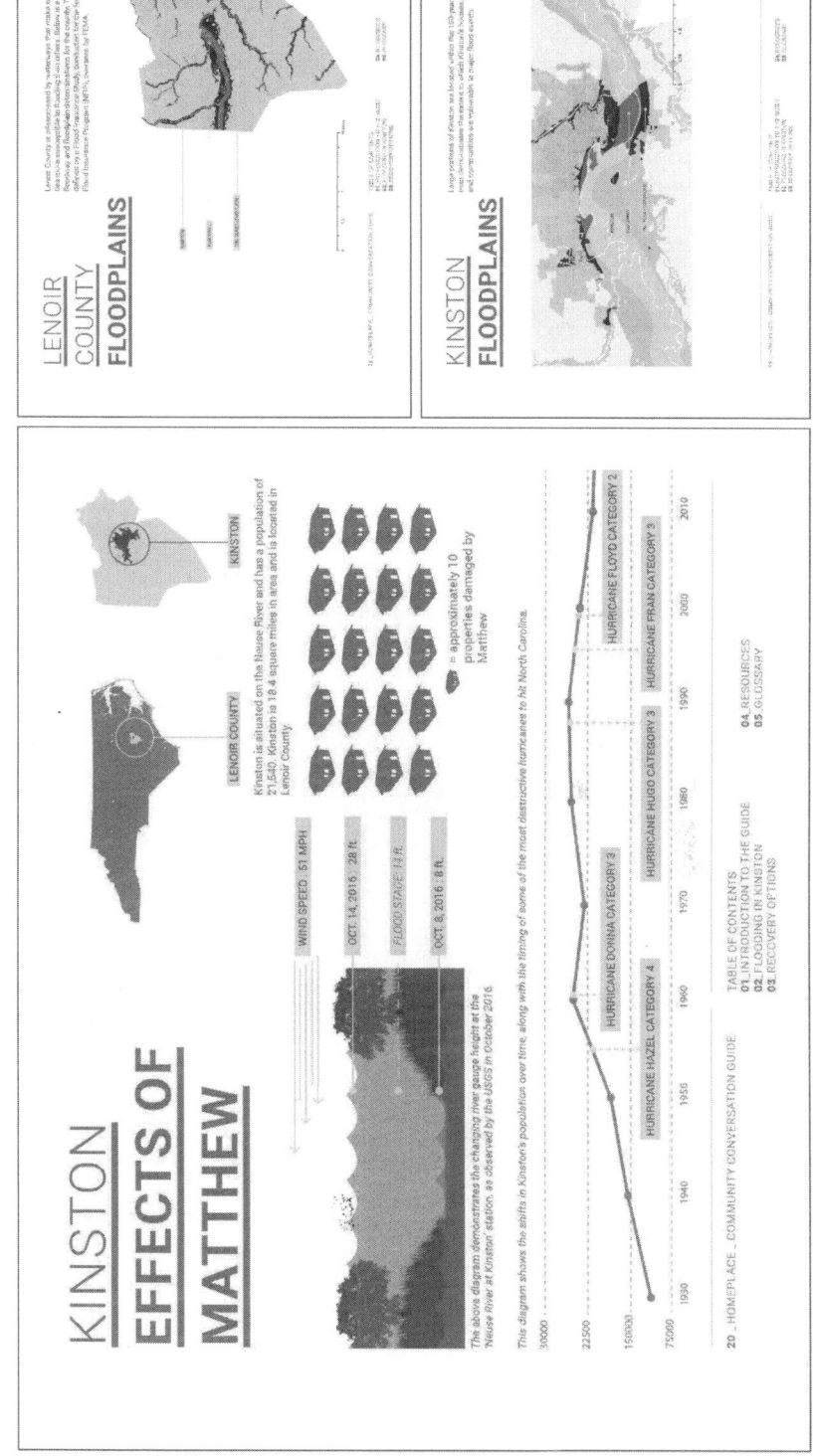

Figure 10.11
Why communities flood. Image courtesy of the Coastal Dynamics Design Lab

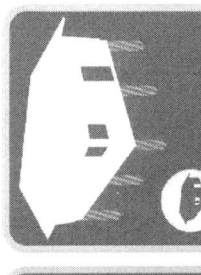
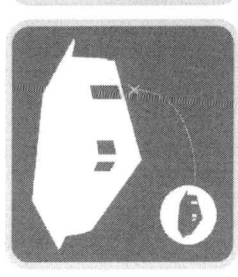
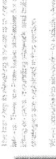
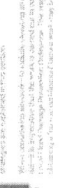

Figure 10.12

Options for residents, relocating, or elevating. Image courtesy of the Coastal Dynamics Design Lab

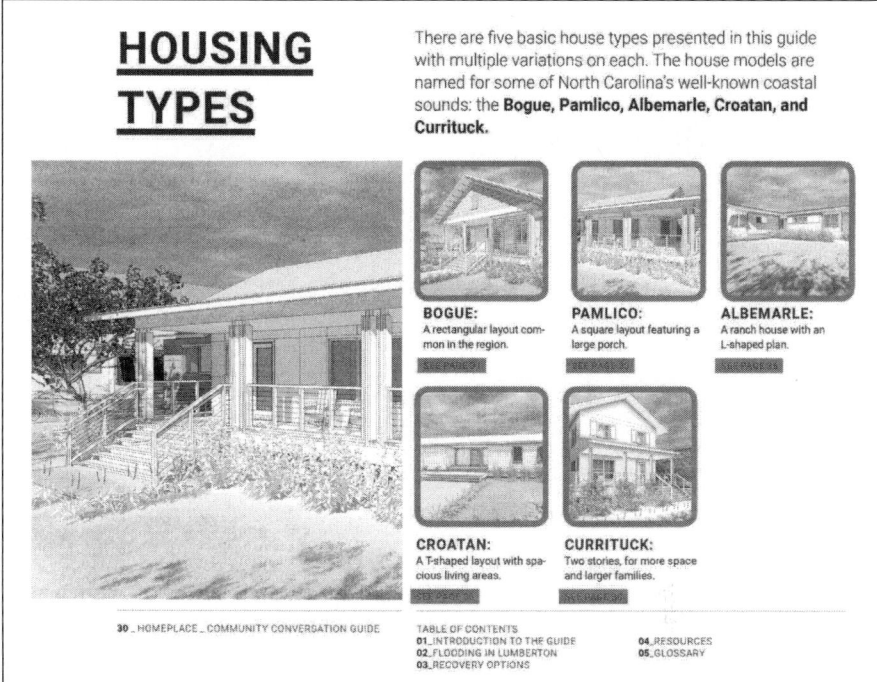

Figure 10.13

Housing types. Image courtesy of the Coastal Dynamics Design Lab

areas undergoing transformation" (Fox et al., 2019). In order to realize these benefits vacant land needed to be evaluated along with the entire community's landscape for larger strategies to emerge. Identifying areas of a community that were most vulnerable to the impacts of flooding, most ecologically valuable, and most connected to existing resources underpinned the strategies the CDDL identified in *FloodPrint*.

For sustainability to become more central to design considering all aspects of the design process as part of a larger system—ecological, social, economic, and some combination of all of those—is a significant paradigm shift, but one that is becoming more inherent in all aspects of design. Considering design action also as part of a continuum that is affected by the environment in which it exists, and potentially as a design that can respond to that environment, holds many exciting opportunities for radical innovation. Looking for inspiration and knowledge in the natural environment holds many possibilities for rethinking and re-understanding the man-made environment and to shift the paradigm from people (and by extension design) trying to control nature, to one where design works alongside to enhance natural capabilities. These are the types of projects that hold the most possibility for a future earth that is resilient and capable of far-reaching survival and thriving.

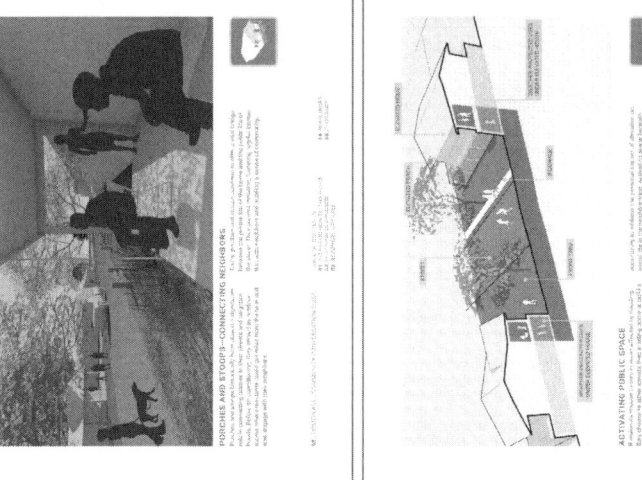
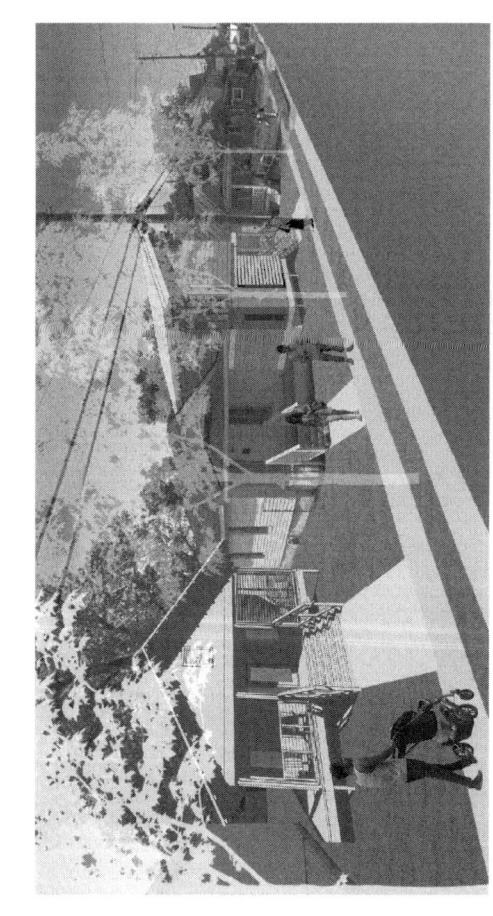

Figure 10.14

The neighborhood scale. Image courtesy of the Coastal Dynamics Design Lab

Creating resilient futures

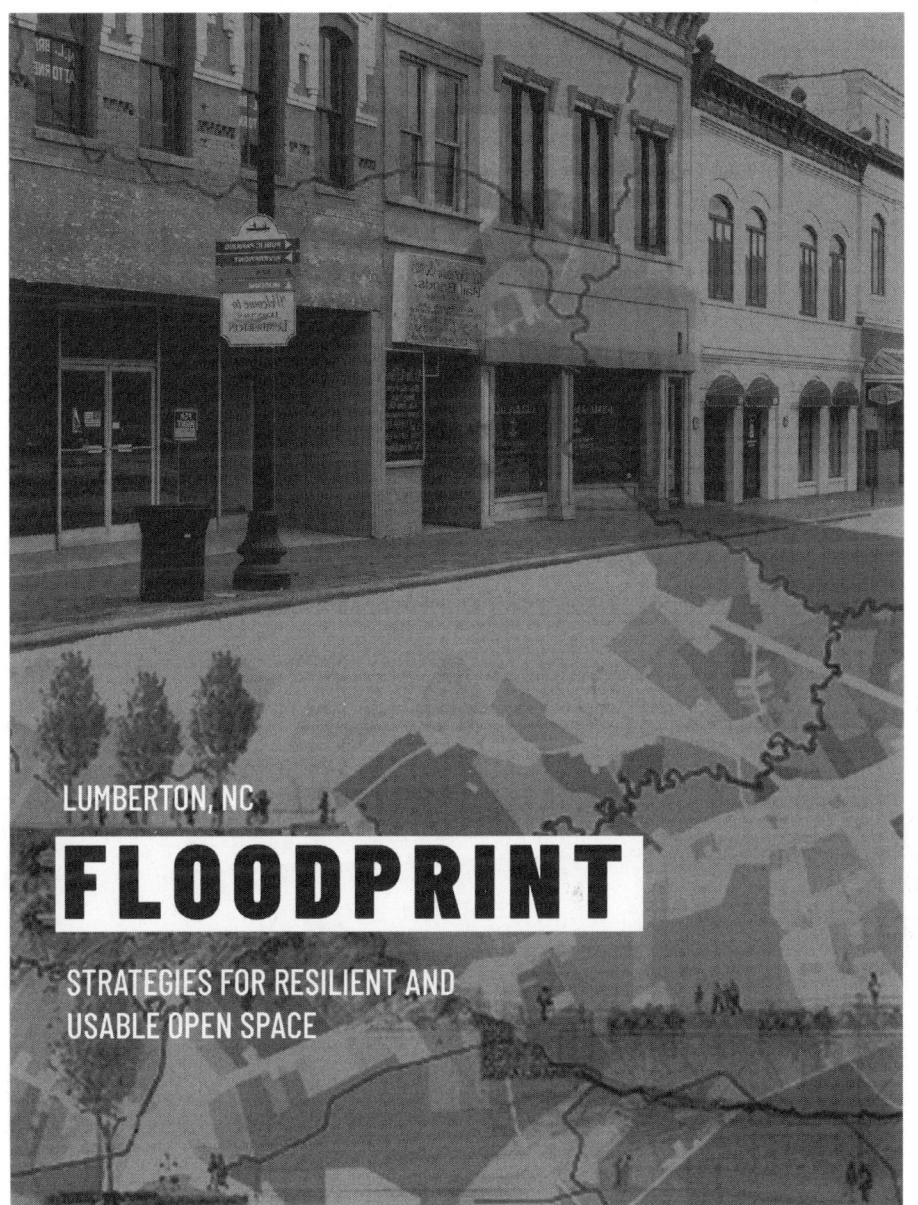

Figure 10.15

FloodPrint cover. Image courtesy of the Coastal Dynamics Design Lab

Creating resilient futures

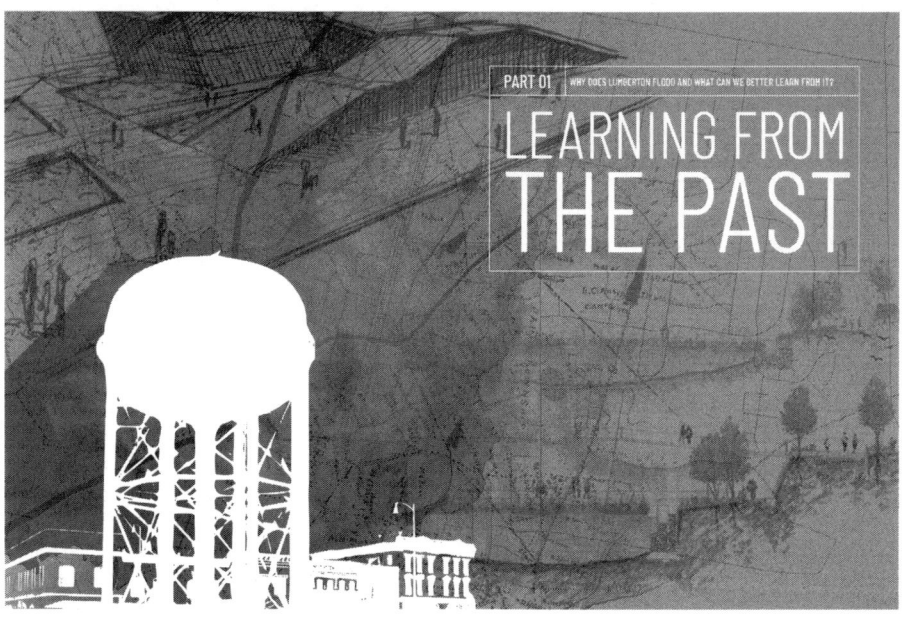

Figure 10.16

Section break, Learning from the past. Image courtesy of the Coastal Dynamics Design Lab

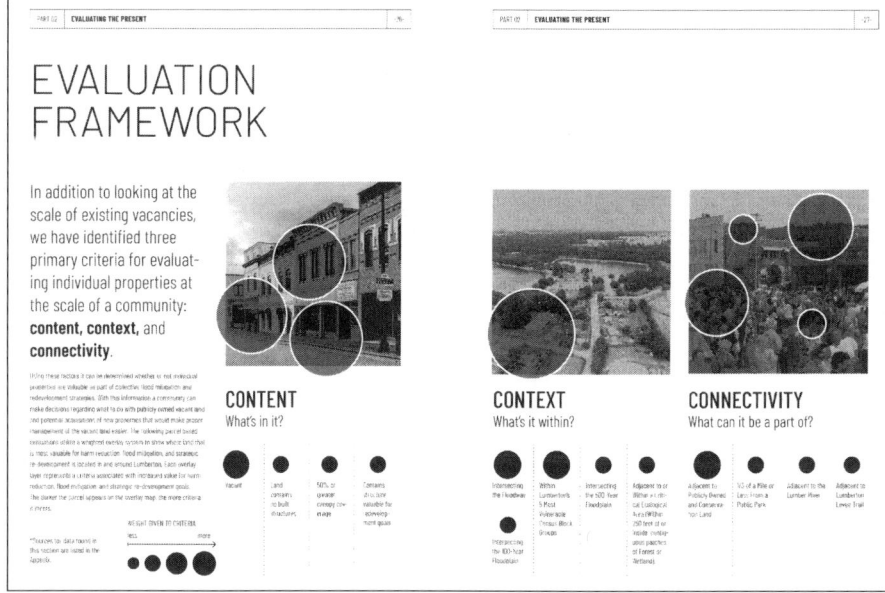

Figure 10.17

Evaluation framework. Image courtesy of the Coastal Dynamics Design Lab

Creating resilient futures

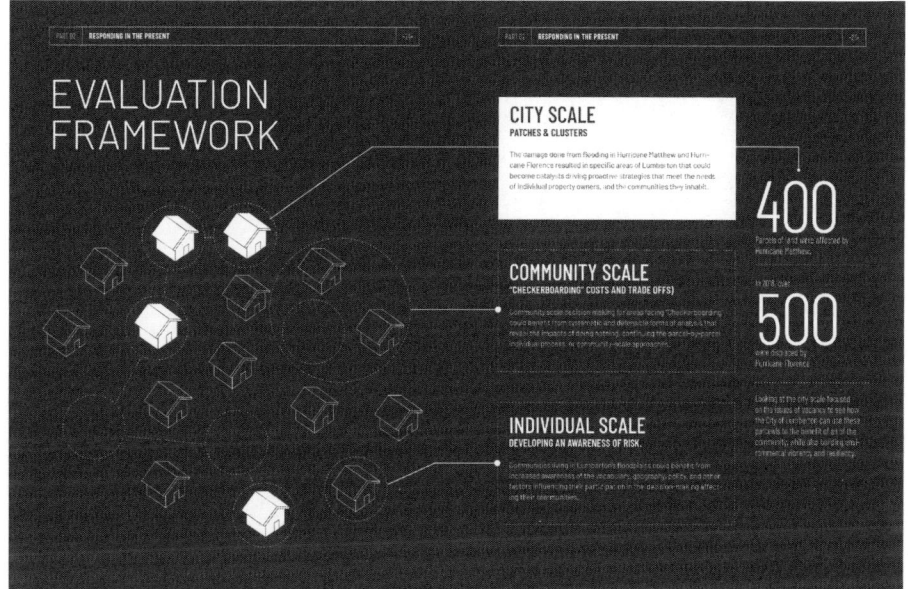

Figure 10.18

Evaluation framework. Image courtesy of the Coastal Dynamics Design Lab

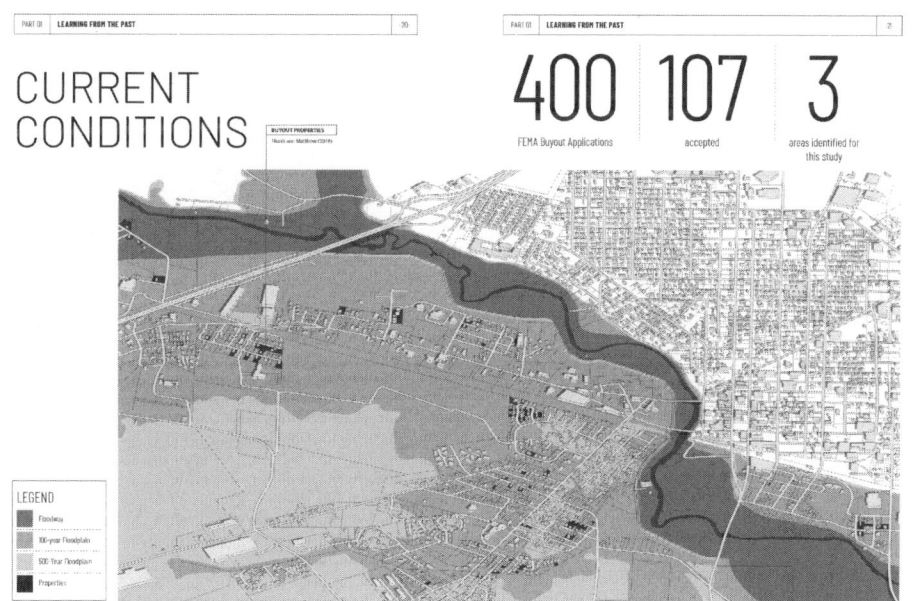

Figure 10.19

Current conditions. Image courtesy of the Coastal Dynamics Design Lab

References

Boone, Kofi, Fox, Andrew, and Hill, David. *HomePlace*. Raleigh, NC: NC State University College of Design, Coastal Dynamics Design Lab Publication, 2018.

Brozan, Nadine. "Emotional Effects of Natural Disasters." *The New York Times*, June 27, 1983. Accessed as digital archive, December 15, 2018.

Doan, Abigail. "Biomimetic Architecture: Green Building in Zimbabwe Modeled After Termite Mounds." *Inhabitant*. November 29, 2012. Retrieved from https://inhabitat.com/building-modelled-on-termites-eastgate-centre-in-zimbabwe/?variation=c. Accessed September 25, 2018.

Fox, Andrew et al. "FloodPrint." *Coastal Dynamics Lab*. 2019. Retrieved from www.coastaldynamicsdesignlab.com/lumberton-floodprint. Accessed March 28, 2018.

McLendon, Russell. "Qatar's Impact on the Environment: How the U.N. Climate Talks in Doha Cast a Spotlight on the Country." *Huffington Post*. November 30, 2012. Retrieved from www.huffingtonpost.com/2012/11/30/qatar-environmental-impact-climate_n_2213298.html. Accessed September 22, 2018.

Thackara, John. *In the Bubble: Designing in a Complex World*. Cambridge, MA: MIT Press, 2005.

Turner, J. Scott and Soar, Rupert C. "Beyond Biomimicry: What Termites Can Tell Us About Realizing the Living Building." *First International Conference on Industrialized, Intelligent Construction (I3CON)*. Loughborough University, May 14–16, 2008.

Part 4

Design and morality
Do the right thing

11 Making change, design as moral mediator

In the introduction, there was an implicit (or maybe explicit) theme: that all design is aimed at changing behavior. A design plan could be aimed at encouraging people to move into a new house or neighborhood, or to stop smoking, or to join a new gym. Previously in the book, we discussed the idea that all design is interactive in some way—whether it's a simple act like reading a poster or opening a door, or a more complex activity like searching through online archives. This chapter builds on the idea that design actually impacts the values that people have and by extension their ongoing behavior—for better and for worse. As some of the examples and case studies will show, design can do this knowingly or unknowingly and have longer-term effects on how we interact with one another. Because of this, designers cannot be divorced from the impact of how their designs encourage new moral and cultural behavior and norms.

This idea may seem daunting and even paralyzing. How can designers foresee *all* of the impacts their design will have? And, wouldn't that pressure prevent them from designing in the first place? One could argue that no one could have foreseen the impact that the car would have on travel, pollution, gas consumption, or the scarcity of oil. But, we now see all of the implications that the invention of the car has. Do the positives outweigh the negatives? This is the question that designers today face, and a critical one to integrate into design education and practice. We know that wicked problems don't have single solutions, just better and worse ones. We also know that the complexity of design problems necessitate an examination that involves different scales, orientations, and timelines. In addition, these examinations need to include the assumptions that design solutions are based upon—assumptions guided by individual experience of the designer, or the client, or even the community itself.

Let's take the housing bubble that burst in the U.S. in 2007 (Hardaway, 2011) but then continued to slide downward until it reached is low point in 2012. On the surface, that was a banking and mortgage industry problem. They sold sub-prime mortgages to people who couldn't really afford them, and without taking into real account the possibility that the current economic conditions would change. As a result, there was unprecedented new housing construction in many parts of the country. The "market" (and by this I mean, people) wanted new houses, rather than living in old ones and renewing them. And the design industry responded by developing new plans for homes and communities. Technology also played a large role as new software applications were developed at an exponential rate that allowed consumers to take virtual tours, see houses as soon as they went on the market, link to mortgage companies and get bids online—generally reducing the process time and making it much easier to find and finance a loan. And the communication directed at consumers was generally focused on how easy this process was. Rather than focusing on making the complexity of the loan process easier to understand so that consumers could make more informed decisions about what would be a financially healthy decision, advertising and marketing focused on making the process "digestible," removing critical pieces of information that customers needed to have. This is not to blame this crisis on advertising, marketing, and interface designers, but rather to help emphasize the influential role design has in a much larger system that impacts the behaviors of the people whom we "serve." Designers have not traditionally questioned the moral outcomes of the work that they are doing, unless it is incredibly obvious—designing a gun, for instance. And in a small part, this chapter aims to encourage designers to start questioning more deeply the outcomes and impacts of the work they are engaged in, and to spend more time speculating on the impact of design action. It's not that designers alone could have avoided the burst previously mentioned, but quite possibly could have contributed to a different outcome.

If design is to advance, it needs to learn from its past. We are all quick to jump on the bandwagon of what will address an acute issue or symptom, rather than seeking ways to solve the larger, more chronic issues that are driving the problem in the first place. Design need not limit itself to the symptoms, but that seems to be where the focus continues to reside. For example, the cigarette ads of the early 20th century claimed the positive benefits of smoking—often employing the trusted endorsement of a doctor to set customers at ease. After much research, experimentations, and litigation there is now common acknowledgment of the connection between cigarettes and cancer, lung disease, and other deadly ailments. But a quick survey of vapor cigarette ads shows a similar language of safety and harmlessness that were implicit (or explicit) 80 years ago. A 2016 report by the surgeon general shows an almost 900% increase in high school students using e-cigarettes between 2011 and 2015 (US Department of Health and Human Services, 2016), even as traditional cigarette smoking has reduced among the same group. This supports the conclusion that young people might be believing these messages, even as studies show that vaping can still become a gateway to traditional cigarette smoking (Baker, 2015). Here is an opportunity to learn from the power of language, endorsement, and responsibility that designers hold, and to think about what they are "prescribing" through their activity of creation. It is not the designer's job alone to think through these implications, but the propositional nature of design activity positions the designer in a unique position to influence the direction of design action, as well as to challenge the assumptions that drive desired outcomes.

Making change, design as moral mediator

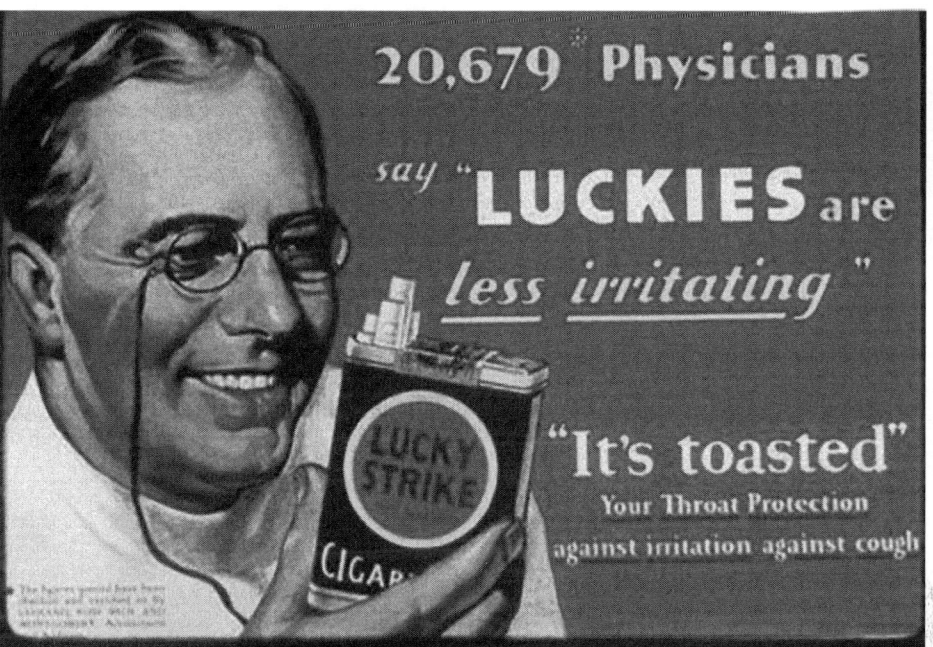

Figure 11.1
Cigarette ad, circa 1930

Design as a moral mediator

Many contemporary theories in design attempt to understand how design objects and environments affect values and behaviors. Emerging from fields outside of design such as philosophy, social work, and art, these theories can help designers think about what they are designing and how they are engaging in the activity of design in new and powerful ways. They extend the reach of design beyond an activity and towards a philosophy in and of itself. What is common about these theories is the impact of design artifacts and environments in shaping the way people understand their world and other people within it. In each of these theories, design is but a piece of a larger puzzle that includes economic, political, environmental, and social policies and norms.

Technical objects as moral mediators

One of the core theories we can look to understand designs effect on values and behaviors comes from the philosopher Bruno Latour (2002) who argued that technical objects act as *moral mediators*. This means that our engagement with objects can change our moral intentions. Latour uses the gun as an example of this, specifically in relation to the statements, *guns kill people vs. people kill people*. Latour argues that neither of these statements are true and overlook an important relationship between the two agents. The gun does not have the ability to kill someone on its own—without a human agent pulling the trigger. Nor is the person as easily able to kill without the gun. Latour suggests that it is the relationship

161

between the two agents that contributes to the ultimate action. This interaction contributes to a shift in behavior and values on the part of the person. And for the gun, it transforms a tool that doesn't kill into a tool that kills. It turns an angry person who will not kill, into an angry person who will. In this way, the object has an influence over the moral decisions and behavior of the person using it and, Latour argues, actually changes moral intentions. Latour might argue that the introduction of the cell phone into a social situation actually transforms our moral behavior and inserts a different value system than if it were not there—making physical and in-person connections less important than the snippets of curated life that we see on Facebook and Twitter.

Peter-Paul Verbeek builds on Latour's ideas on his 2008 article, "Morality in Design," looking at the ways design and designers respond to technological objects mediating moral experiences. Verbeek argues that the major problem with the way ethics has been addressed in design focuses on the artifact and less on what users do as a result of engaging with it: "When technologies are used, they always help to shape the context in which they fulfill their function. They help shape human actions and perceptions, and create new practices and ways of living" (92). In other words, the objects that people interact with have an active effect on the decisions that they make. The objects alone do not have a life, but they do initiate a behavior, and suggest a use for them that in turn affects how users perceive and interact with them. And most dramatically, change the way that we perceive our world and how to behave within it.

While neither Latour nor Verbeek discuss the built environment explicitly, it's not hard to make the leap to include design decisions made in that realm. For instance, how do the design of roads encourage or discourage speeding? How might a home design illuminate energy consumption? Or how might a neighborhood plan motivate accountability for collective safety? At these moments, it is the designer who is in the position to advocate for new ways of thinking that consider the moral implications of design interventions.

Urban space as moral agents

The shifts in city and urban planning that emerged in the last 50 years are a particularly poignant example of design's impact on moral judgments and behavior. In *The Death and Life of Great American Cities* (1961), the activist Jane Jacobs argued that 1950s urban renewal was founded on a false premise that compartmentalization of people, classes, and urban uses would help improve the quality of life in city environments. Rather than the utopia that planners envisioned for these urban islands, they were often met by decay because they failed to take into account the complexity of the people who were to inhabit them. Why? Jacobs argued that:

> Cities are an immense laboratory of trial and error, failure and success, in city building and city design. This is the laboratory in which city planning should have been learning and forming and testing its theories. Instead the practitioners and teachers of this discipline (if such it can be called) have ignored the study of success and failure in real life, have been incurious about the reasons

for unexpected success, and are guided instead by principles derived from the behavior and appearance of towns, suburbs, tuberculosis sanatoria, fairs, and imaginary dream cities—from anything but cities themselves

(8)

The expansion of American suburbia separated classes, concentrated poverty, and denied access to many. It imposed an order that discouraged casual interaction and the development of community through personal relationships. Defining "mixed" communities as adjacencies rather than integrative, planners failed to see the negative outcomes of being able to peer over the fence, but not gain access. Jacobs further argued that "These amputated areas typically develop galloping gangrene" (4). Jacobs was critical of the philosophy of utopian urban planning—evidenced by Ebenezer Howard's Garden City or Daniel Burnham's City Beautiful—in favor of a practical philosophy that emphasized the needs and wants of the people living in urban neighborhoods. Jacobs was particularly critical of these utopian philosophies because they separated working space from living and cultural space and created schematics that were beautiful and organized, but lacked an authenticity for what actually made city living work because they refused to look at what was already working. From the vantage point of today, we have witnessed many of the failures of this philosophy. The housing project Pruitt–Igoe in St. Louis—first occupied in 1954 and torn down in 1972—was evidence of many of Jacobs's claims. A large, geographically isolated

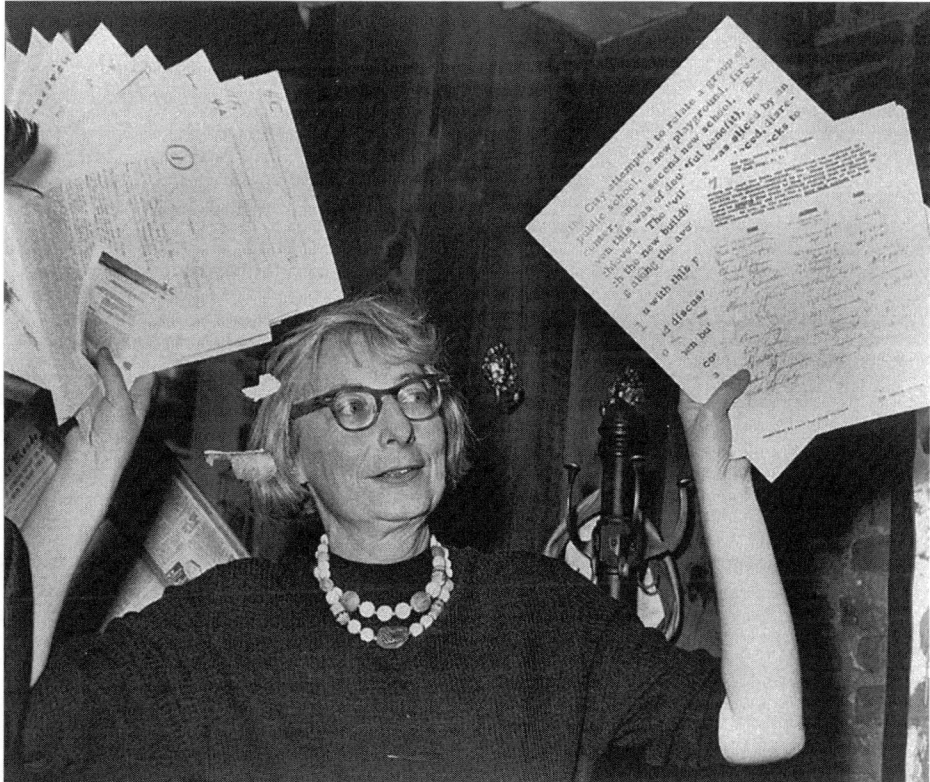

Figure 11.2

Jane Jacobs,
Library of Congress

and vertical low-income housing project, it was an infamous as a bastion of crime and poverty and proved to many that the built environment does have a dramatic effect on the behavior of those who live within it—but not always the affect that the designer has in mind. The design of Pruitt–Igoe included elevators that stopped on alternate floors, along with small corridors and galleries that were supposed to encourage "'individual neighborhoods' within each building" (Bristol, 2015). Instead, these spaces became dangerous intersections between families and gangs and increasingly tenants felt unsafe. Pruitt–Igoe shows the power of design as a *moral agent* by affecting the moral decisions that people made within them. Again, design and architecture are not the only culprits. Public policy, segregation, and economic and social disenfranchisement all played a part in the downfall of Pruitt–Igoe. But from a design perspective, it provides a powerful example of what happens when you design for people without engaging them in the process. Jacobs's seminal work has contributed to a large-scale shift in the way that we "plan" urban environments, and has even led some to question whether urban planning can exist at all.

With her mentor Walter H. Whyte (see Chapter 4), the author of *The Social Life of Small Urban Spaces* (1980), Jacobs proposed an alternative theory of planning that included community involvement and the examination of how successful urban communities actually worked. Her observations of successful urban districts like the North End in Boston illuminated the importance of diversity of business, variety of use, and integration of public and private space. Additionally, Jacobs advocated tirelessly for community involvement and partnership in the planning process. Her work has led to a theory of community-based city planning and architecture called placemaking. According the group,

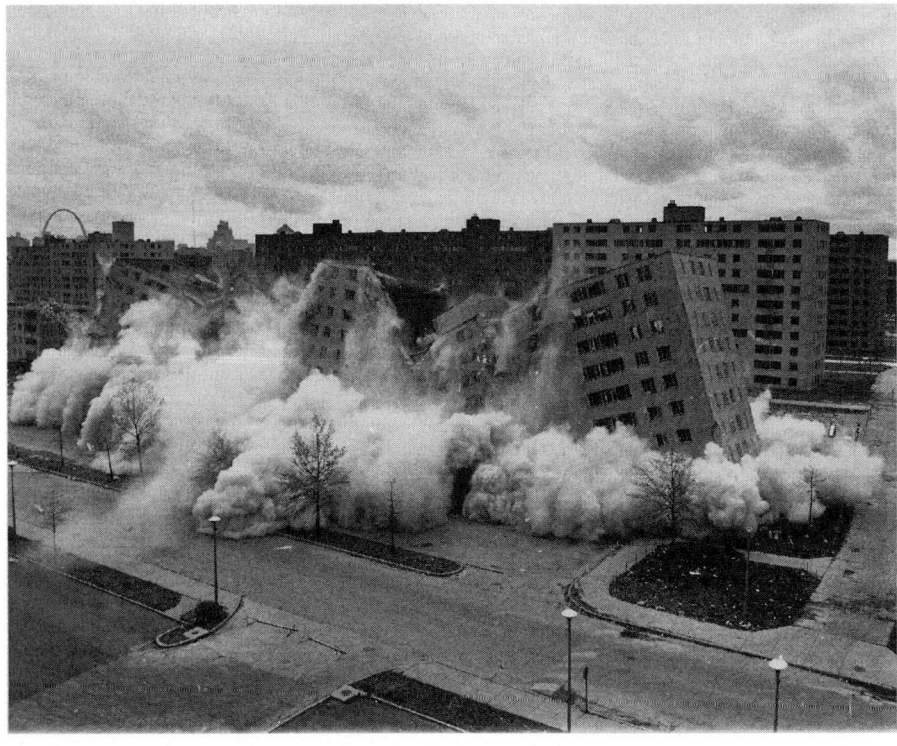

Figure 11.3

Pruitt–Igoe, US Department of Housing and Urban Development

Project for Public Spaces—started by a contemporary of Whyte and Jacobs—placemaking is "More than just promoting better urban design, Placemaking facilitates creative patterns of use, paying particular attention to the physical, cultural, and social identities that define a place and support its ongoing evolution" (Project for Public Spaces, 2007). Community-based placemaking is a complex approach to urban development primarily because it challenges the idea of the master plan. Theories of placemaking focus on the positive impacts of integrating community participation into the design and planning process, and the simple power of observation. Placemaking advocates argue that community involvement encourages place-attachment—which creates a bond between people and the places that they occupy. By encouraging place-attachment, placemaking improves ownership, agency, and the reclaiming of space—not by planners and policymakers, but by the people who live in and manage them every day. Jacobs argued this self-governance was a core aspect to healthy neighborhoods, and the real goal of urban planning. Placemaking also aims to move design and planning beyond the physical space and into the cultural one. How can spaces help people trust each other more? Feel more accountable? Build stronger communities? The National Endowment for the Arts (NEA) in the United States has built on this to consider how peacemaking might use creative endeavors to enhance the attachment to community. As the NEA has defined it:

> Communities across our nation are leveraging the arts and engaging design to make their communities more livable with enhanced quality of life, increased creative activity, a distinct sense of place, and vibrant local economies that together capitalize on their existing assets. The NEA defines these efforts as the process of creative placemaking.
>
> (Markusen and Gadwa, 2010)

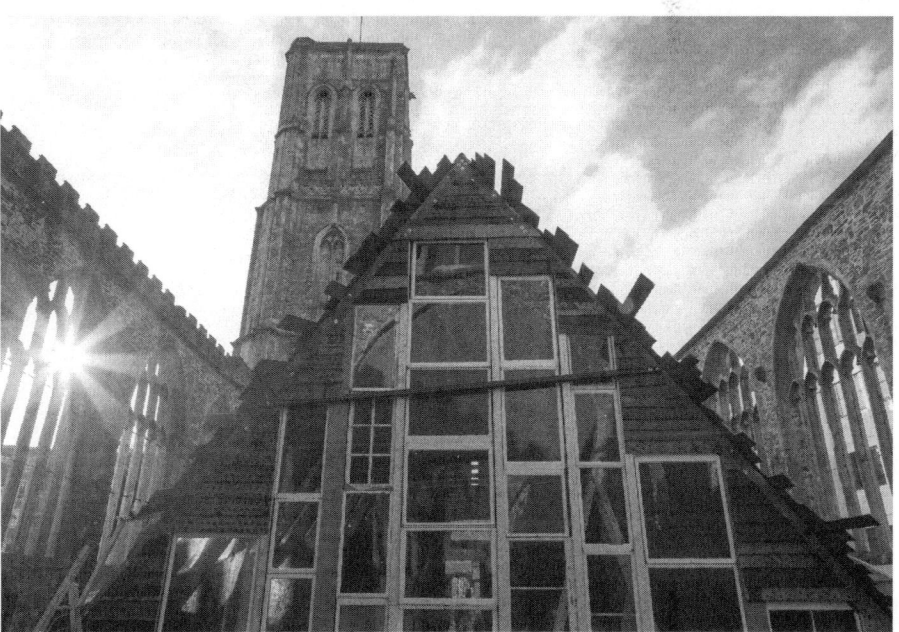

Figures 11.4–11.5

Theaster Gates's Sanctum. Image courtesy of Max McClure

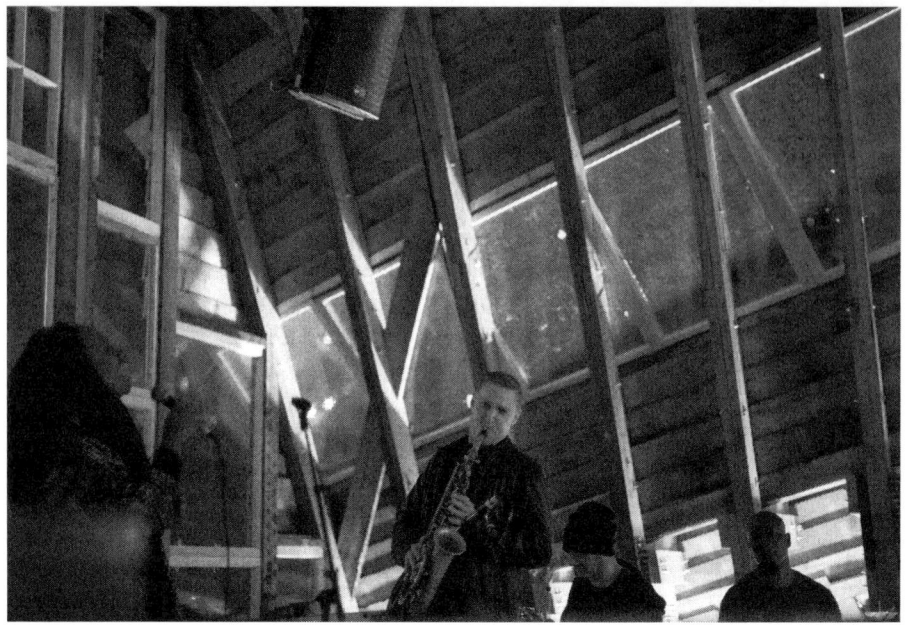

Critics of creative placemaking, however, argue that in many cases it is just a band-aid solution that is unsustainable because the communities are not fully included in the process in a way that creates mutual ownership, or worse leads to gentrification and displacement. That's not true of a vast creative placemaking project in the South Side of Chicago that has been initiated and supported by Theaster Gates to revitalize and reactivate a part of the city that is notorious for crime and poverty. Gates is using "redemptive architecture" to revive the Greater Grand Crossing area on the South Side of Chicago without displacing the residents who are currently living there. The buildings and spaces involved in this project include a community arts center, archive, library, performance center, museum gallery—sometimes in different buildings and sometimes co-located in a single space. In addition to the more permanent buildings, Gates has also used temporary projects, such as *Sanctum*, which was an aesthetically haphazard looking structure that augmented a bombed out Bristol, UK church, to temporarily activate spaces through architecture and performances. "During its occupancy in the bombed shell of Temple Church, the work acted as a gathering spot for artists and musicians within the public, amplifying voices and establishing relationships that would have otherwise inactivated" (Hoare, 2016). The purpose is not only to activate the physical environment and make it look more beautiful and alive, but also to activate the social fabric of the area, and make current residents proud of their environment.

Environments as moral projections

Jacobs suggested that the relationships, trust, and social fabric necessary for self-governance many times took place in the spaces in between work and home—the sidewalks, the cafes,

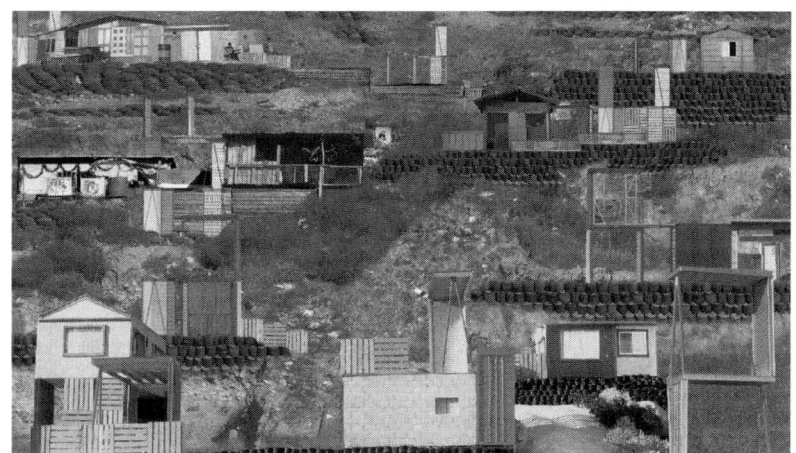

Figures 11.6–11.8

Manufactured Sites, Estudio Teddy Cruz + Fonna Forman

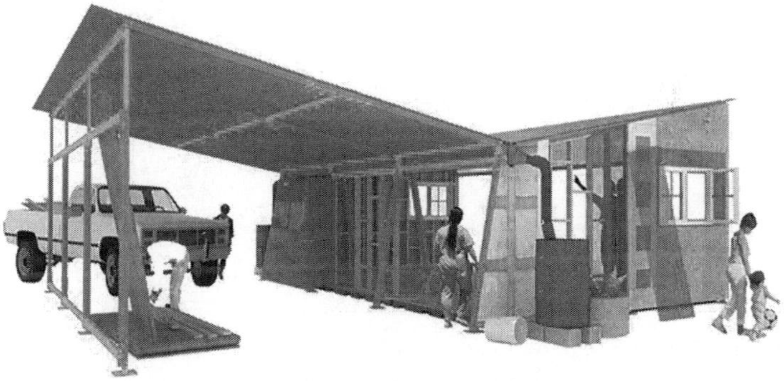

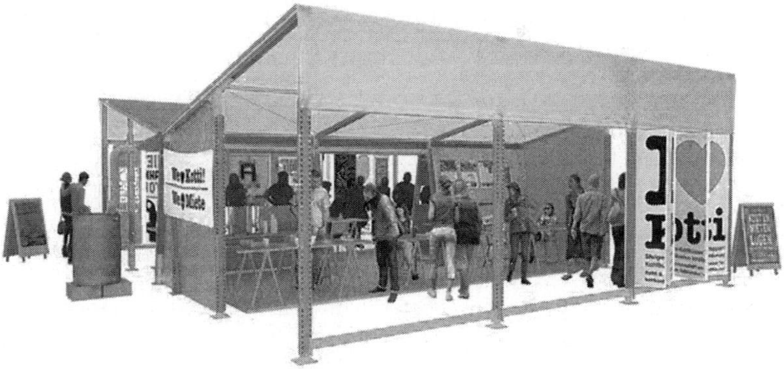

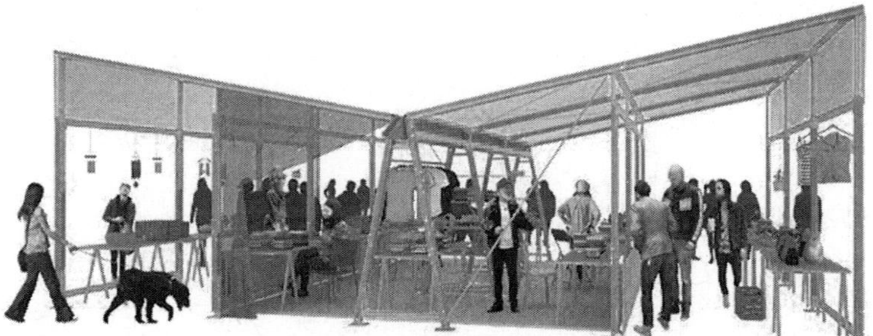

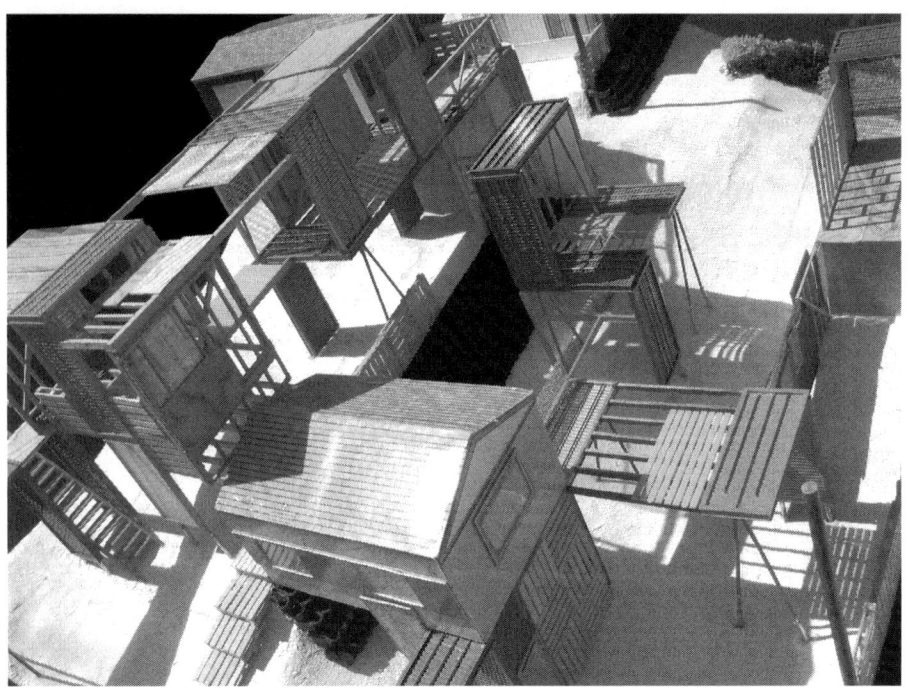

the neighborhood stores, and parks. These spaces in between are otherwise known as interstitial space and can take many forms. They can be "behind-the-scenes" and out of site to a building's users, functioning as integral components that hold mechanical systems, like the space between floors. They can also be the physical space that connects two spaces together—a corridor or hallway, for instance. A somewhat newer and more theoretical concept has elaborated on the physicality of interstitial space as having a social component—a social interstice. The art critic and educator Nicolas Bourriaud has suggested that spaces such as a contemporary art gallery can act in this socially interstitial capacity because "it creates free areas, and time spans whose rhythm contrasts with those structuring everyday life, and it encourages an inter-human commerce that differs from the 'communication zones' that are imposed upon us" (1998, 16). Bourriaud further suggests that people are more open to new ideas in these spaces, and willing to engage with others and with new concepts. Building on his concept, and extending this concept beyond the art exhibition, provides new paradigms for designers to consider how these interstitial spaces are activated—not used just as in-between zones (as Jacobs argued many were doing) but in making them places where people can engage with each other and with new, formative ideas. In this way, design can engage in *moral projections*—by reimagining norms and foundational assumption guiding the way that people work and live. By being outside of the norms of everyday life, designers can help users and visitors engage in a new vision of the world, and life—challenging the social and political norms that we take for granted, and showing what might be.

While he has not claimed that as his goal, that activation of interstitial space is exactly what the architect and activist Teddy Cruz, previously mentioned in Chapter 7, has done with many of his projects. Focusing on the border between San Diego and Tijuana,

Cruz's projects attempt to reimagine the relationship that exists as a result of the border. Namely, the separation and hierarchy the border is a reminder of. His project, *Learning from Tijuana*, looks closely at the disparity and tension between these two countries. In many ways, Cruz is reimagining a social interstice through this very project. Namely, that of a top-down relationship between the two countries. Cruz identifies the creative use that emerges from economic necessity mixed with an influx of discarded materials and waste streaming across the border from San Diego into Tijuana. As Cruz states, "one city builds itself from the waste of another." But Cruz's real mission is to reframe this relationship—so the necessity of invention evident in Tijuana infiltrates San Diego. A particularly compelling example of Cruz's argument is clearly seen by the automobile tire retaining walls that abound in the Mexican city or the houses that have made their way across the border, intact, and then scaffolded above the markets and businesses that line the streets in Tijuana's neighborhoods. "He has developed an architectural practice that is rooted in the realities of informal settlements and immigrant suburbs, and that is equally engaged with the needs—and innovations—of their residents and the exigencies of their local bureaucracies" (Waldorf, 2009). As Cruz states, "It is, in fact, in the most depressed, disenfranchised and underrepresented neighborhoods that some of the more interesting social and political agendas have begun to emerge" (Waldorf, 2009). Making clear that he is not romanticizing the ingenuity of poverty, Cruz advocates for a bottom-up approach to urban planning—one that is a negotiation between those who need, use, and live in urban environments and those who plan, organize, and monitor those spaces.

The real issue that Cruz is challenging through his work is the assumptions that affluent and privileged cultures of consumption base their design principles upon. Namely that materials and resources are limitless, that design and urban planning must always start with a "clean slate" and that design interventions need to replace existing systems, rather than building upon them.

References

Baker, Holly. "E-Cigarettes and Subsequent Tobacco Use in Adolescence." *The Lancet Oncology*, 16(13), October 2015, p. e481.
Bourriaud, Nicholas. *Relational Aesthetics*. Dijon: Les Presse Du Reel, 1998.
Bristol, Katherine. "The Pruitt-Igoe Myth." *The Journal of Architectural Education*, 44(3), 2015, pp. 163–171.
Hardaway, Robert. *The Great American Housing Bubble: The Road to Collapse*. Santa Barbara, CA: Praeger, 2011.
Hoare, Ben. "Sanctum." *The Seen: Chicago's International Online Journal of Contemporary and Modern Art.* January 20, 2016. Retrieved from http://theseenjournal.org/art-seen-international/sanctum-theaster-gates/. Accessed September 22, 2018.
Jacobs, Jane. *The Death and Life of Great American Cities*. New York: Random House, 1961.
Latour, Bruno. "Morality and Technology: The End of the Means." *Theory, Culture & Society*. London, Thousand Oaks and New Delhi: Sage Publications. Vol. 19(5/6), 2002, pp. 247–260.

Markusen, Ann and Gadwa, Anne. "*Creative Placemaking.*" The Mayors' Institute on City Design. Washington, DC: Markusen Economic Research Services and Metris Arts Consulting, 2010.

Project for Public Spaces. "What is Placemaking?" Project for Public Spaces, 2007. Retrieved from www.pps.org/article/what-is-placemaking. Accessed September 22, 2018.

US Department of Health and Human Services. *E-Cigarette Use Among Youth and Young Adults: A Report of the Surgeon General.* US Department of Health and Human Services, 2016.

Verbeek, Peter-Paul. *Moralizing Technology: Understanding and Designing the Morality of Things.* Chicago: The University of Chicago Press, 2011.

Verbeek, Peter-Paul. "Morality in Design: Design Ethics and the Morality of Technological Artifacts." In P.E. Vermaas, P. Kroes, A. Light, and S. Moore, editors. *Philosophy and Design: From Engineering to Architecture.* New York, NY: Spring, 2008, pp. 91–103.

Waldorf, Caleb. Interview with Teddy Cruz. *Triple Canopy*, 2009. Retrieved from http://apubliclibrary.org/cw/posts/interview-with-teddy-cruz/. Accessed September 22, 2018.

Whyte, William H. *The Social Life of Small Urban Spaces.* New York: Project for Urban Spaces, 1980.

12 Narrative design thinking

Asking designers to consider the moral implications of design action might ruffle the feathers of many. It's much cleaner (and far less daunting) to see designers' roles as communicating other points of view, messages, or strategies. But I would argue that designers' capacity for recognizing problems at different scales, and formulating alternative plans and propositions is exactly the reason their role is so critical. The capacity to imagine alternatives to existing conditions also gives designers an astute ability to recognize intended and unintended consequences. By exploring the three fundamental ways that morality and design are integrated we can better understand how designers might respond.

1. By changing people's behaviors, design ultimately changes values and therefore acts as a *moral mediator*;
2. Because it is a visual and material artifact, design can bring light to current values and norms and therefore act as a *moral agent*;
3. By acknowledging design's role in changing values and norms, design can integrate *moral projections* to encourage a more fundamental understanding of short and long-term impacts.

One critical way that designers should consider the moral dimension of their work is by divorcing themselves from the nuts and bolts of the everyday design process. The focus on intervention, innovation, and ideation that drive the designers need to improve existing conditions overwhelms the ability to see the ultimate, and longer-term impact of those solutions. The rest of this chapter will be dedicated to the methods that designer might employ to speculate and imagine these longer-term impacts and the moral dimension of designs strategies.

The Storytelling Animal

Design that is focused on bridging the gap between users' values and behaviors requires theories, research methods, and practical application that focus on exposing the links between statements and actions; thoughts and words; and ideals and realities. For designers interested in finding and exposing those connections, narratives—and the many forms narratives may take—provide such an opportunity. Those in the humanities and social sciences would largely agree that narratives and stories have an incredibly powerful effect on human cognition and world view. Jonathan Gottschall, author of *The Storytelling Animal: How Stories Make us Human* (2013), argues that "We are, as a species, addicted to stories. Even when the body goes to sleep, the mind stays up all night telling us stories" (xiv). The idea that design tells a story is more readily accepted in certain fields of design than others. Graphic designers—working largely with text and visual- or image-based narratives, have a generally easier time understanding the narrative capacity of their work. An architect might have more trouble articulating how Falling Water tells a story about a region and a country. But they both do. Through the creation of something from nothing, design occupies an "imaginative realm called Neverland. Neverland is your home and before you die, you will spend decades there" (Gottschall, 2013, xv). Design, like fiction, "subtly shapes our beliefs, behaviors, ethics—[and] powerfully modifies culture and history" (Gottschall, 2013, xvii). Designers interested in the moral implications of their design proposals can look to three principles of storytelling to encourage new insight and focus on outcomes and impacts. Firstly, the inclusion of the user in the research, ideation, and testing process can "tell us what we can't hear, and show us what we can't see" (Brown, 2009, x). Secondly, using strategies that encourage imagination and speculation focused on future-casting—whether focused on a future problem or the outcomes of the design proposal—can unleash the constraints of practicality and open the possibility for new interpretations and assumptions. And thirdly, creating immersive and playful environments allow designers and users to act out certain behaviors and imagine how those behaviors might impact, or be impacted by, a design.

Design research methods: using narratives to understand the moral dimension of a design problem

Narrative research

Narrative research is a qualitative research method that is valuable in uncovering morals and values in users interaction with design objects because it focuses on the lived experience and the interpretation of meaning. Through narrative research, designers "engage with people and seek to hear, record and understand their life experiences as stories. Stories in narrative research are typically first person, oral accounts of events" (Crouch and Pearce, 2015, 105). Through narrative research, designers seek out participants' stories, collecting oral histories or narratives from current and potential users. These stories are often collected in small groups or even individual interactions, recorded by the designer and then transferred and interpreted into a metanarrative that the designer uses to position or guide a proposal. It is through these histories and stories that researchers uncover common themes, language, values, wants, and needs. By allowing the research participant to define the boundaries of their contribution, these narratives can often go in directions that the designer-researcher might not initially foresee, which can be powerful in breaking down any assumptions that the designer-researcher might have about the link between action, behaviors, and values.

Culture probes

Like narrative research, culture probes can be an important design research methodology for illuminating the values and behaviors of users because it is based on inspirational and creative information gathering, rather than a systematic analysis of data. While traditional surveys and usability research focus on having users tell or explain why they are making certain choices, culture probes are used by designers to observe behavior, and interpret values. First introduced by Gaver, Dunne, and Pacenti in 1999, culture probes have been embraced by design research because they relocate how data is collected away from the surveyor and towards the participant. The most common of culture probes is a toolkit given to participants that might include materials such as a camera, journal, marking equipment, map. The participants are then given a task, or asked to document something about their lives. These tasks can be discrete tasks, such as brushing their teeth, more complex, such as their route to work, or more general, such as documenting a "day in their everyday life." Culture probes can also invite an active participation with the user, such as the previous example of the toolkit illustrates, or it can involve passive or even unknowing participation on the part of the user, by capturing and recording a particular element of behavior. An idea for a smart table in a coffee shop included a proposal to record how long coffee mugs sat on the table, what type of reading or working materials were being used by the customers and for how long. While that information can be observed anecdotally, the idea of a culture probe would capture information in a more tangible way, and over a longer period of time, to see if the anecdotal evidence that people came in to work in the morning, and met with friends in the afternoon was accurate. This in turn might give the coffee shop owners data that would inform changes, improvements that they might make to encourage alternate usage. The ultimate goal of the culture probe, like with any design research, it to uncover patterns in the ways that users behave, think, feel, and ultimately value. What is unique about culture probes is the way that this insight is accomplished. When designers focus on the conditions through which users can record and evaluate their experiences, they can be more comfortable, honest and real—giving designers an insight into what are authentic values and behaviors.

Participatory design research

Participatory design, or co-creative design, engages users or stakeholders in the design process. Through direct or indirect narrative, participatory design research is a way to create stories that are useful to both researcher and participant. While not the same

Narrative design thinking

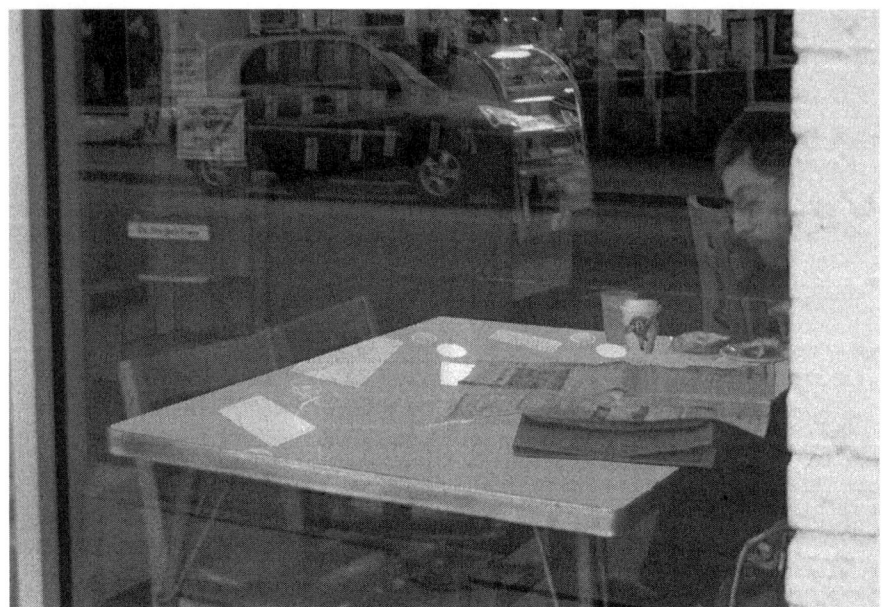

Figures 12.1–12.2

Culture probe prototype capturing coffee shop visitors habits and behaviors through an interactive table. Image courtesy of Cady Bean Smith

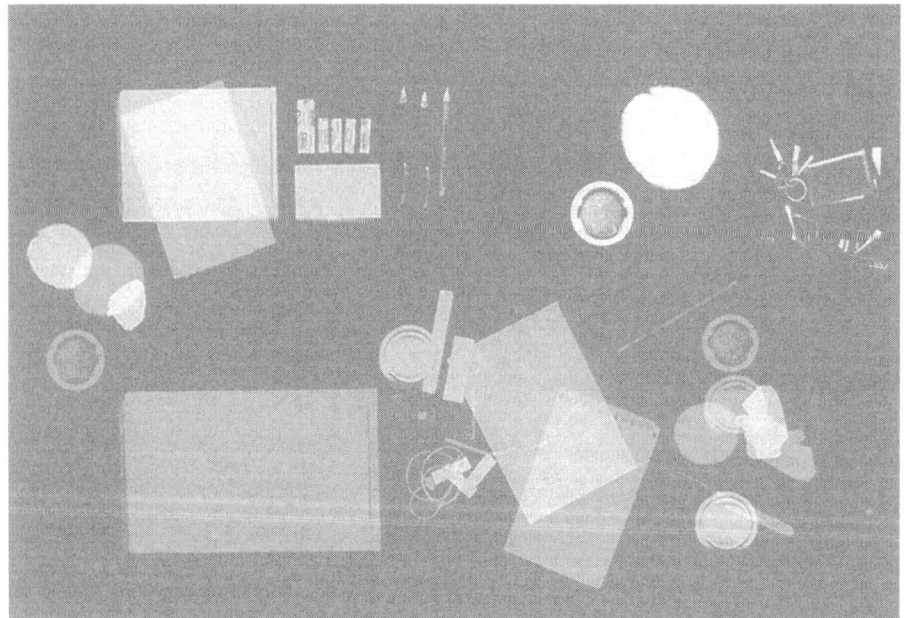

thing, participatory design is linked to action research—a type of research often used in the social sciences to gather information, but also to ultimately influence the behaviors of its participants. Participatory research has its roots in the social sciences, where the aim is not necessarily to change an environment, but because of the inherent nature of design to make change, the link is stronger in this context. As an extension of usability, participatory design was developed to help bring users into the design process—to use their first-hand experience as users of design artifacts to help designers understand how to improve them—what was working, and what was not. Rather than conducting focus groups or surveys where users would tell designers what they thought of a product, or what they needed to have as features of a product, participatory design encouraged them to show designers what they needed. What resulted is a rich aspect of design research that actively engages users in helping to define design problems and to ideate on potential solutions. Theories of participatory design draw heavily on social theorists like Ivan Illich who developed a theory of "convivial tools" (1973) which were tools aimed at helping people work and problem-solve together. One of the pioneers of this method of design—Liz Sanders—has developed "MakeTools" to act as mediators between designers and non-designers (clients, communities or the public at large.) These devices help non-designers speak the language of design, identifying and modeling where problems lie, as well as what solutions might be best to address those problems. In their book, *Convivial Toolbox*, Sanders and P. J. Stappers (2013) refer to this type of research as generative research. Sanders and Stappers argue that people are, in general, seeking out more creative endeavors and point to movements like the DIY movement as support. They see this new context as demanding more involvement from users in co-creating design. Pushing against the old and dominant mindset of the researcher as expert, they argue for design research that equally involves the user in the creation process. "Generative design empowers everyday people and promote alternatives to the current situations" (20). Through generative design tools are developed that help create a "shared design language" and that designers and users (or stakeholders) can use to communication visually and verbally throughout the design process. These tools are ways to construct narratives and stories about the problems that design is trying to address, as well as the stories of how they might be used to improve user and stakeholder situations.

Narrative design thinking methods and process: using stories to understand the moral dimension of a design solution

Personas

A critical component of any narrative are the characters that inhabit it. The development of personas encourage empathy through the vivid personalization of what would normally be an abstract and generic user. They help designers see in detail the motivations, needs, and wants of a specific use and to anticipate what might be easy, hard, enabling, or limiting. Personas are generally an amalgamation of a number of different "types" of users and based on initial research and observations that are then combined and culled into prototypical and simplified personalities. Personas can be generalized

Narrative design thinking

and anonymous—the "speed demon," or the "dillydallier." They can also be specific and personalized, focusing on motivations of a type of user as identified through a particular character. Some design researchers also argue that much more insight can be gained when looking at users that exist on the edge of the user continuum. A concept developed by IDEO and the d.School at Stanford, "extreme" users are particularly insightful because:

> [w]hen you speak with and observe extreme users, their needs are amplified and their work-arounds are often more notable. This helps you pull out meaningful needs that may not pop when engaging with the middle of the bell curve. However, the needs that are uncovered through extreme users are often also needs of a wider population.
>
> (IDEO, 2003)

Examples of extreme users could involve the very old or the very young, those with extreme abilities or limitations, or those with circumstances outside the bounds of normal, everyday life. In the design of a playground, for instance, how does the design change if you consider how it might be used by grandparents who are accompanying their children there, or parkour enthusiasts?

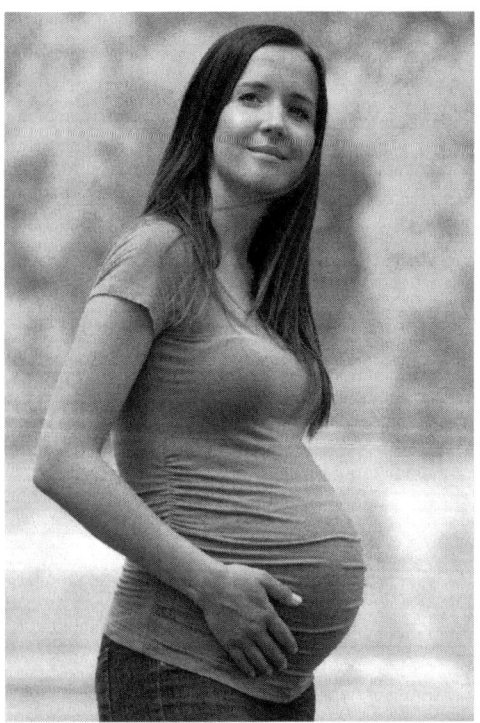

Extreme User:

Jenna Ortiz is 7 months pregnant. She is an avid marathoner and triathalete and competes nationally. Throughout her entire pregnancy she has continued her exercise regimen, but as she has gotten closer to her due date, she has found that many of the exercises she had been doing are uncomfortable. She was also recently diagnosed with moderately high blood pressure as a result of the pregnancy and her doctor wants her to be increasingly careful. She wants to continue her exercise routines so she can resume her training once she has the baby.

Motivations:
- Better knowledge of exercise that is safe for herself and her baby;
- Excercise routines that will help keep her fitness level high;
- Exercise that will help reduce temporary elevated blood-pressure;
- New routines that she can continue post-delivery.

Figures 12.3–12.4

Extreme user persona cards. Created for a project to redesign a gym. Image courtesy of Tania Allen

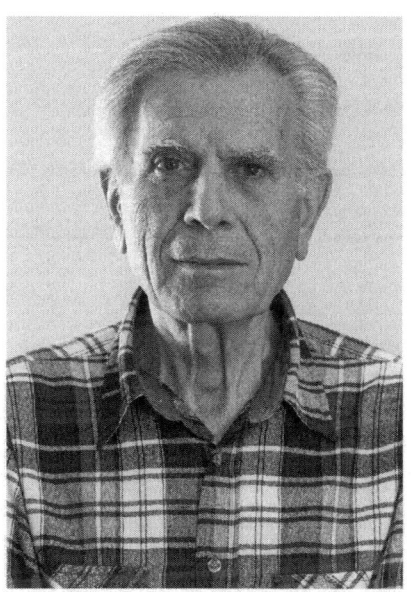

Extreme User:
Dr. Mark Smith holds a PhD in biomedical engineering. As a professor at the local University, he continues to work, even as he is undergoing cancer treatment. He is a widower and has one child who lives in another state so is managing his medical treatment on his own. He has never exercised, but his doctor recommended it to help him reduce stress and increase his recovery from treatment. The cancer treatment that he has received has been hard on his body and he feels particularly vulnerable to pushing himself.

Motivations:
- Exercise routines that will reduce stress;
- Better understanding of how exercise helps with recovery from cancer treatment;
- Exercise that he can easily do at home as well as in the gym;
- Feeling safe in an exercise environment.

Scenarios

One of the most obvious ways to utilize storytelling in the propositional phase of design is through the creation of scenarios. Scenarios give detail to how users behave, react, and interpret certain design actions. They give detail and specificity to who will be using the "product" and frame a way of imagining the outcomes that can be as wild or tame as the designer decides. Scenarios are widely used in user experience design as a way to understand user needs and wants, but can also be used in considering the morality of design experiences. Alan Cooper et al. in *About Face: The Essentials of Interaction Design* (2014) has defined three specific types of scenarios to aid designers in anticipating how users will respond to design proposals: context scenarios, key path scenarios, and validation scenarios. Context scenarios focus on what a user might need to accomplish within the design interaction. Within website design, this might mean completing a task, such as making an online deposit. But if we extend that to include personal and ethical decisions and behaviors, designers can use a similar strategy to imagine what would encourage a user to deposit money into a savings account vs. a checking account, or to start a college fund for their child or to make more responsible spending and savings decisions. Key path scenarios are a second type of scenario that build upon the context scenario to imagine the specific touchpoint that the design will need to include to support the demands outlined by the context scenario. For instance, in website design, this might mean the navigational items, hierarchy, and organization that will help accomplish the task of making the online deposit. When examining design as a moral mediator, this might mean imagining and outlining what that user does and sees that would encourage them to be more reflective in the process of online deposits, and how that encounter might influence both short- and long-term behavior. The third type of scenario

Narrative design thinking

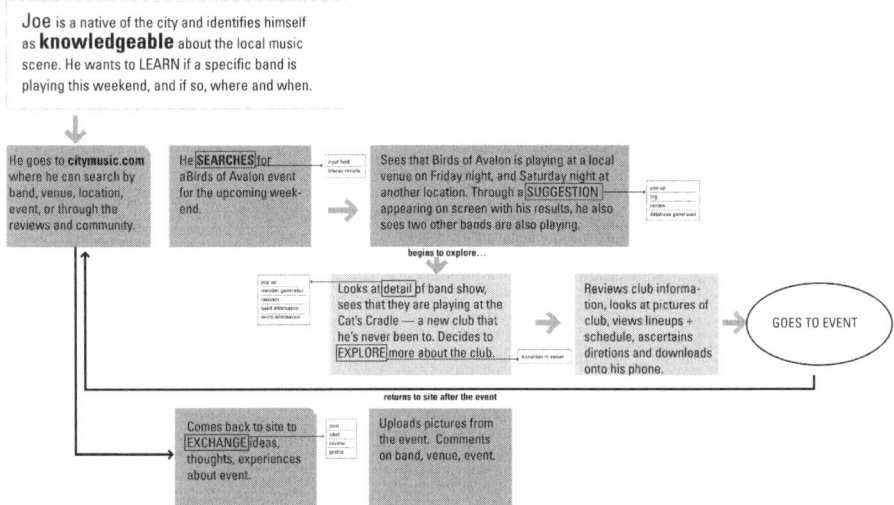

Figure 12.5

Scenario map for a dynamic music application. Created as part of a graduate studio led by Meredith Davis at North Carolina State University. Authors: Tania Allen, Lincoln Hancock, Alberto Rigau, Liese Zahabi

are validation scenarios. These scenarios imagine alternative behaviors and reactions to the design product (or outcome) by asking a series of "what if" questions. In website design, this might take the form of "What if the user doesn't see the deposit checks button?" But in evaluating moral implications of design it might take the form of larger questions, such as "What if the user cannot deposit all of the money into their college fund or savings account? What if the user prefers face to face contact? What if the user is in a financial crisis?" Asking these questions can encourage designers at all stages of the product or environmental design process to look more deeply at the potential impacts of their design decisions. Scenarios can take the form of visual storyboards, or written narratives. They are also analogous to experience maps and can include multiple dimensions and types of information. One of the most insightful of these alternate dimensions comes when designers include emotional or irrational states into the design experiences. The inclusion of these states humanizes the user and the narrative, and uses fundamental aspects of fiction and storytelling to provide vivid and deep imagination on the part of the designer.

Situational and scenario-based personas

The power of scenarios and personas is that they help designers think in specifics, rather than generalities. But, if only focused on demographic information (age, race, gender, etc.) it is easy to rely on stereotypical attributes to characterize a persona. For example, if you are designing an app that allows users to order groceries on their phone and pick up at the grocery store (or have delivered) it might seem natural to identify a persona as a *busy mom with two kids who lives in the suburbs of an American city*. This might reinforce specific ideas about motherhood that include being harried, driving a mini-van stocked with kids, running from playdate to playdate, and not necessarily being

> engaged in a world outside of her children. Building the persona this way relies more heavily on stereotypes of certain values or behaviors that may or may not be accurate or helpful and in many ways reverts back to the generalizations that the persona is attempting to dislodge. It also encourages you to derive behaviors from a type of person, rather than focusing on the behavior itself.
>
> Instead, thinking of a scenario that highlights a particular motivation can force you to move beyond these generalities into a more complex and situationally based set of behaviors. By starting with a scenario, you can start to think of your persona within a particular situation that has its own set of particularities that may or may not be the constant. Much like the "extreme users" mentioned in the usability section, these scenarios can incorporate idiosyncrasies that might reveal unique and innovative discoveries. For example, thinking of Judy who is driving home from a busy day at the office, just picked up her son from camp and realized that she has not gone to the grocery store in a week. She usually likes to cook fresh meals, but is also okay with prepared or frozen food every once in a while. This example begins a narrative that is rich in visuals and might dissuade overt generalizations about your users.

Design fiction

Otherwise known as speculative design, design fiction uses principles of science fiction to imagine future scenarios and how design might respond to these real-world problems. Anthony Dunne and Fiona Raby are pioneers in this field—often working with science fiction writers like Bruce Sterling to bring tangible proposals to what are intangible and imaginative problems. The real power of design fiction is the freedom from the limitations of immediate practicality. In *Speculative Everything* (2013), Dunne and Raby argue that "Design speculation can act as a catalyst for collectively redefining our relationship with reality" (2). What does this mean? It means breaking free from the assumptions in which current beliefs and values are anchored. This could mean changing our perspective on what capitalism is, or should be; or what political systems encourage innovation and quality of life; or where energy comes from; or any other aspect of life that we rest our design decisions upon. Often, design fiction starts out with an extreme scenario—the world cannot produce enough food to feed the population; an epidemic has made it so humans can no longer travel over 20 miles per hour without severe nausea and vertigo; or globalization has forced everyone in the world to adopt a common written and spoken language. These scenarios are then used as starting points to imagine what the outcomes of this scenario might mean and how design might intervene or react. What new symbology could graphic designers create that draws from a multiplicity of written languages to create universal images of communication? How would such a dictate influence culture and communication overall? Much like science fiction, design fiction uses this speculation not to imagine the future (though it does that) but to teach us about today, and to open up new possibilities for how we design our world. Design fiction is "the idea of possible futures and using them as tools to better understand the present, and to discuss the future that people want, and of course, the futures that people do not want" (2).

Narrative design thinking

A design fiction prompt

The scenarios associated with prompts for design fiction should imagine wild futures and can explore some of the underlying issues that design is responding to or even mitigating and encouraging. In an example from a graphic design project, the following prompt was given: "In the future, globalization is central to everyday life. Education, business, popular culture all take place in a multi-national (uni-national) environment. In this context, many are calling for a universal written language or code. But many sides to the debate over globalized communication

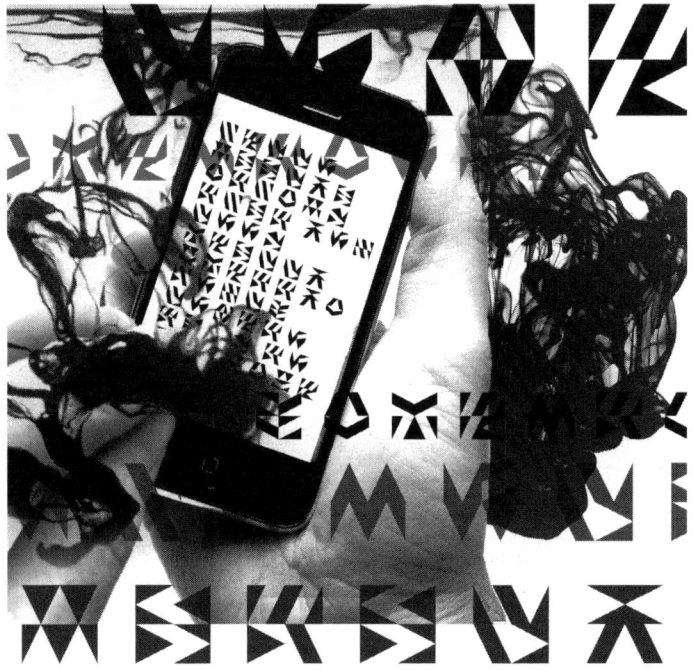

"I will love you until the day I die, Natalya; you are the most perfect woman whom I have had the honor to get to know. Please I must meet you in person."

Figure 12.6

Love Language universal typeface. Image courtesy of Kirsten Benson

> are emerging—primarily how it will impact culture, history, language, and ritual."
> Responses to this prompt took the form of story writing and the design of a modular typeface that imagined what a "universal written language" might look like. Through this project, students examined and evaluated core visual elements of typographic style, but were also challenged to think about the implications of this universal language, especially as it related to dominant cultures and modes of communication. Students studied existing codes such as Morse code and Braille, as well as different the written language of different cultures, such as Arabic, Asian characters, and even Egyptian hieroglyphics. The stories themselves explored the social, political, and economic impacts that such a move might make as a way to more deeply examine what such a design move would mean.

The narrative power of games

Through the creation of fictional worlds—both abstract and vivid—games provide a powerful platform for designers to imagine and test design ideas and their potentially moral, ethical, and behavioral impacts. Jane McGonigal, author of *Reality is Broken: Why Games Make Us Better and How They Can Save the World* has argued that games offer a powerful tool for connecting people and providing immersive experiences in which to play out scenarios that are both *real* and *extreme* (McGonigal, 2011). McGonigal sees the power of games not only in providing an alternate reality and escape for the players, but also in changing behaviors in the tangible, real world. An avid gamer and game designer, McGonigal created a serious multi-player reality game called "World Without Oil," which imagined the first 32 weeks of an oil crisis. Through videos, blog entries, voicemails, and images, over 1,900 players imagined (and lived) a life without oil. Behaviors changed in expected ways—riding bikes or walking to work. But they also changed in more unexpected ways—growing their own food, monitoring and lowering electricity consumption.

> WWO benefited from "the wisdom of crowds"—as more and more people examine a subject, they tend to cause more truthful and insightful ideas to rise to the top . . . the multiplicity of viewpoints tends to reveal aspects to the subject that even experts might overlook.
>
> ("World Without Oil," n.d.)

For designers, using games as a platform for interacting with users, as well as developing design ideas, provides an important opportunity to take on the persona of another and explore the implications of design decisions. As a leader in the field of game theory, McGonigal (2011) has called out four critical features that games contribute to imagining alternative futures and creating positive images of that future. The first is urgent optimism. Games encourage an urge to act immediately with a belief of reasonable hope of success. Games also strengthen social fabric because we like people better after we play a game with them. There is trust involved and bonds are created, because we value

Narrative design thinking

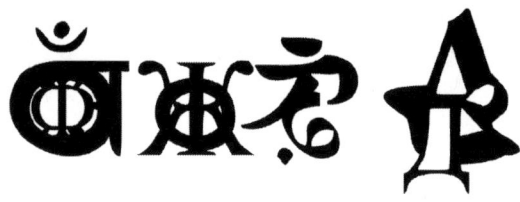

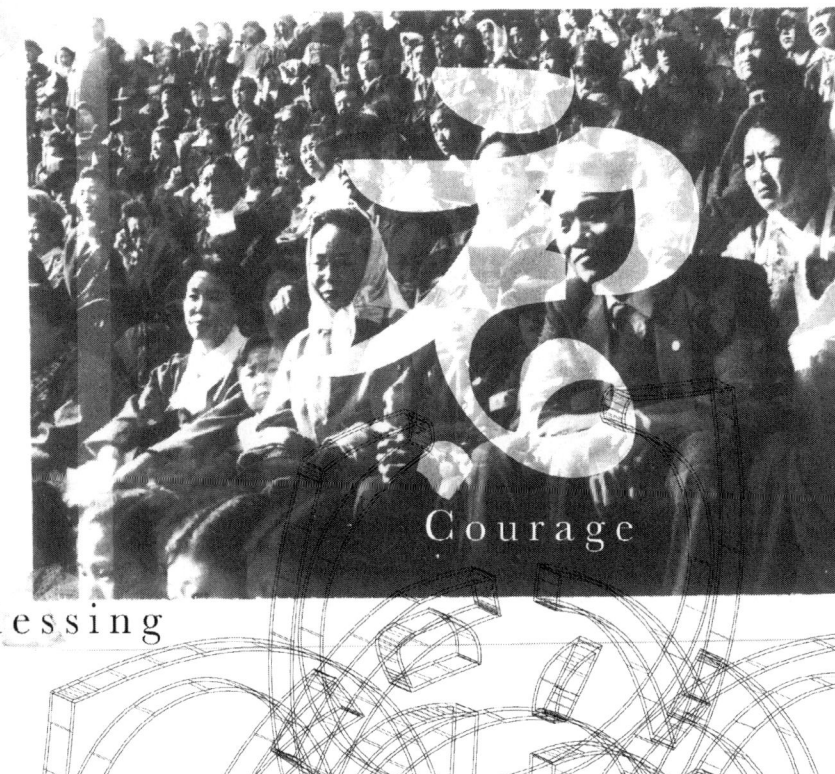

Figures 12.7–12.8

Babble universal typeface. Image courtesy of James Park

the same goals and need to start from a common base if the game is going to be successful. Game playing also encourages a state of "flow"—a term the cognitive psychologist Mihalyi Csikszentmihalyi (2008) has argued is the key to happiness because when we are in a state of flow we are satisfied in our productivity. When playing a game, we're happier working hard. Because it doesn't feel like work. The final feature of games contribution is in their fostering of epic meaning. "Games give us epic and awe-inspiring missions at all scales" (McGonigal, 2008). These missions prove to us that our potential is greater than our reality.

Narratives give us the potential to imagine worlds that don't yet exist as well as to imagine the outcomes of our current situations. They can provide inspiration and warnings through fictional worlds which explore the serious impacts of design interventions. As creative tools, they can help designers be more critical, and to encourage empathy with users in a variety of contexts. Most importantly, they can encourage designers to see things in a new light, and through contexts that might be contemporary or future oriented. In doing so, the interventions that designers make are more discriminating and open-minded.

References

Brown, Tim. *Change by Design*. New York: Harper Business, 2009.
Cooper, Alan, Reimann, Robert, and Cronin, David. *About Face: The Essentials of Interaction Design*, 4th Edition. Hoboken, NJ: Wiley, 2014.
Crouch, Christopher and Jane Pearce. *Doing Research in Design*. London: Bloomsbury, 2015.
Csikszentmihalyi, Mihalyi. *Flow: The Psychology of Optimal Experience*. New York: Harper Perennial Modern Classics, 2008.
Dunne, Anthony and Raby, Fiona. *Speculative Everything: Design, Fiction, and Social Dreaming*. Cambridge, MA: MIT Press, 2013.
Gaver, B., Dunne, Anthony, and Pacenti, Elena. "Culture Probes." *Design Interactions*. January/February, 1999, pp. 21–29.
Gottschall, Jonathan. *The Storytelling Animal: How Stories Make us Human*. Wilmington, MA: Mariner Books, 2013.
IDEO. "Extreme User." *IDEO Method Cards*. San Francisco, CA: William Stout, 2003.
Illich, Ivan. *Tools for Conviviality*. New York: Perennial Library, 1973.
McGonigal, Jane. *Reality is Broken: Why Games Make Us Better and How They Can Change the World*. New York: Penguin Books, 2011.
Sanders, Elizabeth and Stappers, P. J. *Convivial Toolbox: Generative Research for the Front End of Design*. Amsterdam: BIS Publishers, 2013."World Without Oil." Retrieved from http://writerguy.com/wwo/metahome.htm. Accessed September 22, 2018.

13 Creating stories together
Case studies of narrative design thinking

If our addiction to stories is as intense as Jonathan Gotschall (2012) claims, then creating conditions in which users can participate in the active construction of narratives has a powerful potential for understanding the impacts of design proposals on moral and ethical grounds. When designers are working in partnership with clients and communities they get a first-hand perspective of the users or consumers beyond the research phase and into an ongoing partnership with those who are using, adapting, and evolving their design. This, in turn, helps designers see below the surface into how these users behave, what they value and how a design decision might reinforce or re-route those values. Thinking about design in this way is more like thinking about designing conditions, rather than artifacts. These conditions can encourage users to see their surroundings in a new way, to challenge their own assumptions about what they know and how they understand space and place and encourage the public to speculate on the future of their environment.

Designing in a time of crisis: design as tool for empowerment

We often think of the role of the designer as improving conditions for others. Because of this, the need for empathy is a predominant strategy for designers to learn as a critical part of the process. Getting into the minds of others, especially those that have different experiences, is a large part of this chapter, and using storytelling and narrative strategies has been previously advocated as an effective way to engage in cultivating the empathy that is so critical for designers. But, what happens when it is the designer herself who needs the empowerment? How might design be used as a tool for working through traumatic situations for the designer?

After the devastating hurricane that hit Puerto Rico in September 2017, one design professor at a small private college there faced this very dilemma. After being called back to teaching less than a month after Maria hit, the curriculum that had been established for the semester was immediately irrelevant. Without power, or the tools and materials students were used to, the activity of design took on a new importance. It became about working through the stresses that the students were trying to overcome in the wake of the devastation. And, in trying to empower the students to be resilient visionaries for their community.

The collaboration between Dr. María Mater O'Neill, an adjunct professor of Graphic Design from Puerto Rico and Lesley-Ann Noel, a design professor at a university in Trinidad and Tobago, used strategies that Noel had been developing to help elementary school children in Trinidad and Tobago use design thinking to empower and enhance their own education. Specifically, Noel's strategy used elements of critical pedagogy theory, critical utopian action research, and a framework proposed by Ira Shor (1992) for empowering education that encouraged students to become thinking citizens, change agents, and social critics. Shor proposed that empowering pedagogy must be participatory, affective, problem-posing, situated, multicultural, dialogic, desocializing, democratic, researching, interdisciplinary, and activist (Noel and O'Neill, 2018). Noel built on these concepts in her elementary design curriculum as well as in the suggestions that she made for O'Neill's post-Hurricane María class. In this approach, she proposed that the discussion and reflection during the design process are significant in the development of solutions to local problems. O'Neill then used a resiliency toolkit, *Bound by Design*, that she had developed through her dissertation, as a way to adapt Noel's theories in a practical way. Noel and O'Neill set the theme of the class around a future Puerto Rico in 2054 so the students could use a utopian or dystopian narrative about Puerto Rico as a point to develop the design stories. As O'Neill explained it, Noel's framework and looking at the near future (rather than the immediate present) were very effective in getting

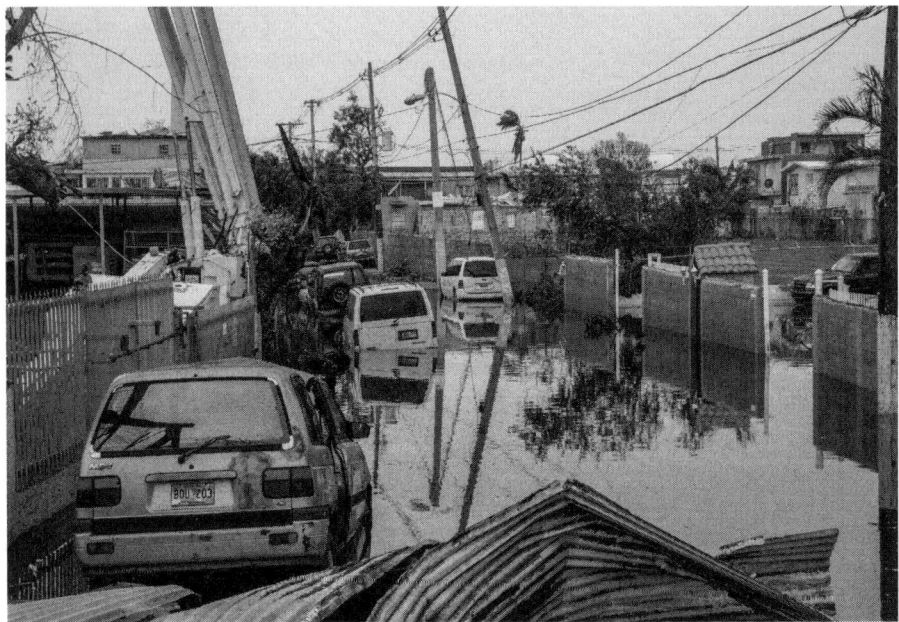

Figure 13.1

Puerto Rico, post Hurricane Maria

the students to step outside of their immediate experience and trauma without trying to absolve or ignore it. This became an effective launching point. Then when the students were ready, they were able to come back down to earth to put their larger-picture theories and ideas into a specific, community-based, and intimate context.

The aim of the revised "post-María" curriculum was to provide a platform for students to share and build on the experience of the crises of Hurricane María, and loss of their homes and displacement, and to create a forum for hope and action in the design studio, while students collectively dealt with their loss and grief. The desired outcomes for this course were a) the cathartic discussions and reflections of the students and b) design activity where students developed and proposed solutions to some of the challenges that they had identified, using design theory and theoretical concepts such as critical utopian action research and design fiction. Students were encouraged to use narrative to envision a utopian or dystopian future. Critical discussions surrounded these choices and the implications that each perspective might have on the outcome of the project, and

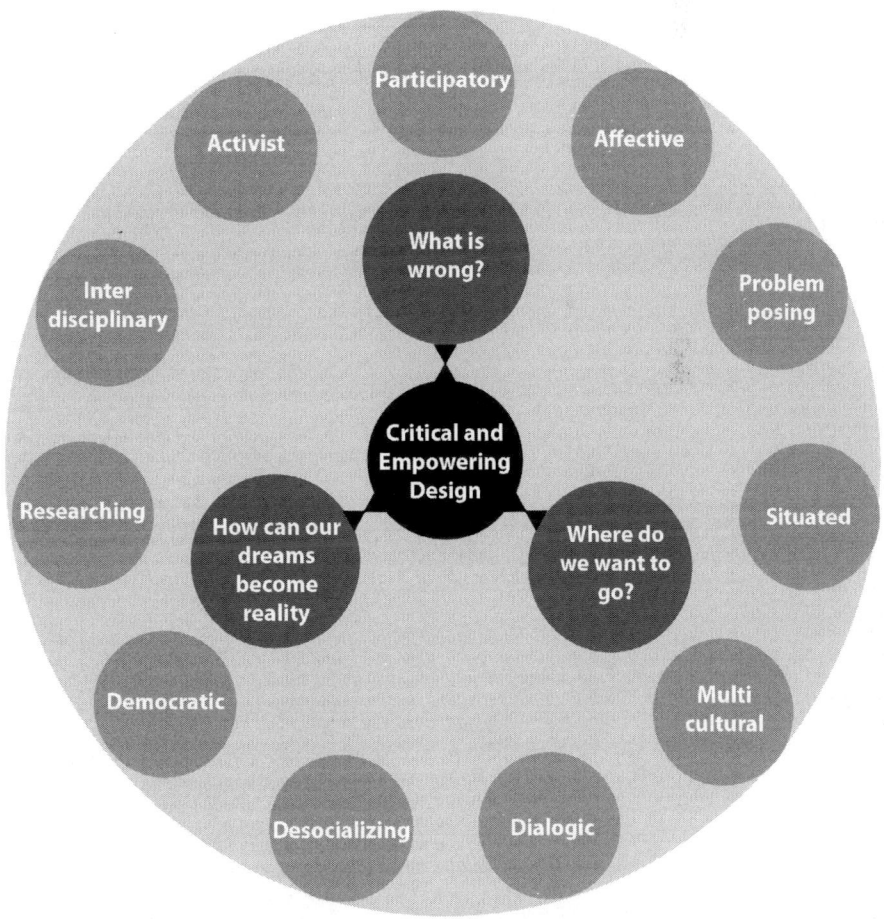

Figure 13.2

Noel's diagram for empowering education, based on Ira Shor's framework. Image courtesy of Lesley-Ann Noel

Framework for Empowering Design Education

the future of the community. The course outline was divided into four parts as follows: understanding what happened, thinking about Utopia, making in times of catharsis, and reflection and critique. Ultimately, the students devised a final prototype that responded to a critical issue and operated in part as a cathartic tool for themselves and those in the community. Themes emerged through the project, and students were able to see how their own methods of coping with the disaster were similar and different to their peers. Some of these themes included inside/outside where the difference between being immersed in the disaster versus looking at it from the outside informed the level of investment one had in fixing it; moving beyond "survival mode;" mobility; emotional regulation and others.

To help with the prototyping process, O'Neill also introduced students to "disruptive hypotheses" cards which were based on Luke Williams's (2010) concept of the same name. Five key questions helped them think about innovative ways to interact with and sell, among other things, new products or services. The purpose of this step was to write a disruptive hypothesis by discarding clichés or standard beliefs that dictate the way people think about a particular user experience. These also got them thinking about an actionable plan for impacting the future of Puerto Rico in the face of this disaster.

Finally, students engaged in deep and prolonged reflection about the challenges that they faced in the creative process. Many had lost stability in their living situations, or lost computers and tools usually used to help them in the design process. Because of the

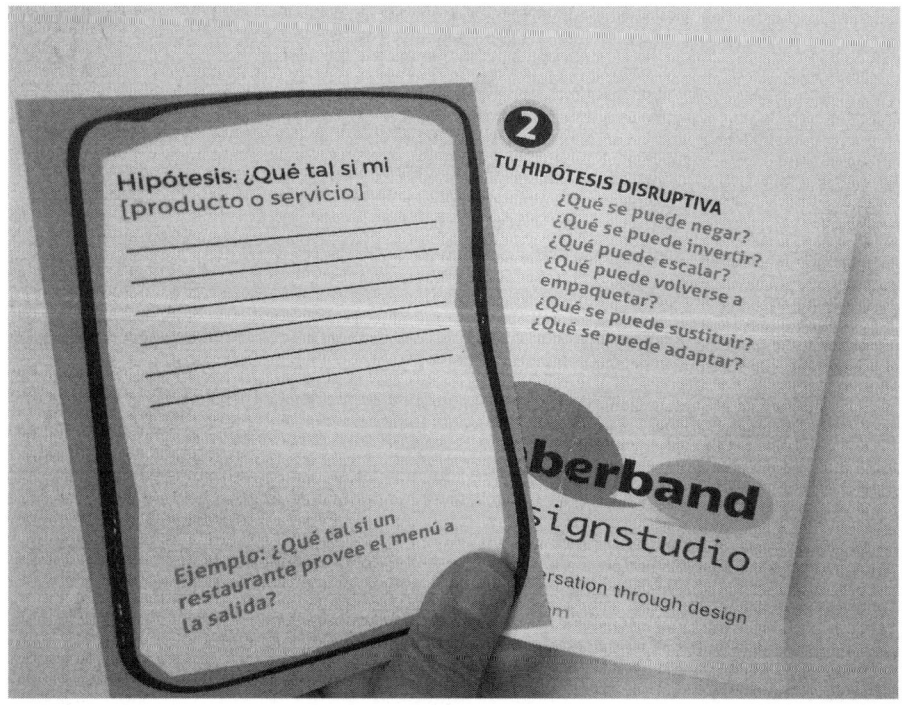

Figure 13.3

Disruptive hypothesis cards. Image courtesy of María O'Neill instability of the electrical grid, much of the design work had to happen off the computer, which (while often frustrating) also encouraged students to use the craft of making as a way to think through how they created visual designs in a different way than the approach typical for them. O'Neill also engaged in much of the design process alongside the students, which also removed the typical hierarchy of the studio environment and encouraged the students to engage in a process of mutual discovery alongside O'Neill, which also empowered the process and the final project.

Advocating through design

Public interest design attempts to balance social, economic, and sustainable impacts inherent in any design intervention. Particularly relevant to architectural practice, public interest design challenges architects and designers to look beyond those who have access to design services, and extend practice to those who really need it—who are living in conditions that are unhealthy, untenable, and actively limiting access to resources, infrastructure, and livelihood. A leader in the field, Bryan Bell explains that "it differentiates itself from other design practices because of its deep commitment, public participation and democratic decision making" (Abendroth and Bell, 2015, 1). As suggested by the name, public interest design is also committed to using design

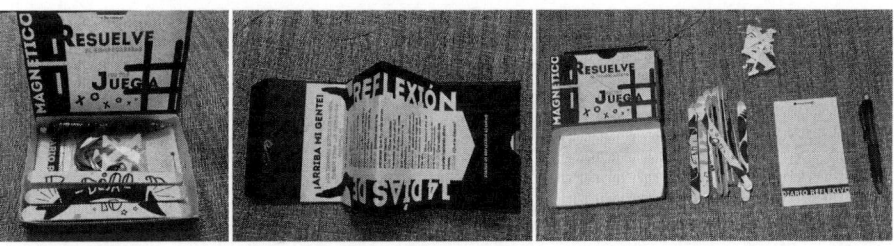

Figure 13.4

"One day at a time" toolkit with a puzzle and simple daily tasks to strengthen self-motivation. Image courtesy of María O'Neill

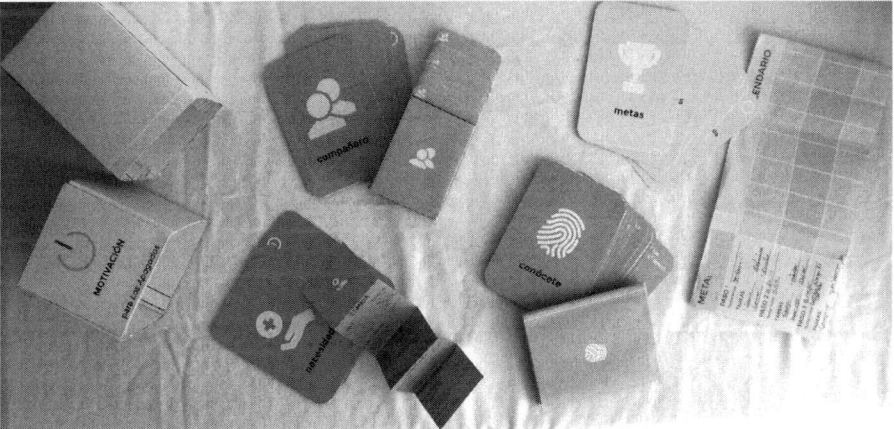

Figure 13.5

Apagados card game strengthens social relationships, logistics skills, and self-reflection. source: Image courtesy of María O'Neill practice as a systematic approach to solving problems that impact not just a select and certain population, but that also address root problems and causes—problems which are usually most visible at the lower levels of socio-economic populations. In contrast to traditional design practice that identifies and isolates a particular problem within a larger issue, public interest design sees the necessity of cultivating and sustaining ongoing relationships to affect longer-lasting, permanent change. In this way, those engaging in public interest design are actively engaging in ongoing effort to identify the link between values, and behaviors from an external and internal perspective, and to identify the multiplicity of sources that are encouraging or influencing the proliferation of a problem.

Through Community Food Lab, Erin White is taking such a systematic and systemic approach to public health, by focusing on the role that design and architecture play in access to fresh, healthy food. In addition to engaging in design projects such as creating school gardens, or reimagining convenience stores with healthy food, Community Food Lab:

> treats the entire food system as an opportunity for design thinking to identify new and unseen value for the health, economy and sustainability for communities, businesses and organizations . . . [and] recognizes the significant threats facing local and global food systems, the awesome complexity of these problems, and the urgent need to make change, now.
>
> (White, n.d.)

Through community engagement, partnerships with local officials, governments, and leaders, Community Food Lab recognizes the importance of advocacy and relationships in cultivating lasting and enduring change in the way that we produce, transport, purchase, and consume food. Since the middle of 2013, Community Food Lab has been developing and sharing a concept for a Food Corridor in Raleigh, North Carolina that relies on collaboration and engagement. As Community Food Lab describes it, this project "can be imagined as a civic engagement project, a food justice initiative, and a catalyst for the local and regional food systems" (White, n.d.). Community Food Lab sees the Raleigh Food Corridor as connective tissue in a city, linking diverse parts of the city around the shared economic, social, and ecological benefits of local food projects. By connecting the vision and common values of a top-down plan with the flexibility and responsiveness of grassroots energy and action, the Raleigh Food Corridor is designed for community impact and inclusive development. The space and shape of the Corridor will evolve over time, as the shared vision expands and shifts when diverse new projects emerge to meet neighborhood needs and shape new ideas. Through its work and attention on self-generated community projects, Community Food Lab is redefining the role of the designer from the traditional visualizer and planner of a strategy, into developer of the strategy itself. By looking at the Raleigh Food Corridor as a system, Community Food Lab recognizes the role that infrastructure, business, government, education, and community perspective play in food production and consumption.

Creating stories together

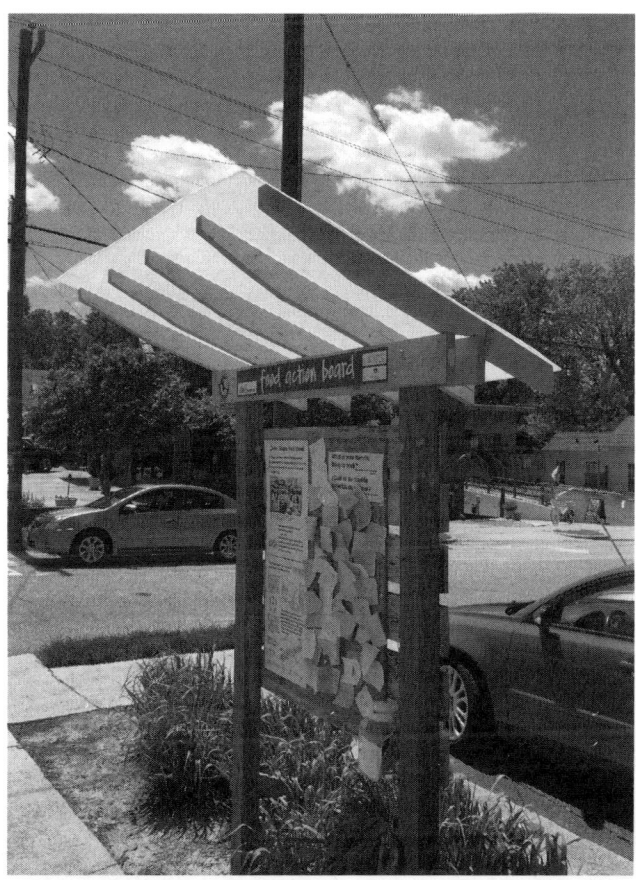

Figure 13.6

Community Food Lab, Raleigh Food Corridor community board. Image courtesy of Community Food Lab

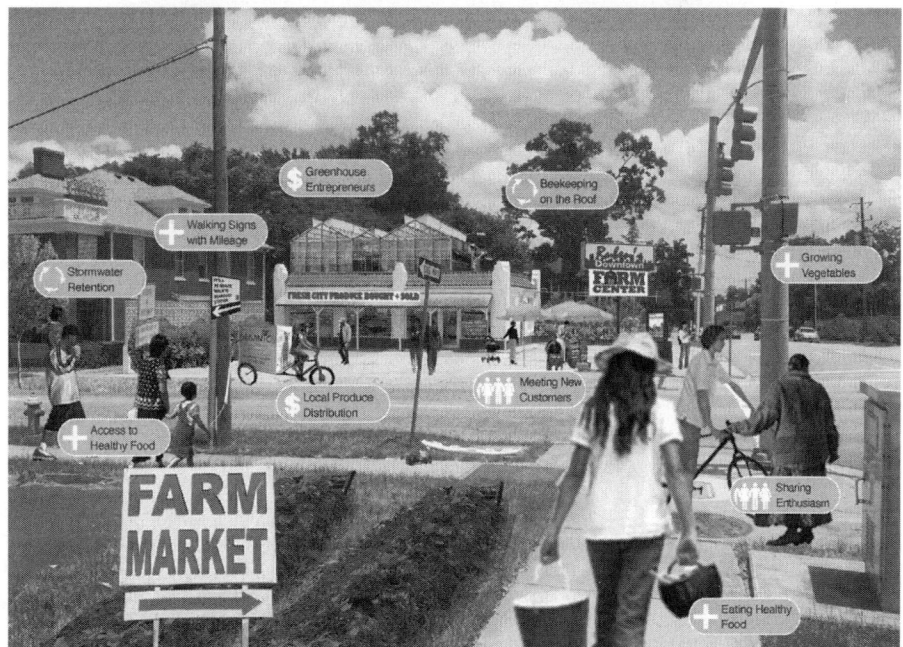

Figure 13.7

Community Food Lab, Raleigh Food Corridor tendering. Image courtesy of Community Food Lab

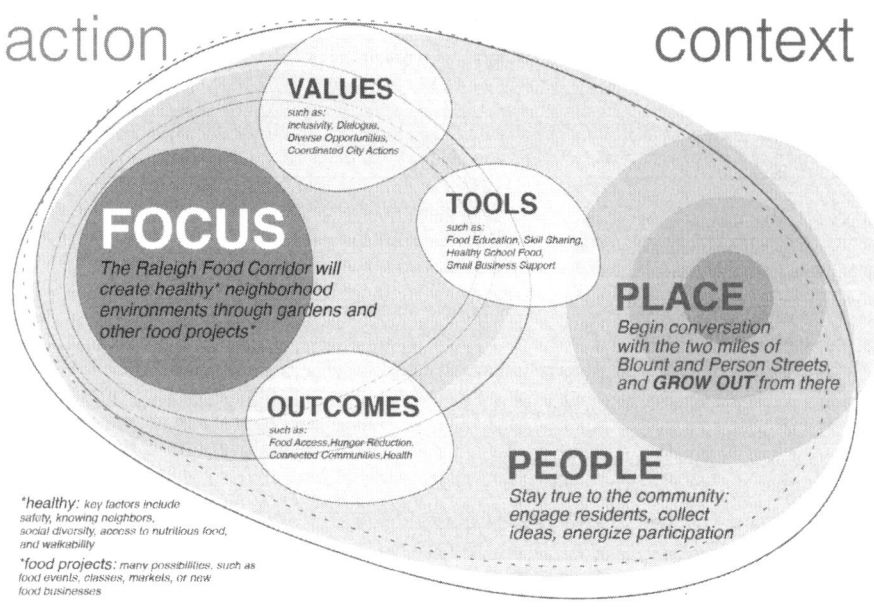

Figure 13.8

Community Food Lab, Food Corridor strategy. Image courtesy of Community Food Lab

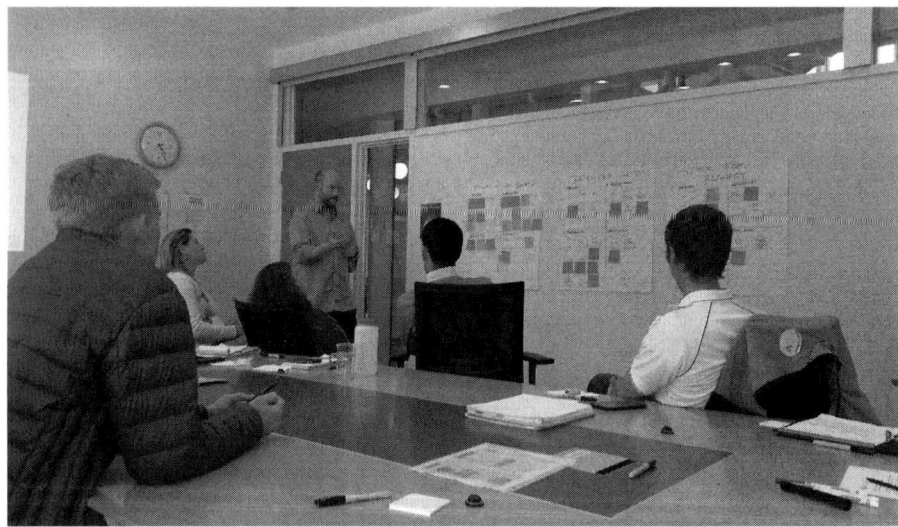

Figure 13.9

Community Food Lab, Food Corridor meeting. Image courtesy of Community Food Lab

In addition to larger studies like the Raleigh Food Corridor, Community Food Lab also looks as specific sites and instances where food production and consumption can increase community engagement, health, and education. In another project, White and his team worked with the Durham Public Schools to create a learning farm for students, teachers, and community members. The Durham Public Schools Hub Farm is a 30-acre site supporting experiential farm, garden, and outdoor education for students throughout the Durham school district. As a mixed educational resource, the farm is a model of flexible programming and activity that uses its landscape of fields, ponds, and woods for education at all grade levels and alongside many community partners.

In creating a vibrant farm and outdoor education site for Durham Public Schools, Community Food Lab worked with a collaborative team of partners and advisors to build a phased site plan, a network of supportive and invested stakeholders, and initial grant funding to support key site improvements. In close collaboration with Landscape Architect Katherine Gill of Tributary Land Design, Community Food Lab led a multi-pronged design approach to early planning that combined education and curriculum opportunities, creative funding strategies, landscape design, and diverse community engagement.

Over 18 months, they worked with partners to create a stable advisory board, initial site management team, and action plan designed for incremental growth of the project. In the two years after their involvement, the HUB Farm has continued to grow in size and reach. A collaboration with an NCSU Design/Build studio culminated in an innovative floating classroom. Up to 300 students per week visit the Farm, engaging in all aspects of the site. In addition, the Farm runs a CSA box program and operates a seasonal on-site farm stand. Plans are in place to obtain GAP certification for the Farm, which would allow produce to be used directly in DPS cafeterias.

The strategy that Community Food Lab has developed in partnership with community activists and stakeholders ranges from discrete and specific interventions, like a community food board and planter garden bus stops to more systems-based research and evaluative mapping of the larger corridor area. What is particularly unique about Community Food Lab's approach is the understanding that systemic change needs the collaboration and thinking of a variety of different stakeholders, and that the answer to the wicked problems they are facing is not always a traditional design intervention, but sometimes is more rooted in advocacy and community building.

To see more information about this and other Community Food Lab projects that use mapping and visualization as a research tool, go to community foodlab.org.

A new type of tactical urbanism

In many ways, Community Food Lab can be seen as a new form of tactical urbanism. Building on theories of placemaking, tactical urbanism calls for small scale interventions in public space with the aim of making them more lively, usable, and enjoyable for those who engage and live in them. Like both public interest design and relational design, tactical urbanism relies on the participation of users to build and ultimately own the design experience. "Tactical Urbanism is an approach to neighborhood building using short-term, low-cost and scalable interventions and policies . . . It makes use of open and iterative development processes, the efficient use of resources, and the creative potential unleashed by social interaction" (Lydon and Garcia, 2015, 2). While tactical urbanism is initially conceived within a specific context or environment, it is often transferrable—with strategies originating in one city quickly adapted and embraced by other cities that see its value to help address common issues. Examples of tactical urbanism range from repurposing empty dumpsters into planters and urban gardens, to transforming public stairways into large-scale piano keys, to pop-up bike lanes. Recently, the mayor of New York City engaged in an experiment of tactical urbanism by turning Times Square into a pedestrian mall using simple barriers. This intervention in public space allowed visitors, business owners, government officials, and residents to experience this urban space quite differently than the normal everyday reality of traffic congestion, overly crowded sidewalks, and as a liminal, transitional space rather than a destination.

One of the most well-known examples of tactical urbanism is Parking Day. Starting as a yearly event in San Francisco, Parking Day was conceived by Rebar Art + Design in 2005 when they converted a parking space into a mini-public park in an area of San Francisco underserved by public green space. Parking Day soon spread across the country and is now recognized as a national U.S. event on the third Saturday of September. With roots in the Parking Day events, Parklets are now being created in many urban settings as a way to reuse urban space and introduce green space into areas in more permanent ways. Through the creation of these semi-permanent parks, city officials, residents, visitors, business owners, and others can envision and experience new forms of urban infrastructure at a scale that is low-stakes, but real. As examples of tactical urbanism, these projects provide real and engaging spaces for designers and the public to imagine urban futures together.

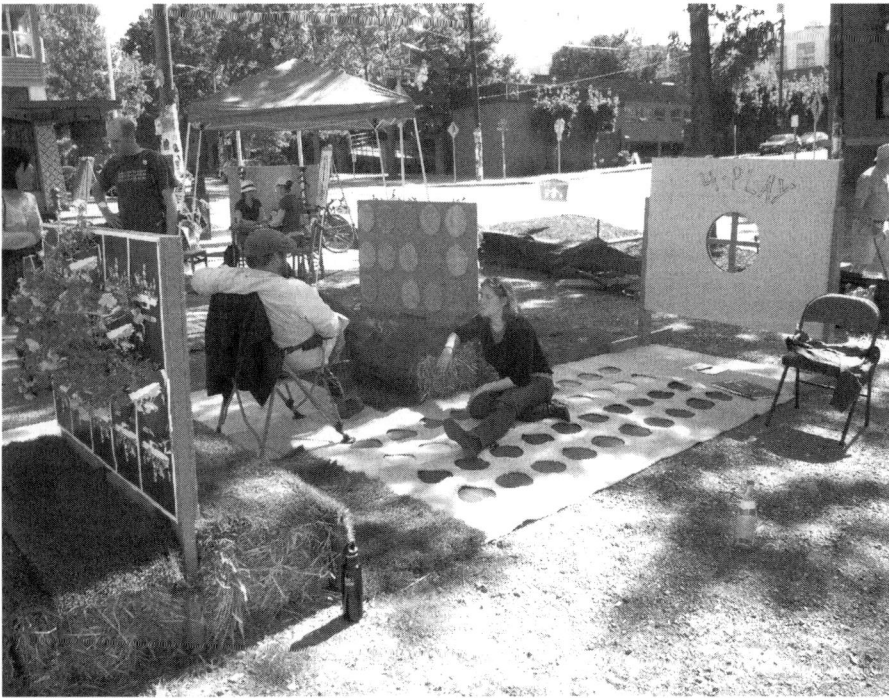

Figure 13.10
Parking Day, Seattle 2009. Image courtesy of Joe Mabel

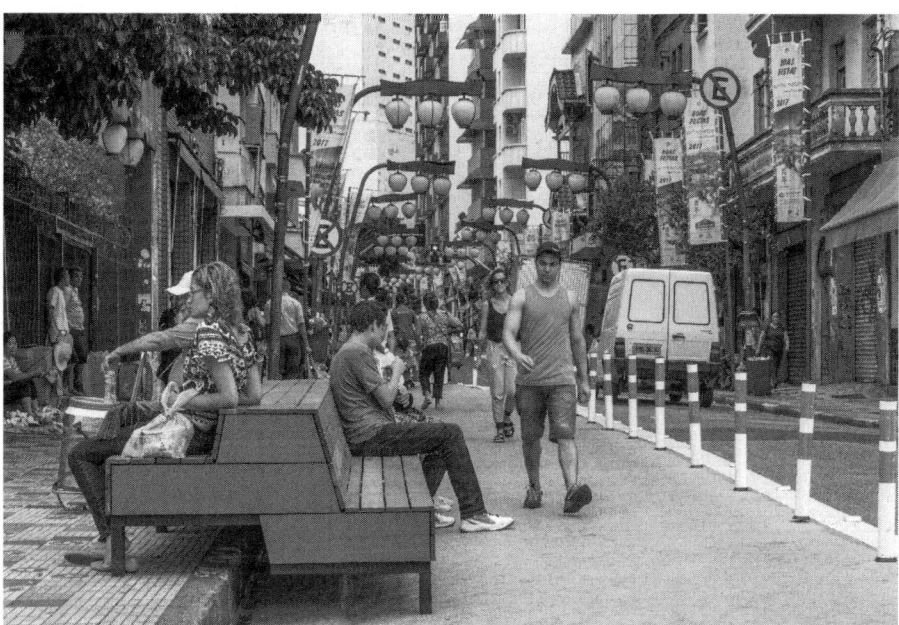

Figure 13.11

Pedestrian Lane in Sao Paolo, Brazil. Image courtesy of Alf Ribeiro/ Shutterstock

Creating conditions for both designers and users to consider design from moral and ethical dimensions includes a focus on the behavior that certain design strategies encourage and discourage. Utilizing methods that uncover or unpack these perspectives, and the behaviors that they engender, cannot happen in isolation from the people for whom designers create. To that end, designers have to reach outside of their comfort zone and actively engage individuals and communities in an open dialogue about how design improves, persuades, encourages, and potentially hampers values in order to improve collective conditions of which we are all a part. Additionally, designers must constantly challenge their own assumptions and biases about what they know, and how that affects what they propose. This can only be done by a progressive investigation of situations, contexts, and methods that constantly remix relationships between what is viable, what is necessary, and what is instrumental.

References

Abendroth, Linda and Bell, Bryan. *Public Interest Design Practice Guidebook: SEED Methodology, Case Studies, and Critical Issues*. Abingdon, UK: Routledge, 2015.

Bleecker, Julian. "Design Fiction: A Short Essay on Design, Science, Fact and Fiction." *Near Future Laboratory*. Retrieved from http://blog.nearfuturelaboratory.com/2009/03/17/design-fiction-a-short-essay-on-design-science-fact-and-fiction/March, 2009. Accessed September 21, 2018.

Gotschall, Jonathan. *The Storytelling Animal: How Stories Make Us Human*. Boston, MA: Houghton Mifflin, 2012.

Lydon, Mike and Garcia, Anthony. *Tactical Urbanism: Short-term Action for Long-term Change*. Washington, DC: Island Press, 2015.

Noel, Lesley-Ann and O'Neill, María. "Puerto Rico 2054: Design Pedagogy in a Time of Crisis." *Design Research Society 2018 Catalyst*. June 25–28, 2018, Limerick, Ireland doi: 10.21606/dma.2018.351, 2018.

Shor, Ira. *Empowering Education: Critical Teaching for Social Change*. Chicago, IL: The University of Chicago Press, 1992.

White, Erin. "Raleigh Food Corridor." *Community Food Lab*. Retrieved from http://communityfoodlab.org/projects/2014/5/23/raleigh-food-corridor. Accessed September 21, 2018.

White, Erin. "Restoring a Healthy Relationship with Food." *The News and Observer*. September 20, 2016. Retrieved from www.newsobserver.com/opinion/letters-to-the-editor/article102982657.html. Accessed September 21, 2018.

Williams, Luke. *Disrupt: Think the Unthinkable to Spark Transformation in Your Business*. Upper Saddle River, NJ: Pearson FT Press, 2010.

14 Conclusion
Putting it all together—design futures

Design is not what it used to be. No longer can we say that we are delivering products or even solutions. Today, designers are consultants, and mediators—problem-framers and solvers. The way that designer think about and practice design is changing and as such will constantly need to adapt to that reality. Designers can't merely come up with "a solution" but instead need to increasingly focus energies on deliberating, evaluating, and being critical not just about the solutions that are being proposed, but also on the questions that are being asked. As Don Norman (2013) argues, "It is all too easy to see only the surface problems, and never dig deeper to address the real issues" (218). This reality only becomes more prominent as the design process becomes more decentralized and reliant on user participation in the creation and adaptation of design.

Throughout this book, I have tried to encourage an approach to design that challenges our assumptions about the proposals that we make in design, and that creates a role for designers that is both critical and creative, and uses research and design thinking not only to support a design solution, or answer, but also maybe more importantly to challenge our own belief in the proposals that we are making.

Because of the emphasis of design thinking as a unique process and methodology, many design practitioners and academics have argued for design as an independent domain, one that is truly unique from other disciplines. I get this motivation. By separating it from other disciplines, design becomes uniquely its own thing—no longer is it reliant on the processes and methods of others disciplines to help define it. This perspective gives it credibility, validates it as a discipline and makes it equal to the other modes of inquiry that are currently shaping it. The problem with this perspective is that design is distinctly integrative in nature. Designers need to understand various perspectives that exist in the world—and to be able to speak many different "languages" in order to translate these ideas in meaningful ways. In the future, I hope to see a field of design that is fully integrated with other domains and disciplines, and one where the research and thinking that takes place in design is seen to be as valuable as those practiced in the humanities and sciences. I hope to see as much, or more time, spent on the research process, and engaging in critical research, as on the ideation process, where we can continue to put efforts to improve the field.

Putting it all together

Design as literacy-making

As a part of this social activity, and directly related to the desire of design and technology to make our lives easier and more convenient, automation becomes more and more central to the goal of design. From autocorrect to GPS mapping applications to self-driving cars, the future of design will rely more and more on processes that are automated for users. Nicholas Carr (2015) would argue that this has a "degeneration effect" that dulls our skills, makes us complacent and overshoots critical parts of learning and practice where explicit knowledge becomes tacit knowledge. By allowing our technology to take over tasks that we might think are menial, we are changing ourselves, and our ability to think, learn, and behave in a certain way. As designers, thinking about the role that design plays in this automation is critical for the future.

Issues of automation can be both physical in nature—like technology that washes our dishes, or vacuums our floors, or reminds us to take our medicine. It can also be cognitive in nature—like the creation of echo chambers that exist when social media platforms only show us images and comments from people who believe similar ideas to us. They can encourage confirmation bias and a diminished ability (or desire) to critically evaluate what we are reading and believing. As a result, the future of design must also take on the evaluation of the impact that this automation has on the people who use it. And as technology continues to move in the direction of automation, quite possibly the role of design will rest on combatting its negative effects, and to make users more literate about how technology is affecting their experiences, what it is exposing them to, and how it is contributing to their understanding of the world. As some of the projects in this book have shown, more and more designers are using their interest and ability to engage in projects that allow users control over their own experience while at the same time making the experience more transparent.

In the 2018 book, *Algorithms of Oppression: How Search Engines Reinforce Racism*, author Safiya Noble argues that Google and other search engines reinforce stereotypes and biases of the people who are designing those algorithms. While sometimes subtle, Noble argues that advertising and other commercial aspects direct how users gain access to information and reinforce negative and positive stereotypes. For example, entering "beautiful" into a search engine primarily returns images of white women, usually scantily clad. "The platform exists because it's made by people . . . and the people who make it are biased, and they code their biases into search" (Illing, 2018). To this end, the future of design is quite possibly aimed at revealing these biases and intentionally counteracting them through the very technology that has supported them in the first place.

Design as a social activity

In 1923, John Dewey argued for a paradigm shift in art and the way it is understood and critiqued. His seminal book, *Art as Experience* (1934), was particularly critical of artistic critique that focused only on evaluating formal components of a piece—the colors, the production, the composition. Instead, Dewey argued that art was really an experience—one that was more like a dialogue between the viewer and the composition. As an "expressive object" art didn't *state* a meaning, but rather *expressed* it. In this expression, there are a host of interrelated components that are all contributing to its meaning. The viewer does not come to the object as a "blank slate" but with previous experiences that affect the way that they respond to and interact with the piece, and contributes to their understanding of the artist's intentions.

A similar trajectory can be seen in design. The way that many designers discuss the intention of their work has shifted from questions like, "What the user will do?" to "How the user might engage?" and from a specific type of experience as engineered by a designer to a host of experiences that might be suggested or precipitated by the design object. Some might argue that this is a failure of design, but I would argue quite the opposite. For designers to understand their work as part of a dialogue influences the design output in much more nuanced ways, and relieves the designer from the burden of needing to control every aspect of the experience. And even more than relieving a burden, it actually opens up a host of opportunities for new approaches to design and design interventions. This also shifts the idea of design objects and experiences as contributing to a system—not removed from but part of a living world. As discussed in the previous section, it can also broaden the context through which designers consider the impact of their work, and engage in more critical dialogue around it.

Susan Yelavich, co-author of *Design as Future-Making* (2014) might characterize this shift in design as:

> designs social nature, or . . . the social relationships embedded in and mediated by the spaces, places, messages and things encountered every day . . . less concerned with design per se than with how and where design can contribute to conversations larger than itself.
>
> (12)

As such, the future of design is reliant more on how designers understand the idea of the social and of society in general. Engaging with people as a social activity means opening up practices of design that focus on the interpretation of meaning as well as habits and behaviors.

One of the places this can be seen most readily and explicitly is in the work of designers on social justice issues and most explicitly the work of Shepard Fairey and the work that he created and shared in the US as a response to the anti-immigration legislation put forth in 2016. Fairey first got notoriety as a street artist responsible for the Obey posters that popped up around the US in the early 2000s. He gained further recognition for creating the iconic image of Barack Obama's Hope campaign in 2008. Throughout his career, a large part of his work has centered on the social realm, and on sharing his work with others. In response to the immigration debate, not only did Fairey create a series of images that responded to the legislation, but he also put them out on a public platform for download and use by the public. People could print and use them as signs and banners to protest the legislation, and they did, becoming important images defining the movement.

Putting it all together

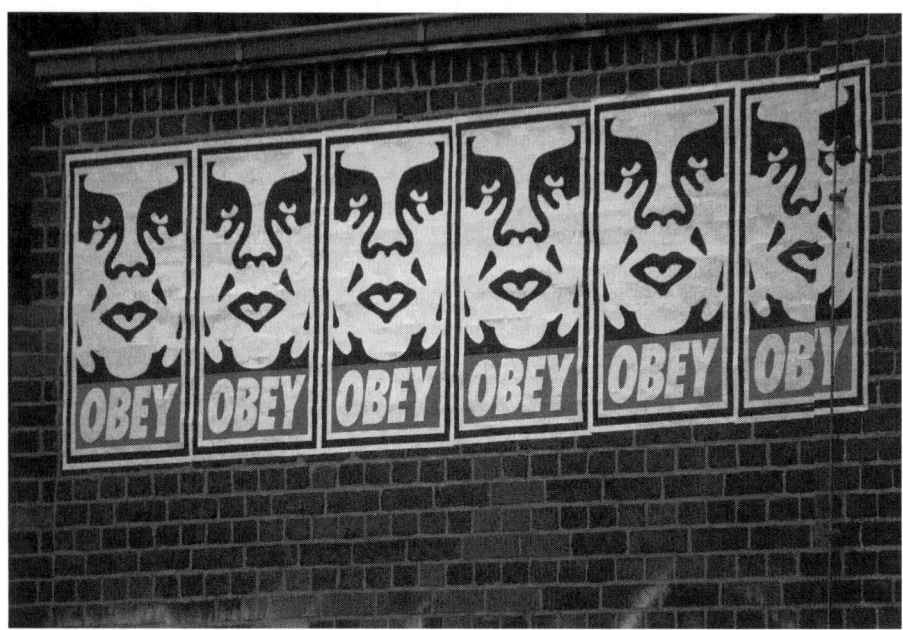

Figure 14.1

Obey posters by Shepard Fairey. Juli Hansen/ Shutterstock.com

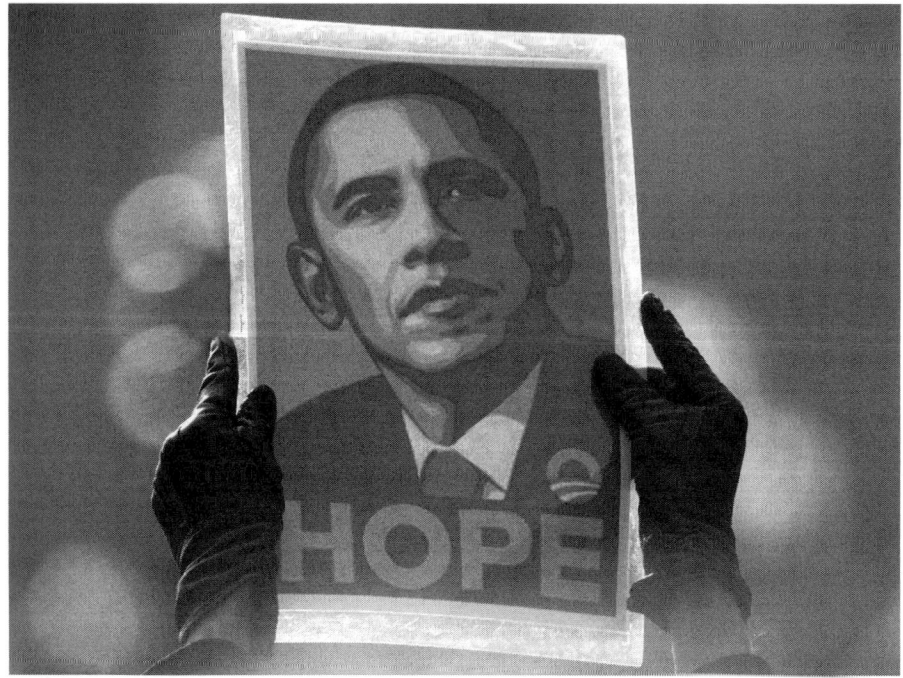

Figure 14.2

Hope campaign sign by Shepard Fairey

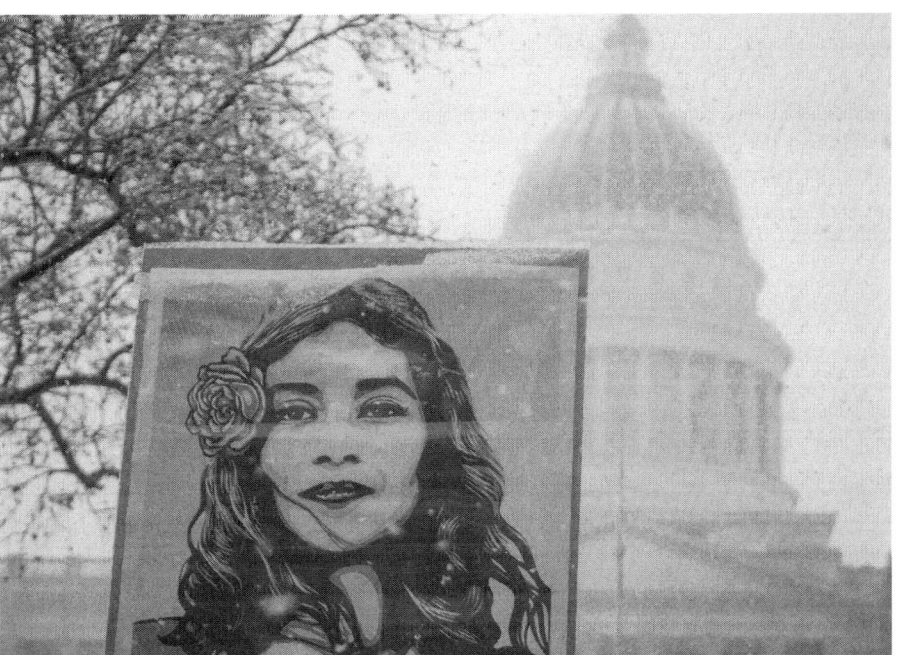

Figure 14.3

Pro-immigration sign by Shepard Fairey

The paradox of impact

Designers are future-makers. But designers also need to continually acknowledge their role as one piece in a very large puzzle that makes the world a different place tomorrow than it was today. While the idealism and utopianism that often characterize design solutions are valuable in the sense that they allow us all to see what might be in a perfect work, it might be more beneficial to start to consider design as moving from "*the* solution" to "*a* solution." At a conference on Design Studies at Parsons in 2013, Hugh Dubberly of Dubberly Design Office also argued for change in the end result of design from "almost perfect" to "good enough for now" and for an integrative approach to design that shifts from the mechanical to the biological (Dubberly, 2013). What this basic shift does is help designers see the products, services, and experiences they design as one piece in a larger, ever-evolving, and shifting system—some pieces of which they have some control over and some which they don't. Designers can work against this, or they can embrace it and capitalize on it, and use what is unique to design—the ability to take what is abstract and make it concrete to help explore and experiment with what these futures might hold for us all.

The paradox of impact is that while design shapes the world in profound ways, it is also being shaped by the world. Design as a process necessarily interfaces with many other systems to shape and redefine the world and our human experience within it. Designers and design in general is, however, uniquely situated to be critical mediators between the various entities, forces, and agendas that are constantly at work in developing the future that we collectively and individually want.

The graphic designer and co-principle of 2x4, Michael Rock illuminates this paradox in at 2016 *New York Times* article entitled, "The Accidental Power of Design." Focusing on the bathroom debate that arose in 2016 after a local city ordinance in Charlotte, North Carolina allowed people to use the bathroom corresponding to their gender identity, Rock argued that the construct of bathroom division was primarily one reinforced, and to some extent, pushed forward by design. It became the norm, and one that design reinforced without much thought. The separation of bathrooms was sacred, but only because we decided it was. As Rock argued, "design solidifies, and naturalizes, things that start off as opinions, stories and traditions, supplying form to the fictions by which we live." But as the "bathroom debate" deepened, it also illuminated the arbitrariness of those norms and traditions.

> What seems self-evident can no longer be imagined as arbitrary. It's only when our belief systems shift, and culturally we experience a seismic disruption, that we suddenly recognize the underlying fictions on which our designed world is built. Design always depicts, and manifests, the things that matter to us . . . until they don't.
>
> (Rock, 2016)

All in all, the future of design is about acknowledging the critical role that design has in everyday experience, and also the bias that is inherent in all design. Rather than absolving designers of responsibility by hiding behind a cloak of objectivity, making the subjectivity of the design more transparent increases its authenticity, believability, and challenges designers to take a stand regarding their own role in design impacts and outcomes.

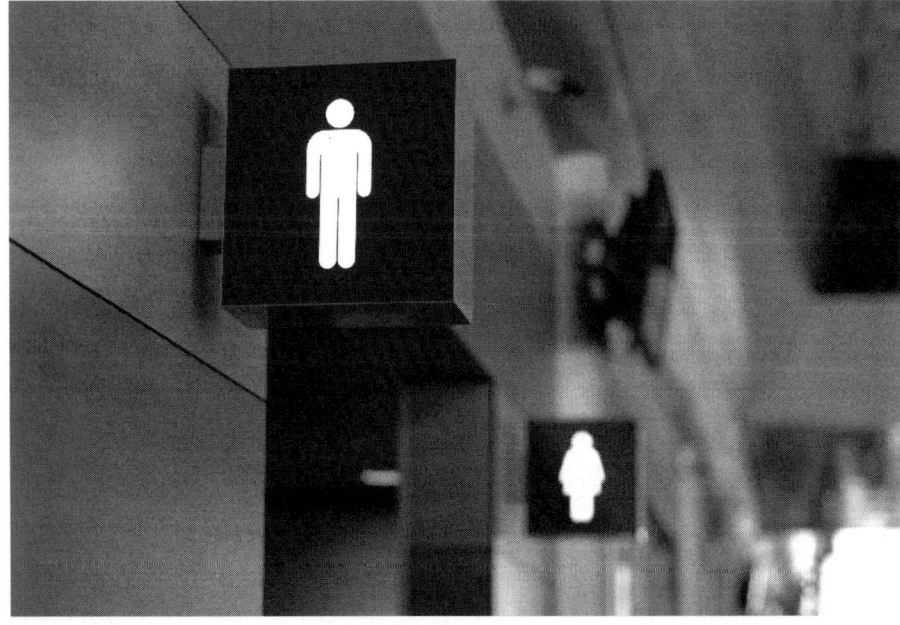

Figure 14.4

Gender-specific bathroom signs

Putting it all together

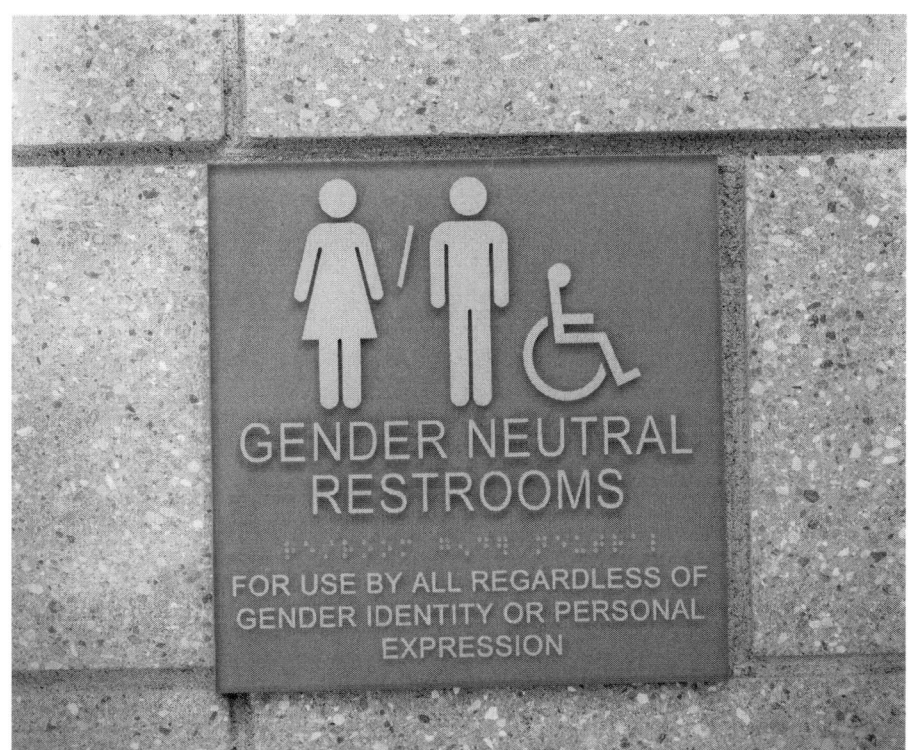

Figure 14.5
Gender-neutral signs

Figure 14.6
Gender-neutral signs that take on a political tone

203

References

Carr, Nicholas. *The Glass Cage: How Our Computers Are Changing Us*. New York: W.W. Norton & Company, 2015.

Dewey, John. *Art as Experience*. New York: Perigee Books, 1934.

Dubberly, Hugh. "A Systems Perspective on Design Practice." *Negotiating the Terrain of Design Studies: Research, Reflection, Practice.* Parson's School of Art and Design History and Theory New York, March 2, 2013. Panel Discussion.

Illing, Sean. "How Search Engines are Making Us More Racist (Interview with Safiya Umoja Noble)." April 6, 2018. Retrieved from www.vox.com/2018/4/3/17168256/google-racism-algorithms-technology. Accessed March 27, 2019.

Noble, Safiya. *Algorithms of Oppression: How Search Engines Reinforce Racism*. New York: NYU Press, 2018.

Norman, Donald A. *The Design of Everyday Things*. New York: Basic Books, 2013.

Rock, Michael. "The Accidental Power of Design." *The New York Times*. September 15, 2016. Retrieved from www.nytimes.com/2016/09/15/t-magazine/design/bathroom-debate-accidental-power-of-design.html. Accessed September 30, 2018.

Yelavich, Susan and Adams, Barbara, editors. *Design as Future-Making*. London: Bloomsbury Academic, 2014.

References

Introduction

Blauvelt, Andrew. "Towards Relational Design." *Design Observer*, 2008. Retrieved from: https://designobserver.com/feature/towards-relational-design/7557. Accessed September 12, 2018.

Brown, Tim. *Change By Design*. New York: Harper Business, 2009.

Buchanan, Richard and Margolin, Victor, editors. *Discovering Design: Explorations in Design Studies*. Chicago, IL: University of Chicago Press, 1995.

Buchanan, Richard and Margolin, Victor, editors. *The Idea of Design*. Cambridge, MA: MIT Press, 1996.

Cross, Nigel. *Designerly Ways of Knowing*. Basel: Birkhäuser Architecture, 2007.

Kelley, Tom. *The Art of Innovation*. New York: Currency, 2001.

Lawson, Bryan. *How Designers Think: The Design Process Demystified, 4th edition*. Oxford: Architectural Press, 2005.

Norman, Donald. *The Design of Everyday Things*. New York: Basic Books, 2013.

Poggenpohl, S.H. "Time for Change: Building a Design Discipline." *Design Integrations: Research and Collaboration*. Bristol, UK: Intellect Books, 2009.

Poggenpohl, Sharon Helmer and Keichi Sato, editors. *Design Integrations: Research and Collaboration*. Bristol, UK: Intellect Books, 2009.

Simon, Herbert. *The Sciences of the Artificial*. Cambridge, MA: MIT Press, 1996.

Stickdorn, Marc and Jakob Schneider. *This Is Service Design Thinking: Basics, Tools, Cases*. Hoboken, NJ: Wiley, 2012.

Thackara, John. *In the Bubble: Designing in a Complex World*. Cambridge, MA: MIT Press, 2005.

Part 1

Altmann, J. "Observational Study of Behavior: Sampling Methods." *Behaviour*, 48, 1974, pp. 227–265.

American Pediatric Association. "Parent Child Reading and Story Time Promote Brain Development Prior to Kindergarten." August 3, 2015. Retrieved from www.aap.org/

References

en-us/about-the-aap/aap-press-room/Pages/Parent-Child-Reading-and-Story-Time-Promote-Brain-Development-Prior-to-Kindergarten.aspx. Accessed March 28, 2019.

Andreou, Alex. "Anti-Homeless Spikes: 'Sleeping Rough Opened My Eyes to the City's Barbed Cruelty'." *The Guardian*. February 18, 2015. Retrieved from www.theguardian.com/society/2015/feb/18/defensive-architecture-keeps-poverty-undeen-and-makes-us-more-hostile. Accessed November 30, 2018.

Burns, Brian. *People Want Toast Not Toasters*. Ottawa: BuschekBooks, 2012.

Campanella, Thomas. "Jane Jacobs and the Death and Life of American Planning." *Places Journal*. April 2011. Retrieved from https://placesjournal.org/article/jane-jacobs-and-the-death-and-life-of-american-planning/?cn-reloaded=1. Accessed September 21, 2018.

Cooper, Alan, Reimann, Robert, and Cronin, David. *About Face 3: The Essentials of Interaction Design*. New York: Wiley & Sons, 2007.

Cross, Nigel. "Designerly Ways of Knowing: Design Discipline Versus Design Science." *Design Issues*, 17(3), 2001, pp. 49–55.

Crouch, Christopher and Pearce, Jane. *Doing Research in Design*. London: Bloomsbury, 2015.

Diffrient, Niels, Tilley, Alvin R., Bardagly, Joan C. *Humanscale*. New York: Henry Dreyfuss Associates, 1974.

Dreyfuss, Henry. *Designing for People*. New York: Simon & Schuster, 1955.

Emerson, Robert M., Fretz, Rachel I., and Shaw, Linda L. *Writing Ethnographic Field Notes*. Chicago, IL: University of Chicago Press, 2nd Edition, 2011.

Geertz, Clifford. *The Interpretation of Man*. New York: Basic Books First Edition, 1977.

Geertz, Clifford. *The Interpretation of Cultures*. New York: Basic Books, 1973.

Gibson, James J. *The Ecological Approach to Visual Perception*. Abingdon, UK: Taylor & Francis, 2015. Classic Edition.

Grocki, Megan. "How to Create a Customer Journey Map." *UX Mastery*. September 16, 2014. Retrieved from https://uxmastery.com/how-to-create-a-customer-journey-map/. Accessed February 26, 2019.

Gunn, Wendy, Otto, Ton, and Smith, Rachel C., editors. *Design Anthropology: Theory and Practice*. London: Bloomsbury, 2013.

Hayes, Michael. "Incrementalism and Public Policy-Making." *Oxford Review*. April 2017. DOI: 10.1093/acrefore/9780190228637.013.1.

Herman Miller. "Our designers: Charles and Ray Eames." Retrieved from www.hermanmiller.com/designers/eames/. Accessed March 28, 2019.

Hrastinski, Iva and Wilbur, Ronnie B. "Academic Achievement of Deaf and Hard-of-Hearing Students in an ASL/English Bilingual Program." *Journal of Deaf Studies and Deaf Education*, 21(2), April 2016, pp. 156–170.

Jones, Karen. *Sign Me a Story: Shared Reading in American Sign Language With Interactive Animated Narration*. North Carolina State University Master's Thesis, 2017.

Lupton, Ellen. *Beautiful Users: Designing for People*. New York: Princeton Architectural Press, 2014.

Marshall, Aarian. "Alphabet is Trying to Reinvent the City, Starting with Toronto." *Wired*, October 17, 2017. Retrieved from www.wired.com/story/google-sidewalk-labs-toronto-quayside/. Accessed February 26, 2019.

Meers, Chris. "Prototypes – The Beginner's Guide" *The UX Review*. May 10, 2013. Retrieved from https://theuxreview.co.uk/prototypes-the-beginners-guide/. Accessed February 26, 2019.

Norman, Donald. *The Design of Everyday Things*. New York: Basic Books, 2013.

Oudshoorn, Nelly and Pinch, Trevor, editors. *How Users Matter: The Co-Construction of Users and Technology*. Cambridge, MA: The MIT Press, 2003.

Peinhardt, Katherine. "Google's Urban Experiment in Toronto: A Q&A with Sidewalk Labs' Rit Aggarwala." Project for Public Spaces. November 30, 2017. Retrieved from www.pps.org/article/google-urban-experiment-toronto-sidewalk-labs-rit-aggarwala. Accessed September 21, 2018.

Poggenpohl, S.H. "Time for Change: Building a Design Discipline." *Design Integrations: Research and Collaboration*. Bristol, UK: Intellect Books, 2009.

Project for Public Spaces. "What is Placemaking?" Project for Public Spaces, n.d. Retrieved from www.pps.org/article/what-is-placemaking. Accessed September 29, 2018.

Project for Public Spaces. "PPS Involvement in the Place-Led Regeneration of Detroit, MI." Project for Public Spaces, n.d. Retrieved from www.pps.org/projects/pps-involvement-in-the-place-led-regeneration-of-detroit. Accessed September 29, 2018.

Sauro, Jeff and Lewis, James. *Quantifying the User Experience: Practical Statistics for User Research*. Waltham, MA: Elsevier, 2012.

Schön, Donald. *The Reflective Practitioner: How Professionals Think in Action*. New York: Basic Books, 1983.

Sidewalk Toronto. Retrieved from https://sidewalktoronto.ca/. Accessed March 28, 2019.

Simon, Herbert. *The Sciences of the Artificial*. Cambridge, MA: MIT Press, 1996.

Story, Molly Follette. "The Principles of Universal Design." In Wolfgang F.E. Preiser and Elaine Ostroff, editors. *Universal Design Handbook*, Second edition. New York: McGraw-Hill, 4(1–6), 2011, pp. 4.3–4.11.

Strauss, Claudia and Quinn, Naomi. *A Cognitive Theory of Cultural Meaning*. Cambridge: Cambridge University Press, 1997.

Tunstall, Elizabeth. "Decolonizing Design Innovation: Design Anthropology, Critical Anthropology, and Indigenous Knowledge." In Wendy, Gunn, Ton Otto, and Rachel C. Smith, editors. *Design Anthropology: Theory and Practice.*. London: Bloomsbury, 2013.

Wahid, Arif Rahman and Atmodiwirjo, Paramita. "Storyboard as a Representation of Urban Architectural Settings." *International Conference on Architectural Education in Asia*. SHS Web Conference (eduARCHsia 2017). Volume 41, 2018.

Whyte, W.H. *The Social Life of Small Urban Spaces*, Reprint edition. New York: Project for Public Spaces, 2001.

Part 2

Bhargava, Rahul et al. "Data Murals: Using the Arts to Build Data Literacy." *The Journal of Community Informatics*. October 26, 2016.

Blauvelt, Andrew. "Towards Relational Design." *Design Observer*. November 3, 2008. Retrieved from https://designobserver.com/feature/towards-relational-design/7557. Accessed September 22, 2018.

References

Bloch, Matthew, Keller, Josh, and Park, Haeyoun. "Vaccination Rates for Every Kindergartener in California." *The New York Times*. February 6, 2015. Retrieved from www.nytimes.com/interactive/2015/02/06/us/california-measles-vaccines-map.html. Accessed September 22, 2018.

Bogost, Ian. *Persuasive Games: The Expressive Power of Videogames*. Cambridge, MA: The MIT Press, 2010.

Bolter, Jay David and Gromala, Diane. *Windows and Mirrors: Interaction Design, Digital Art, and the Myth of Transparency*. Cambridge, MA: The MIT Press, 2005.

Bolter, Jay David and Grusin, Richard. *Remediation: Understanding New Media*. Cambridge, MA: The MIT Press, 1999.

Bouikidis, Aphrodite. "3 Ways Social Entrepreneurship Can Create a Resilient Ecosystem in Greece." *Forbes*, November 6, 2014. Retrieved from www.forbes.com/sites/ashoka/2014/11/06/3-ways-social-entrepreneurship-can-create-a-resilient-ecosystem-in-greece/. Accessed June 10, 2015.

Carr, Nicholas. *The Glass Cage: How Our Computers Are Changing Us*. New York: W.W. Norton & Company, 2015.

Corner, James. "The Agency of Mapping: Speculation, Critique and Invention." In Denis Cosgrov, editor. *Mappings*. London: Reaktion Books, 1999, pp. 231–242.

Cross, Nigel. "Designerly ways of knowing: design discipline versus design science." *Design Issues*, 17(3), 2001, pp. 49–55.

Crouch, Christopher and Jane Pearce. *Doing Research in Design*. London: Bloomsbury, 2015.

DeBono, Edward. *Lateral Thinking: Creativity Step by Step*. New York: Harper Colophon, Reissue edition, 2015.

Dewey, Caitlin. "How the Internet's Most Earnest Evangelist Became its Fiercest Critic." *The Washington Post*. October 25, 2015.

D'Ignazio, Catherine. "This Online Game Forces You Out of Your Bubble by Taking You to Places You've Never Heard Of." *Huffington Post*. October 4, 2014. Retrieved from www.huffingtonpost.com/catherine-daignazio/terra-incognita_b_5643012.html. Accessed September 22, 2018.

D'Ignazio, Catherine and Bhargava, Rahul. "DataBasic: Design Principles, Tools and Activities for Data Literacy Learners." *The Journal of Community Informatics*, 12(3), 2016, pp. 83–107.

Druckery, Timothy. "Relational Architecture: The Work of Rafael Lozano Hemmer." *Debates & Credits. Media / Art /Public Domain*. Amsterdam: De Batie Centre for Culture and Politics, 2003, pp. 69–72.

Gerolympou-Karadimou, Alexandra. "Στοές και περάσματα στην αγορά." ["Arcades and passages in the market."] *Parallaxi Magazine*, January 1, 2014. Accessed June 10, 2015. Retrieved from http://parallaximag.gr/thessaloniki/stoes-kai-perasmata-stin-agora. Accessed March 1, 2019.

Greenfield, Adam. *Everyware: The Dawning Age of Ubiquitous Computing*. San Francisco, CA: New Riders Publishing, 2006.

Greenfield, Adam. *Radical Technologies: The Design of Everyday Life*. New York: Verso, Reprint edition, 2018.

Groat, Linda and Wang, David. *Architectural Research Methods.* Hoboken, NJ: Wiley, 2013.

Hager, Thomas. *The Alchemy of Air: A Jewish Genius, a Doomed Tycoon, and the Scientific Discovery that Fed the World but Fueled the Rise of Hitler.* New York: Broadway Books, 2009.

Harris, Jonathan. "We Feel Fine" and "Network Effect." (n.d.). Retrieved from http://number27.org/networkeffect. Accessed March 1, 2019.

Holzer, Jenny. "Truisms, 1978–87." *The Museum of Modern Art, MoMA Highlights.* New York: The Museum of Modern Art, 2004.

Kelly, Kevin. *What Technology Wants.* New York: Penguin Books, 2011.

Koukoumakas, Kostas. "Στις στοές της Θεσσαλονίκης." ["In the arcades of Thessaloniki"] *Kathimerini,* February 2, 2015. Retrieved from www.kathimerini.gr/801932/article/ta3idia/sthn-ellada/stis-stoes-ths-8essalonikhs. Accessed June 10, 2015.

Lay, Stephanie. "Uncanny Valley: Why We Find Human-Like Robots and Dolls so Creepy." *The Guardian.* November 13, 2015.

McKim, Robert. *Experiences in Visual Thinking.* Boston, MA: Cengage Learning, 2nd edition, 1980.

McLuhan, Marshall. *Understanding Media: The Extension of Man.* Cambridge, MA: The MIT Press, Reprint edition, 1994.

Novak, Joseph D. and Gowin, D. Bob. *Learning How to Learn.* Cambridge: Cambridge University Press, 1984.

Patsarika, Maria. *Iconic or Ironic? Multiple Perceptions of the Baltic Centre for Contemporary Art, Newcastle upon Tyne.* International Centre for Cultural and Heritage Studies, the University of Newcastle. Unpublished MA dissertation, 2005.

Reagle, Joseph. *Good Faith Collaboration: The Culture of Wikipedia.* Cambridge, MA: The MIT Press, Reprint edition, 2012.

Rose, David. *Enchanted Objects: Innovation, Design, and the Future of Technology.* Scribner, Reprint edition, 2015.

Rosenberg, Elissa. "Walking in the City: Memory and Place." *Journal of Architecture,* 17(1), 2012, pp. 131–149.

Seedat, Mohamed. "Oral History as an Enactment of Critical Community Psychology." *Journal of Community Psychology,* 43(1), 2014, pp. 22–35.

Shaviro, Steven. *Connected or What It Means to Live in a Networked Society.* Minneapolis, MN: University of Minnesota Press, 2003.

Tenner, Edward. *Why Things Bite Back: Technology and the Revenge of Unintended Consequences.* New York: Vintage, Reprint edition, 1997.

Yan, Holly, Simon, Darran, and Vercammen, Paul. "California Wildfires Have Destroyed 1,000 Structures . . . and Counting." cnn.com. December 12, 2017. Retrieved from www.cnn.com/2017/12/11/us/california-wildfires/index.html. Accessed September 22, 2018.

Zwicky, Fritz. "The Morphological Approach to Discovery, Invention, Research and Construction." In Fritz Zwicky and Albert Wilson, editors. *New Methods of Thought and Procedure: Contributions to the Symposium on Methodologies.* Berlin: Springer-Verlag, 1967.

References

Part 3

Benyus, Janine M. *Biomimicry: Innovation Inspired by Nature*. New York: Harper Perennial, 2002.

Boone, Kofi, Fox, Andrew, and Hill, David. *HomePlace*. Raleigh, NC: NC State University College of Design, Coastal Dynamics Design Lab Publication, 2018.

Braungart, Michael and William McDonough. *Cradle to Cradle*. New York: North Point Press, 2002.

Brownell, Blane and Swackhamer, Marc. *Hypernatural: Architecture's New Relationship with Nature*. New York: Princeton Architectural Press, 2015.

Brozan, Nadine. "Emotional Effects of Natural Disasters." *The New York Times*, June 27, 1983. Accessed as digital archive, December 15, 2018.

Cooper Hewitt Archive. "Design for the Other 90%." Cooper Hewitt Design Museum. 2007. Retrieved from http://archive.cooperhewitt.org/other90/other90.cooperhewitt.org/about/index.html. Accessed December 15, 2018.

Cosco, Nilda, Moore, Robin, and Islam, Mohammad Zahirul. "Behavior Mapping: A Method for Linking Preschool Physical Activity and Outdoor Design." *Official Journal of the American College of Sports Medicine*, 2010, pp. 513–519.

Doan, Abigail. "Biomimetic Architecture: Green Building in Zimbabwe Modeled After Termite Mounds." *Inhabitant*. November 29, 2012. Retrieved from https://inhabitat.com/building-modelled-on-termites-eastgate-centre-in-zimbabwe/?variation=c. Accessed September 25, 2018.

Fox, Andrew et al. "FloodPrint." Coastal Dynamics Lab. 2019. Retrieved from www.coastaldynamicsdesignlab.com/lumberton-floodprint. Accessed March 28, 2018.

Illich, Ivan. *Tools for Conviviality*. New York: Perennial Library, 1973.

Jennings, Ken. "The Real Story Behind Dubai's Palm Islands." Condé Nast Traveller. November 23, 2015. Retrieved from www.cntraveler.com/stories/2015-11-23/the-real-story-behind-dubai-palm-islands. Accessed September 22, 2018.

Lopate, Phillip. "Above Grade: On the High Line." *Places Journal*. November 2011. Retrieved from https://placesjournal.org/article/above-grade-on-the-high-line/. Accessed September 22, 2018.

Mathur, Anuradha and da Cunha, Dilip. *Mississippi Floods: Designing a Shifting Landscape*. New Haven, CT: Yale University Press, 2001.

McLendon, Russell. "Qatar's Impact on the Environment: How the U.N. Climate Talks in Doha Cast a Spotlight on the Country." *Huffington Post*. November 30, 2012. Retrieved from www.huffingtonpost.com/2012/11/30/qatar-environmental-impact-climate_n_2213298.html. Accessed September 22, 2018.

Meadows, Donella. *Thinking in Systems: A Primer*. White River Junction, VT: Chelsea Green Publishing, 2008.

Papanek, Victor. *Design for the Real World: Human Ecology and Social Change*. Chicago, IL: Chicago Review Press, 2nd Edition, 2005.

Sanders, Elizabeth B.N. "From User-Centered to Participatory Design Approaches." In Jorge Frascara, editor, *Design and the Social Sciences: Making Connections*. New York: Taylor & Francis, 2002.

Scientific American. "Use It and Lose It: The Outsize Effect of U.S. Consumption on the Environment." *Scientific American*. (n.d.). Retrieved from www.scientificamerican.com/article/american-consumption-habits/. Accessed September 22, 2018.

Smith, Cynthia, editor. *Design For The Other 90%*. New York: Editions Assouline; ND Marginalized ed. edition, 2007.

Stellar, Daniel. *The PlayPump: What Went Wrong? State of the Planet*. Columbia: Earth Institute, Columbia University. July 1, 2010.

Sundararajan, Arun. *The Sharing Economy: The End of Employment and the Rise of Crowd-Based Capitalism*. Cambridge, MA: The MIT Press, 2017.

Thackara, Jonathan. *In the Bubble: Designing in a Complex World*. Cambridge, MA: MIT Press, 2005.

Troubled Water. Frontline. WGBH Educational Foundation, 2010.

Turner, J. Scott and Soar, Rupert C. "Beyond Biomimicry: What Termites Can Tell Us About Realizing the Living Building." *First International Conference on Industrialized, Intelligent Construction (I3CON)*. Loughborough University, May 14–16, 2008.

Van Rees, Hellen, et al. "Textile Waste and Haptic Feedback for Wearable Robotics." *Design Research Society Catalyst*. University of Limerick, June 25–28, 2018.

Yin, Robert K. *Case Study Research: Design and Methods*. Thousand Oaks, CA: Sage Publications, 4th Edition, 2008.

Part 4

Abendroth, Linda and Bell, Bryan. *Public Interest Design Practice Guidebook: SEED Methodology, Case Studies, and Critical Issues*. Abingdon, UK: Routledge, 2015.

Baker, Holly. "E-Cigarettes and Subsequent Tobacco Use in Adolescence." *The Lancet Oncology*, 16(13), October 2015, p. e481.

Blauvelt, Andrew. "Towards Relational Design." *Design Observer*, 2008. Retrieved from: https://designobserver.com/feature/towards-relational-design/7557. Accessed September 12, 2018.

Bleecker, Julian. "Design Fiction: A Short Essay on Design, Science, Fact and Fiction." *Near Future Laboratory*. Retrieved from http://blog.nearfuturelaboratory.com/2009/03/17/design-fiction-a-short-essay-on-design-science-fact-and-fiction/March, 2009. Accessed September 21, 2018.

Bourriaud, Nicholas. *Relational Aesthetics*. Dijon: Les Presse Du Reel, 1998.

Bristol, Katherine. "The Pruitt-Igoe Myth." *The Journal of Architectural Education*, 44(3), 2015, pp. 163–171.

Brown, Tim. *Change by Design*. New York: Harper Business, 2009.

Buchanan, Richard and Margolin, Victor, editors. *Discovering Design: Explorations in Design Studies*. Chicago, IL: University of Chicago Press, 1995.

Buchanan, Richard and Margolin, Victor, editors. *The Idea of Design*. Cambridge, MA: MIT Press, 1996.

Carr, Nicholas. *The Glass Cage: How Our Computers Are Changing Us*. New York: W.W. Norton & Company, 2015.

References

Cooper, Alan, Reimann, Robert, and Cronin, David. *About Face: The Essentials of Interaction Design*, 4th Edition. Hoboken, NJ: Wiley, 2014.

Crouch, Christopher and Jane Pearce. *Doing Research in Design*. London: Bloomsbury, 2015.

Csikszentmihalyi, Mihalyi. *Flow: The Psychology of Optimal Experience*. New York: Harper Perennial Modern Classics, 2008.

Dewey, John. *Art as Experience*. New York: Perigee Books, 1934.

Druckrey, Thomas. "Relational Architecture: The Work of Rafael Lozano Hemmer." *Debates & Credits. Media/Art/Public Domain*. Amsterdam: De Batie – Centre for Culture and Politics, 69, 2003.

Dubberly, Hugh. "A Systems Perspective on Design Practice." *Negotiating the Terrain of Design Studies: Research, Reflection, Practice*. Parson's School of Art and Design History and Theory New York, March 2, 2013. Panel Discussion.

Dunne, Anthony and Raby, Fiona. *Speculative Everything: Design, Fiction, and Social Dreaming*. Cambridge, MA: MIT Press, 2013.

Gaver, B., Dunne, Anthony, and Pacenti, Elena. "Culture Probes." *Design Interactions*. January/February, 1999, pp. 21–29.

Gottschall, Jonathan. *The Storytelling Animal: How Stories Make us Human*. Wilmington, MA: Mariner Books, 2013.

Hardaway, Robert. *The Great American Housing Bubble: The Road to Collapse*. Santa Barbara, CA: Praeger, 2011.

Hoare, Ben. "Sanctum." *The Seen: Chicago's International Online Journal of Contemporary and Modern Art*. January 20, 2016. Retrieved from http://theseenjournal.org/art-seen-international/sanctum-theaster-gates/. Accessed September 22, 2018.

IDEO. "Extreme User." *IDEO Method Cards*. San Francisco, CA: William Stout, 2003.

Illich, Ivan. *Tools for Conviviality*. New York: Perennial Library, 1973.

Illing, Sean. "How Search Engines are Making Us More Racist (Interview with Safiya Umoja Noble)." April 6, 2018. Retrieved from www.vox.com/2018/4/3/17168256/google-racism-algorithms-technology. Accessed March 27, 2019.

Jacobs, Jane. *The Death and Life of Great American Cities*. New York: Random House, 1961.

Latour, Bruno. "Morality and Technology: The End of the Means." *Theory, Culture & Society*. London, Thousand Oaks and New Delhi: Sage Publications. Vol. 19(5/6), 2002, pp. 247–260.

Lydon, Mike and Garcia, Anthony. *Tactical Urbanism: Short-term Action for Long-term Change*. Washington, DC: Island Press, 2015.

Markusen, Ann and Gadwa, Anne. "*Creative Placemaking*." The Mayors' Institute on City Design. Washington, DC: Markusen Economic Research Services and Metris Arts Consulting, 2010.

McGonigal, Jane. *Reality is Broken: Why Games Make Us Better and How They Can Change the World*. New York: Penguin Books, 2011.

Noel, Lesley-Ann and O'Neill, María. "Puerto Rico 2054: Design Pedagogy in a Time of Crisis." *Design Research Society 2018 Catalyst*. June 25–28, 2018, Limerick, Ireland doi: 10.21606/dma.2018.351, 2018.

Norman, Donald. *The Design of Everyday Things*. New York: Basic Books, 2013.

Poggenpohl, S.H. "Time for Change: Building a Design Discipline." *Design Integrations: Research and Collaboration*. Bristol, UK: Intellect Books, 2009.

Project for Public Spaces. "What is Placemaking?" Project for Public Spaces, 2007. Retrieved from www.pps.org/article/what-is-placemaking. Accessed September 22, 2018.

Sanders, Elizabeth and Stappers, P. J. *Convivial Toolbox: Generative Research for the Front End of Design*. Amsterdam: BIS Publishers, 2013. "World Without Oil." Retrieved from http://writerguy.com/wwo/metahome.htm. Accessed September 22, 2018.

Shor, Ira. *Empowering Education: Critical Teaching for Social Change*. Chicago, IL: The University of Chicago Press, 1992.

Thackara, John. *In the Bubble: Designing in a Complex World*. Cambridge, MA: MIT Press, 2005.

US Department of Health and Human Services. *E-Cigarette Use Among Youth and Young Adults: A Report of the Surgeon General*. US Department of Health and Human Services, 2016.

Verbeek, Peter-Paul. *Moralizing Technology: Understanding and Designing the Morality of Things*. Chicago, IL: The University of Chicago Press, 2011.

Verbeek, Peter-Paul. "Morality in Design: Design Ethics and the Morality of Technological Artifacts." In P.E. Vermaas, P. Kroes, A. Light, and S. Moore, editors. *Philosophy and Design: From Engineering to Architecture*. New York: Spring, 2008, pp. 91–103.

Waldorf, Caleb. Interview with Teddy Cruz. *Triple Canopy*, 2009. Retrieved from http://apubliclibrary.org/cw/posts/interview-with-teddy-cruz/. Accessed September 22, 2018.

White, Erin. "Raleigh Food Corridor." *Community Food Lab*. Retrieved from http://communityfoodlab.org/projects/2014/5/23/raleigh-food-corridor. Accessed September 21, 2018.

White, Erin. "Restoring a Healthy Relationship with Food." *The News and Observer*. September 20, 2016. Retrieved from www.newsobserver.com/opinion/letters-to-the-editor/article102982657.html. Accessed September 21, 2018.

Whyte, William H. *The Social Life of Small Urban Spaces*. New York: Project for Urban Spaces, 1980.

Williams, Luke. *Disrupt: Think the Unthinkable to Spark Transformation in Your Business*. Upper Saddle River, NJ: Pearson FT Press, 2010.

"World Without Oil." Retrieved from http://writerguy.com/wwo/metahome.htm. Accessed September 22, 2018.

Conclusion

Carr, Nicholas. *The Glass Cage: How Our Computers Are Changing Us*. New York: W.W. Norton & Company, 2015.

Dewey, John. *Art as Experience*. New York: Perigee Books, 1934.

Dubberly, Hugh. "A Systems Perspective on Design Practice." *Negotiating the Terrain of Design Studies: Research, Reflection, Practice*. Parson's School of Art and Design History and Theory New York, March 2, 2013. Panel Discussion.

References

Illing, Sean. "How Search Engines are Making Us More Racist (Interview with Safiya Umoja Noble)." April 6, 2018. Retrieved from www.vox.com/2018/4/3/17168256/google-racism-algorithms-technology. Accessed March 27, 2019.

Noble, Safiya. *Algorithms of Oppression: How Search Engines Reinforce Racism*. New York: NYU Press, 2018.

Norman, Donald A. *The Design of Everyday Things*. New York: Basic Books, 2013.

Rock, Michael. "The Accidental Power of Design." *The New York Times*. September 15, 2016. Retrieved from www.nytimes.com/2016/09/15/t-magazine/design/bathroom-debate-accidental-power-of-design.html. Accessed September 30, 2018.

Yelavich, Susan and Adams, Barbara, editors. *Design as Future-Making*. London: Bloomsbury Academic, 2014.

Index

Accessibility 51–53
Affordances (Anti, Hidden and False) 12–15, 39–40
Altman, Jeanne 24
Analogies 78–79
Anderson, Wes 130
Anti-solutions 129–130

Backwards Systems 129–130
Bell, Bryan 189
Benyus, Jane 130
Bhargava, Rahul 98–100
Biomimicry 130–134, 141
    Behavioral 130
    Genetic 131
    Epigenetic 131
Blauvelt, Andrew 2, 96
Bogost, Ian 68–69
Bolter, Jay David 62, 67
Bookmooch 118
Bound by Design 187
Bourriaud, Nicolas 168
Braungart, Michael 112, 114
Brown, Tim 1
Brownell, Blaine and Swackhamer, Marc 130
Burnham, Daniel 163
Burns, Brian 9
Buchanan, Richard 4

Carr, Nicholas 61, 212
CGI Technology 62
Chornyak, Brooke 39–44
City Beautiful 163
Coastal Dynamics Design Lab 145–155
Community Food Lab 190–193
Convivial Toolbox 175
Cooper, Alan 34, 177
Cooper Hewitt 116
Corner, James 123
Creative Placemaking 165
Critical Cartography 75
Cronin, David 34
Cross, Nigel xii, 1, 20
Crouch, Christopher 20, 26, 86
Cruz, Teddy 96, 167–169

Csikszentmihalyi, Mihalyi 183
The Culture of Wikipedia 61

da Cunha, Dilip 113, 114
Databasic.io 98–101
DeBono, Edward 78
Decolonizing Design 16
Defensive (Hostile) Architecture 13
Desalination Process 91, 115
Design Anthropology 16–17
Design for the Other 90% 116–118
Design Fiction 179–181, 187
Design As Future Making 199
Design as a social activity 198
Design Thinking, Definitions of
    Designers and 1–2
    Empowering Education 186
    Experiential Design Thinking 19
    Networked Design Thinking 71–74
    Ecological Design Thinking 121
    Narrative Design Thinking 171–172
Design Thinking, Methods
    Concept Mapping 78
    Critical Cartography 75
    Design Fiction 179–181, 187
    Extreme Users 176–177
    Game-based 181–183
    Lateral Thinking 78–79
    Personas 176
    Prototyping 36–37
    Scenarios 177–178
        Context Scenarios 177
        Key path Scenarios 177
        Validation Scenarios 177–178
    Storyboarding 32–33
    User Journey Mapping 32–33
    Visual Thinking 78
Dewey, John 198
Diffrient, Niels 10
D'Ignazio, Catherine 96–99
Diller, Scofidio + Renfro 123
Disney, Walt xi
Disruptive Hypothesis 188
Doha, Qatar 152

index

Dreyfuss, Henry 10–11
Dubberly, Hugh 201
Dunne, Anthony 173, 179

Eames, Charles 39, 112
Eames, Ray 112
Eastgate Centre 141, 143–144
Emans, Denielle 138–139
Empathy, and Design 15, 53, 175, 183, 185
Empowering Design Education 186–188
Extreme Users 176–177

Fairey, Shepard 199–200
Field Visits 22–23
Field Operations (James Corner's) 123–124
Food Systems and design 189–193
Flows (Systems) 128
    Inflows 128–129
    Outflows 128–129
Friends of the High Line 123–124
Forman, Fiona 167–169
Fox, Andrew 146–147

Gamification 68
Garden City 163
Gates, Theaster 165–166
Geertz, Clifford 21, 37
Generative Design 175
Gibson, J.J. 12
Google 44–46, 198
Gotschall, Jonathan 172, 185
Gowin, Bob 78
Greenfield, Adam 60–61
Groat, David 75
Gromala, Diane 67
Grusin, Richard 62
Gulf of Knowledge and Gulf of Execution 11–12

Haber-Bosch Machine 60–61
Hager, Thomas 60
Harris, Jonathan 101–107
The High Line 123–124
Hill, David 146
Howard, Ebenezer 163
Hostile (Defensive) Architecture 13
Human Factors 10–11
Humanscale 11
Hurricane
    Design in Response to 145–155, 185–189
    Katrina 114
    Florence 146
    Maria 185–189
    Matthew 114, 147
Hypermediacy 63

IDEO 11 37, 176
Illich, Ivan 118, 175
Immediacy 62–63
Industrialization 114–115
Internet of Things 65
Interstitial Spaces 168
Isle of Dogs 130

Jacobs, Jane 51, 162–166
Journey Mapping 32–34

Kamvar, Sep 101
Kelly, Kevin 59–60, 64
Kelly, Tom 1

Lateral Thinking 78–79
Latour, Bruno 161–162
Lawson, Bryan 1
Learning from Tijuana 169–170
Lewis, James 24
Life Straw 116
Lopate, Phillip 123–124
Lozano-Hemmer, Rafael 96
Lupton, Ellen 10

Make Tools 175
Margolin, Victor 4
Mathur, Anuradha 113, 114
McDonough, William 112, 114
McGonigal, Jane 181, 183
McKim, Robert 78
McLuhan, Marshall 68
Meadows, Donella 128
MIT Center for Civic Media 96
MIT Media Lab 66, 130
Morality and Design
    Moral Mediators 161–162
    Moral Agents 162–166
    Moral Projections 166–169
Mori, Masahiro 62
Morphology 81

Narrative Games 180–181
Noble, Safiya 198
Noel, Lesley Ann 186–187
Norman, Donald 11–12, 25–26, 31, 197
Novak, Joseph 78

O'Neill, Maria 186–189

Palm Islands, Dubai 112
Papanek, Victor 129
Parking Day 194
Parklet 194
Parsons New School of Design 201
Participatory Design 49, 95, 173–175
Pearce, Jane 86
Pearce Mike 141
Personas 175, 178
    Scenario Based Personas 178–179
Piano, Renzo ix
Placemaking 45–46, 49, 164–166, 193
Play Pump 117–118
Poggenpohl, Sharon 4, 9
Problem-Framing 71–72
Procedural Rhetoric 66–69
Project for Public Spaces 44, 46–47, 165
Prototyping, Prototypes 36–37
Pruitt-Igoe 163–164
Public Interest Design 189–190

Raby, Fiona 173, 179
Radical Technologies 60–61
Reagle, Joseph 61
Rebar Art + Design 194
Redemptive Architecture 166

Reimann, Robert 34
Relational Design 2, 95–96
Remediation 63
Research Methods
    Behavior Mapping 126–128
    Case Study Research 122–126
    Case Study, Creating a 125–126
    Correlational Research 76–77
    Culture Probes 173
    Ethnographic Research 21–24
    Experimental and Quasi-experimental Research 20–21
    Field Visits (conducting) 22–23
    Narrative Research 172–173
    Observational Research 24–25
    Participatory Design Research 173–175
    Phenomenological Research 122
    Sampling (in Experimental Research) 24–25
    Sampling (in Behavior Mapping) 127
    Surveys and Interviews 25–26, 28–29
    Survey Instrument (Designing) 28–29
    Usability Testing (Conducting) 31–32
Rock, Michael 202
Rose, David 66

Sanctum (Project) 166
Sanders, Liz 175
Sauro, Jeff 24
Scenarios 177–179
    Context Scenarios 177
    Key Path Scenarios 177
    Validation Scenarios 177–178
Schemas 15
Schneider, Jakob 1
Schon, Donald 17
Sciences of the Artificial 5
Shaviro, Steven 68
Sidewalk Labs 46–51
Sidewalk Toronto 46–51
Silk Pavilion 130–131
Simon, Herb 5
Stappers, P.J. 175
Stempeck, Matt 96
Stickdorn, Marc 1
Stocks (in Systems) 128
Storyboarding 34–36
Substitution Myth 61
Sterling, Bruce 179
Sundararajan, Arun 118
Surveillance (and Technology) 68
Survey Instrument 28–29
Sustainability and Design
    Contextual Systems 112–114
    Behavioral Systems 114–115
    Human Systems 116–118
    Convivial Systems 118
Systems Thinking, definitions of
    Contextual Systems 112–113
    Behavioral Systems 114–115
    Human Systems 116–117
    Convivial Systems 118
Systems Thinking, Methods of
    And Design Thinking 128–129
    Backwards Systems 129–130
    Natural Systems (see also Biomimicry) 130–134

Tactical Urbanism 193–194
Technological Systems
    Open systems 64–65
    Closed Systems 64–65
Technology and Design
    Transparency and 67–68
    Material Network and 68–69
    Living Network and 64–66
    Ubiquity of 61–63
Tenner, Edward 64
Terra Incognita 95–98
Textile Reflexes 131–134
Thackara, John 2, 111, 137, 145
Thessaloniki, Greece 90–95
Tools for Conviviality 118
Tunstall, Elizabeth (Dori) 16, 17

Uncanny Valley 62
Urban Design 44–51
Usability and Design
    Physical Experiences and 10–11
    Cognitive Experiences and 13–16
    Cultural Experiences and 16–17
    Tests 31–32
Utopia, and Design 185–189

Van Rees, Hellen 131–134
Verbeek, Peter Paul 162
Virginia Commonwealth University 152
Visual Thinking 78

Wang, Linda 75
White, Erin 190–193
Whyte, William H. 44–47, 164, 165
Wikipedia 61
Williams, Luke 188
Worst-Case Scenarios 129–130

Yelavich, Susan 199
Yin, Robert K. 122

Zuckerman, Ethan 96
Zwicky, Fritz 81

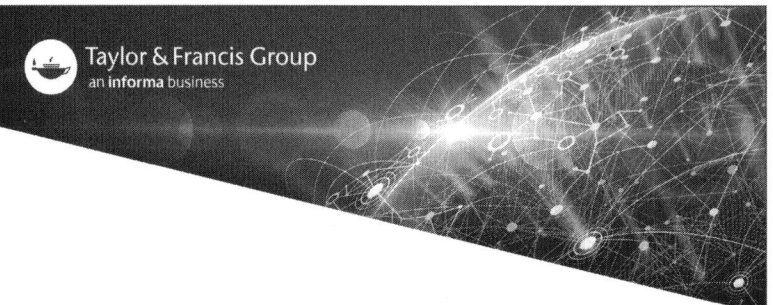